The question why certain kinds of legal institutions are found in certain kinds of societies has been little explored by anthropologists. In this book Katherine Newman examines a sample of some sixty different preindustrial societies, distributed across the world, in an attempt to explain why their legal systems vary.

The key to understanding this variation, Professor Newman argues, is to be found in economic organization. Adopting a Marxian, or materialist, approach, she draws on original ethnographic sources for each culture in order to investigate how legal processes and institutions regulate basic aspects of economic life in societies with differing types of economic organization. She also examines the commonalities of law *within* various preindustrial "modes of production" and shows that the patterning of legal institutions arises from underlying tensions in production systems.

In offering an explanation of the distribution of legal institutions across preindustrial societies, as well as for the sources of conflict in such societies, the book makes an important contribution to the comparative study of legal systems. It will interest anthropologists and other readers concerned with the operation and development of legal institutions.

Katherine Newman is Assistant Professor of anthropology at Columbia University in New York. She received her Ph.D. in Anthropology at the University of California, Berkeley, where she subsequently taught in the School of Law.

Law and economic organization

Law and economic organization

A comparative study of
preindustrial societies

Katherine S. Newman
Department of Anthropology
Columbia University

Cambridge University Press

Cambridge
London   New York   New Rochelle
Melbourne   Sydney

Published by the Press Syndicate of the University of Cambridge
The Pitt Building, Trumpington Street, Cambridge CB2 1RP
32 East 57th Street, New York, NY 10022, USA
296 Beaconsfield Parade, Middle Park, Melbourne 3206, Australia

First published 1983

Printed in the United States of America

Library of Congress Cataloging in Publication Data
Newman, Katherine.
Law and economic organization.
Revision of thesis (Ph.D.) – University of
California, Berkeley, 1979.
Bibliography: p.
Includes index.
1. Ethnological jurisprudence. I. Title.
K190.N48   1983   340'.115   83–7169
ISBN 0 521 24791 8 hard covers
ISBN 0 521 28966 1 paperback

This book is dedicated to my parents,
Evelyn and Charles Newman,
for their support and encouragement

Contents

Figures and tables

Figures

Tables

Acknowledgments

This book was originally written in 1979 as a doctoral dissertation for the Department of Anthropology at the University of California, Berkeley. Its present form reflects my association in the intervening years with the Jurisprudence and Social Policy Program at Berkeley and the Department of Anthropology at Columbia University. The opportunity to work with faculty and students in each of these settings has contributed a great deal to the development of the ideas presented here. It is a pleasure to acknowledge my debt to them.

Brent Berlin first encouraged my interest in the topic of evolution through the unlikely avenue of his own research in the field of ethnoscience. Though his substantive interests are quite removed from my own, the approach to comparative analysis that this book represents owes a great deal to his example. Berlin's insistence on data-based verification of abstract theory has shown me the virtues of his own brand of "dust-bowl empiricism." I appreciate his support and advice over the years.

My association with Philip Selznick was probably the high point of my years as a student and teacher at Berkeley. He gave freely of his time and intellectual energy and provided me with many thoughtful criticisms of this work.

Jack Potter and Aram Yengoyan introduced me to much of what I know about Marxist theory in anthropology. Burton Benedict, Gerald Berreman, and David Mandlebaum listened to my ideas and offered their own throughout the years. Rae Lesser Blumberg guided me in cross-cultural data analysis through the example of her own research on sexual inequality and by giving generously of her time and advice.

Susan Allen-Mills, my editor at Cambridge University Press, patiently saw this work through the review process and offered the kind of encouragement and professional advice that every author needs, but which is often hard to come by. I am also grateful for the comments of the three anonymous scholars who reviewed this book for Cambridge. Although the errors in this book remain my responsibility, I am certain there are fewer of them as a result of the careful reading they gave the original manuscript.

It is a curious fact that this book was originally written in Berkeley, which for all its virtues was not particularly identified with a historical-materialist tradition in anthropology. Columbia University was better known as a crucible of evolutionary-materialist research, and long before I had any personal contact with the Columbia department I thought my work was more closely associated with the traditions of that faculty. I have had the distinct good fortune to learn firsthand that the theoretical approach represented in this book is alive and well at Columbia. I am grateful to my colleagues and the graduate students in the anthropology department.

This work could not have been completed without the generous support of the Institute of Human Learning at the University of California, Berkeley, which provided me with a four-year fellowship funded by U.S. Public Health Service Grant GM1207. Graduate students in the present era receive far less support for their education than I did. I am grateful for the assistance I received and hope that future generations will once again be as fortunate.

I also wish to thank the following group of compatriots who have provided intellectual stimulation and friendship: Alex Alland, Jr., Cheryl Crawley, Terry D'Altroy, Leslie Dow, Willett Kempton, Nancy Lutz, Ann Millard, David Neal, Abraham Rosman, Paula Rubel, Colin Sumner, and Kit Woolard.

Finally, I want to express my thanks to Paul Attewell, my husband and colleague, whose support and encouragement could never be adequately acknowledged.

Introduction

Nineteenth-century social theorists believed the history of human society could be understood as the unfolding of natural laws of development. The infinite variety of human societies, technologies, and cultures was seen as governed by common causal principles. Careful observation and analysis could give rise to a science of humans.

In contrast, the twentieth century is an era of skepticism in the social sciences. Discouraged by the failures of the nineteenth-century vision, modern anthropology in particular retreated to a more limited view of its possibilities. Particularism – the careful study of individual cultures – replaced generalization, as twentieth-century scholars sought a more secure footing in empirical evidence than that afforded the grand theorists of an earlier age.

In this effort to ground theory construction in reliable evidence, much of the original quest was forgotten. Those who originally believed that an adequate data base would eventually allow for generalization ended up convinced of the opposite. Historical particularism engendered a passion for specifics, for detail, for careful and excellent scholarship; it took a dim view of abstraction and an even dimmer view of theory as an enterprise. Within anthropology, the result was a wealth of carefully collected data on individual societies, practically untouched by theoretical hands.

Rumblings of dissatisfaction with the particularist strategy have been heard at various points in time during the "post-Boasian" era. Harkening back to the aspirations of the grand theorists, such anthropologists as Leslie White, V. Gordon Childe, Julian Steward, and a whole host of their well-known protégés (including Marshall Sahlins and Elman Service) initiated a return to some of the more important nineteenth-century questions and goals. "Evolutionism," a term held in disrepute between the turn of the century and the mid-1950s, resurfaced in the anthropological vocabulary. The comparative method, another ill-fated child of the "speculative" period, became a "new" means whereby social scientists could attempt to make sense out of particularistic ethnography.

Furious debates erupted over the adequacy of particular theoretical explanations for social evolution, the development of agriculture, the origin of the state, and a host of similar topics. The stridency of the arguments was a healthy sign. It indicated that the new comparative anthropology was far more sensitive to issues of methodology and empirical grounding than its nineteenth-century predecessor.

This renewed interest in comparative and evolutionary research has not been applied evenly across the subfields of anthropology. Anthropology of law, for example, remains dominated by particularism, despite the fact that it has been blessed with a wealth of data that can be subjected to theorizing of the sort now common in political and ecological anthropology. Virtually every important general ethnography has included information regarding dispute-settlement practices. Hundreds of studies have focused specifically on the ways in which the world's cultures deal with internal conflict. Indeed, the data base of legal anthropology constitutes an embarrassment of riches.

The same cannot be said of its theoretical development. We still know very little about why particular kinds of societies exhibit the structures of conflict resolution they do. There has been a dearth of modern *comparative* work attempting to formulate typologies of legal institutions and determine what, if any, systematic causal links may be found between these institutions and the *types* of societies in which they occur.

This is not to say that legal anthropology is devoid of explanatory analysis. However, the dominant trend in the field has been to describe the internal workings of conflict management in particular preindustrial societies. To the extent that generalization *across* societies has been attempted, it has tended toward the most general forms of explanation. From Malinowski on, anthropologists have relied upon a functionalist explanation of law, that law reduces conflict in a society, that it restores equilibrium when the social fabric is torn.

There is nothing particularly objectionable in this as a first stage in theorizing. Unfortunately, this is all too often both the first and last theoretical step. In ethnography after ethnography, the dispute-settlement practices of "face-to-face" societies have been shown to restore broken ties, to make the peace rather than punish. (Indeed, the point is often made that the legal mechanisms they have developed are more sensible than ones we find in our own advanced industrial societies.) But the theory leaves unanswered some important questions: Why are certain kinds of legal institutions found in some societies and very different ones found in others? What explains the variation?

There is a second sense in which the traditional anthropology of law has led us away from fundamental questions. Because the emphasis of functionalist analysis was on law as an equilibrating mechanism, legal anthropologists working in this tradition have tended to concentrate on conflict *resolution* to the detriment of studying the *origins* of conflict. This is clearly seen in the work of Max Gluckman, one of the finest of legal ethnographers. Gluckman's masterful work on the law of the Barotse of Northern Rhodesia (Zambia) showed that in "multiplex societies," where people are bound by multiple social and economic interdependencies, conflict is particularly disruptive and cannot be tolerated if the community is to survive. Barotse judges are therefore oriented toward reconciliation and devoted to "mending" broken ties, not simply punishing offenders (Gluckman 1955). "Multiplexity" therefore explains the character of the Barotse judicial process.

Echoes of this approach can be seen in the work of many prominent legal anthropologists, including Laura Nader's work on "making the balance" in Zapotec dispute management (Nader 1969) and Phillip Gulliver's research on Arusha moots and conclaves (Gulliver 1963), to name only two. The kind of functional analysis proferred by Gluckman and his followers in the Manchester School has become the major analytic tool in contemporary legal anthropology.

The problem with this functionalist emphasis is that it makes strife appear exceptionally destructive, as abnormal or pathological. In focusing on conflict resolution, it tends to downplay the fact that conflict is a chronic phenomenon in these societies – that conflict is not random, but is generated repeatedly and often in stereotypical contexts. The functionalist perspective draws us away from explaining the origins of conflicts and the ways in which legal institutions are adapted to the specific kinds of social cleavages that they address. Thus another neglected part of the anthropology of law consists of the search for causes or sources of conflict in preindustrial societies and asks: Do these sources of conflict vary systematically across different kinds of societies; how do they shape legal institutions? In short, the comparativist believes that a causal explanation of legal development depends on understanding cross-cultural variation in forms of legal institutions, variation in sources of conflict, and the relationship between these two factors and other features of social structure.

Such an enterprise requires us to formulate both hypotheses that specify the connections between these variables and a methodology capable of testing the empirical validity of the hypotheses. To the best of my knowledge, this has yet to be accomplished. This book represents an effort to explore these comparative questions.

In Chapter 1, I examine a number of classical and contemporary theories of legal development from which the aforementioned hypotheses might be generated. As the reader will see, I choose to elaborate and test a materialist theory of comparative legal institutions. For the moment, suffice it to say that the materialist is concerned with the nature of material production in societies and the internal distribution of the fruits of labor. I shall argue that legal systems play a vital role in regulating labor, allocating economic surplus, controlling land and water rights, and other vital aspects of economic life.

The major analytic tool employed toward this end is that of the "mode of production," a concept that will be fully discussed in Chapter 3. Thus the bulk of the book is dedicated to showing a systematic causal link between particular preindustrial modes of production and the legal institutions and substantive law found within them.

This cannot be accomplished without first developing a typology of legal systems, which is the central purpose of Chapter 2. Eight distinct institutional forms are identified, ranging from self-redress to state-level court systems, and are ranked according to a scale of complexity.

Chapter 3 discusses materialist theory in some detail. I construct variables that measure important dimensions of modes of production, and hypotheses are developed that predict the relationship between these variables and the complexity of legal institutions. Using a cross-cultural sample of sixty societies, these hypotheses are tested and the findings interpreted. Chapter 3 therefore speaks to the first of the two deficiencies in traditional legal anthropology discussed in this Introduction: the lack of understanding of the distribution of legal institutions across preindustrial societies.

The second deficiency concerns our need for a better grasp of the sources of chronic conflict. Chapter 4 analyzes data on recurrent patterns of disputes within different modes of production and argues that the content of the disputes and the growth of substantive law stem directly from strains inherent in the social relations of production and from the regularities of stratification discernible in various production systems. The concluding chapter pulls these arguments together and articulates them into a more fully detailed materialist theory of legal development in preindustrial societies.

This book was undertaken with three basic purposes in mind. First, I hoped to contribute some comparative research to the literature of legal anthropology. Second, I intended to add a useful methodological approach to the developing arsenal of analytic techniques in social anthropology. Finally, I wanted to make a contribution to materialist theories of social institutions. These were my intentions. The reader will be the best judge of their success.

1

Theories of legal evolution

We begin by turning to the past. Many scholars have looked for patterns in the historical development of legal systems. In this chapter, I briefly review the contributions of some of the more important early evolutionary theorists – Maine, Durkheim, Marx and Engels, Weber – and the writings of several more contemporary scholars.

Part one: classical theories of legal evolution

The nineteenth- and early twentieth-century legal theorists shared a general evolutionary perspective. They believed that legal systems could be classified on the basis of formal characteristics, including sources of legal authority as well as similarities in organizational form. Classificatory schemes could be ordered; that is, each type of legal system could be ranked in a sequence. The sequence itself need not represent historical time, although this was often thought to be the case. It might, for example, represent increasing legal complexity.

The classical theorists also assumed that the sequence could be understood as the result of some underlying "force" or movement in history. Evolutionary idealists generally located this movement in the unfolding of an internal logic, a logic that necessarily transformed one kind of legal system into the next one in the sequence. Evolutionary materialists tended to locate the motive force outside the institutions themselves. In examining the work of each theorist, it will be important to determine how each of these three principles was manifested, in addition to describing their specific developmental schemes.

Henry Maine: from status to contract

Sir Frederick Pollock's glowing introduction to Maine's most famous work, *Ancient Law*, notes that the book marked a significant turning point in the study of legal history.

> We who are in no way bound to reticence must say that he did nothing less than create the natural history of the law. He showed, on the one hand, that legal ideas and institutions have a real course of development as much as the genera and species of living creatures, and in every stage of that development have their normal characters. (Pollock in Maine 1970:xiv)

The modern reader may find it difficult to imagine that the science of legal history was born as late as the mid-nineteenth century. However, as Pound (1930) points out in *Interpretations of Legal History*, Maine's antecedents were suffused with notions of the "state of nature." Maine (1970:87) argued that the belief in the natural origins of law was an ill-fated romantic notion that retarded the scientific understanding of legal history. *Ancient Law* stands as one of the earliest scholarly efforts to analyze the foundations of modern law historically rather than philosophically.

In the course of his studies, Maine observed a general trend in law that has subsequently been adopted as a truism by most grand theorists. The movement from status to contract, "a shift from legal rights, duties and commands based on personal status to the objectification and codification of law in impersonal statutes having universal application" (Goddard 1969:85), has been recognized as a key feature distinguishing small-scale societies from modern complex societies. Maine was the first to examine the ramifications of this transformation.

One of the most unusual aspects of *Ancient Law* is the wide variety of sources it draws on. Maine made use of unlikely historical sources, such as epic poetry of the Homeric period and tracts of Stoic philosophy, a practice resembling more contemporary methods of cultural reconstruction.[1] Although Maine's use of these texts was ingenious, his use of extant societies to validate his portrait of primitive cultures of a bygone era is even more impressive. His familiarity with Hindu law and custom[2] formed the basis of his quest for the principles of customary law. However, unlike most

---

[1] Maine argued that although these epics were written for other purposes, they constituted a rich source of untainted data on legal culture. Unlike later Greek historians, who had theological interests, the Homeric poems had no particular bias and as such could be taken as a reliable source of "early forms of jural conceptions."

historians, who derived information only from available written records, Maine supplemented these sources by drawing upon an evolutionary methodology: He viewed synchronic variation as evidence for diachronic change. Having researched the early history of property law as far as the legal record could take him, Maine turned to contemporary "primitive" societies for confirmation of his evolutionary hypotheses.

Maine relied upon yet another analytic technique drawn from the social science of his day, the use of "survivals." Tylor (1958:134) described survivals as institutions or practices that "have been carried on by force of habit into a new state of society different from that in which they had their original home" and argued that survivals constituted evidence for social evolution in that they were "proof . . . of an older condition of culture." In *Ancient Law* this methodological tool was used extensively to argue for the historical (as opposed to Natural) origins of certain legal principles.

Maine adopted this approach, particularly when one legal principle appeared not to "fit" into the logical pattern of contemporaneous legal rules. He explained anomalies in law as survivals from a previous era when they did "fit." He then searched for evidence that the legal principle in question was indeed a historical holdover.

One further methodological point should be made about Maine's work. Because he saw his ranking of legal institutions in terms of unilineal evolution – one institutional form metamorphosing into the next – he had to find evidence linking the stages into a sequence.

Historical records documenting the entire sequence for one society would be the strongest evidence for this kind of evolutionary theory. Since this would be hard to find, however, Maine adopted the next best strategy: He "proved" the reality of the sequence by locating transitional forms, societies undergoing a transformation from one stage to another. Thus in Maine's discussion of the evolution of the legal status of married women, he described first the subordination of women to their *blood relations* in primitive societies. Next he noted that in the law of his own time a married

---

[2] Raymond Firth's preface to *Ancient Law* indicates that Maine served as a member of the Viceroy's Council in India following his retirement from the Chair of Civil Law at Cambridge University. Maine lived in India for seven years and was well acquainted with Hindu law.

woman was legally subordinate to her husband. He argued that this change represented an evolutionary development and not simply two different systems, citing the transitional case of Roman law, which declared a married woman's legal status to be that of her husband's "fictive daughter" (1970:149).

Under Roman law, Maine argued, the legal status of women underwent a metamorphosis from subordination by blood to subordination by marriage. The latter form was expressed *in terms of the former*, as evidenced by the use of the concept "fictive daughter." Roman jurisprudence was thus shown to represent the historical transition Maine needed to argue for the veracity of his evolutionary analysis of the "Law of Persons."

Maine's use of historical and literary documents, extant societies, survivals, and transitional cases to substantiate his observation of the movement from status to contract stands as an exemplary application of evolutionary methodology.

Ancient Law portrayed legal history in four distinct stages: (1) primitive law, (2) ancient law, (3) medieval law, and (4) modern law. Each stage was associated with a distinctive type of social system that Maine argued generated both the forms of legal institutions and particular jurisprudential ideas.

Maine observed that primitive societies were organized according to kinship groups. This sort of social organization, which he termed "Patriarchal," vested legal authority in the head of the family. An individual's status derived entirely from membership in a kin group. Descent, and therefore legal right, was traced through the *agnatic* blood line.[3] Maine stressed that where people were subsumed under patriarchal authority, individual legal rights were nonexistent. Dispute settlement within a lineage group was the responsibility of the patriarch, who was "absolutely supreme in his household. His dominion extends to life and death, and is as unqualified over his children and their houses as over his slaves" (Maine 1970:119).

---

[3] Maine's discussion of the significance of agnatic descent, as distinct from cognatic descent, anticipates the findings of twentieth-century British social anthropology to the effect that descent rules are structural mechanisms for ensuring nonambiguous allegiance of offspring. Maine believed that the agnatic descent system ensured a child's loyalty to the father, rather than to both the maternal grandfather *and* the father. He argued that conflicting allegiance would be an unstable influence in a society whose only form of political organization was kinbased.

This represents the original form of primitive or customary law. Legal precepts derived entirely from tradition (rather than from legislation), and the patriarch was the sole source of legal decisions, without recourse to external principles.

In Maine's second phase of customary law, an external source of legal principles and legitimation came into existence: divine inspiration. This development resulted from changes in social organization, which had progressed beyond the isolated kin group to "an aggregation of families," a form of society Maine likened to a "system of small independent corporations" linked together into a loose confederation. Law had to be elaborated in order to govern the relationships between kin groups:

> [Law] is so framed to be adjusted to a system of small independent corporations. It is therefore scanty, because it is supplemented by the despotic command of the heads of households. It is ceremonious because the transactions to which it pays regard resemble international concerns much more than the quick play of intercourse between individuals. (Maine 1970:7)

Once adjudication between families was required, an authority beyond the patriarch was needed. A "fictitious sovereignty" had to be created over the aggregation of families. Religious inspiration of legal decisions was thus understood in terms of the requirements of a more elaborate form of social organization.

The next stage in Maine's typology was that of ancient law; his model was the Roman legal system. Again, Maine's interests revolved around understanding the impact of social change on legal form. In the early days of the Republic, Roman law was codified in the form of the Twelve Decemviral Tables. This written law constituted the civil law of Rome, and its jurisdiction was strictly limited to the citizens of Rome. Although the Tables represented the formal law of the city, jurisconsults elaborated this code in the form of commentaries known as "Responsa Prudentum, the 'answers of the learned in the law.'" The status of these commentaries was officially that of interpretation; that is, they were not considered to be an independent form of legislation. However, over time they came to modify the codes and gained an independent stature nearly equal to the Tables themselves (Maine 1970:32–3). When the civil law failed to cover particular situations in Rome, the jurisconsults expanded the codified law to meet this need.

Although the civil law and the Responses applied only to Roman citizens, in later periods trade relations and immigration created links between Rome and surrounding regions. This necessitated the development of legal doctrine that could handle disputes between Roman citizens and foreigners. Rather than simply expand the jurisdiction of the civil law, the jurisconsults selected "the rules of law common to Rome and to the different Italian communities in which the immigrants were born." (Maine 1970:47). The *Jus Gentium*, as the common law was called, came to regulate relations within the Empire as its borders expanded drawing new communities within.

An illustration of the effects of this political expansion on substantive law may be found in Maine's discussion of the "Law of Persons." In Rome, the patriarchal family consisted of consanguineal kin, those outsiders "adopted" into the family via legal fictions[4], and slaves (who were included by virtue of their common subordination to the patriarch). Although legal rights were still based on family status, the notion of "family" had taken on an expanded range of reference, thus reflecting a transitional form in the movement from status to contract. In primitive law, legal status had been determined exclusively by family ties understood as kin relations. Under ancient (Roman) law, blood ties between relatives no longer constituted the only means of inclusion into the "legal family." For Maine, this development ultimately culminated in the end of the family as the source of legal personae. The breakdown of the blood tie in Rome opened the way for the elaboration of individual and universal rights under law. This evolutionary trend reached fruition in a limited sense under Maine's third stage, feudalism, and became even more significant in modern legal systems, where the dominant legal relationship is that of free contract.

This brief review of *Ancient Law* indicates that Maine saw two significant types of evolutionary development in law. On the one hand, there is the development of institutional forms: Primitive law is characterized by a lack of institutional structure beyond the authority of the patriarch. As the social and economic foundation of primitive societies expands, the structure of the legal system and

---

[4] By "legal fiction," Maine referred to "any assumption which conceals, or affects to conceal, the fact that a rule of law has undergone alteration, its letter remained unchanged, its operation being modified" (Maine 1970:24).

its sources of authority expand as well. Codification and written law appear in the ancient-law period. Here, too, political and economic expansion affect the structural organization of the legal apparatus. What begins as an authoritative code ends up as an elaborate set of responses developed by a functionally distinct body of jurists. Formal legislation makes an initial appearance in Rome and becomes fully elaborate in modern law. In sum, changing socioeconomic circumstances are the prime mover spurring the evolution of law.

The second aspect of Maine's evolutionary theory deals with the concomitant developments in substantive law. It begins as an entirely status-based determination of legal rights but ends up as free contract and a universal–impersonal application of statutes in the modern period. Maine's discussion of testamentary law and property law attests to the generality of the movement from status to contract across various areas of law.

Emile Durkheim: from repressive to restitutive law

In the Introduction to *The Division of Labor in Society*, Durkheim notes that his intentions are twofold: to determine the function of the division of labor and to determine the causes and conditions on which it depends (Durkheim 1933). The significance of Durkheim's work for the student of legal development goes well beyond these goals. *The Division of Labor* demonstrated a correspondence between the forms of social structure and forms of law and provided a causal theory that united the two.

Giddens (1978:27) points out that Durkheim's general ambition was to show that moral codes could be understood in the same way that we understand other "social facts": by describing them, classifying them, and searching for laws that explain their appearance. For Durkheim, explanatory laws of moral facts must be based upon the recognition that "moral codes are grounded in the social conditions of existence, such that forms of morality appropriate to one society would be quite inappropriate in the context of another." The scientific analysis of moral rules will uncover these "conditions and thereby show what are the moral codes demanded by any particular type of society" (Giddens 1978:28).

However, moral phenomena are not directly observable. They can be studied only by examining "external indices" that measure changes on the surface of society indicative of the evolution of underlying moral codes. Legal systems represent just such an index because laws express moral prescriptions in a formal and codified fashion. Consequently, an empirical investigation of variation in legal codes will lead to conclusions about moral evolution (Durkheim 1933:64–8).

Durkheim's interest in moral codes went beyond their intrinsic philosophical status. He was concerned with a larger social issue, one that preoccupied the intellectual leaders of his day (Tonnies, Spencer, Comte, and others), namely, the "nature of social solidarity itself." Lukes (1972:139) notes that Durkheim's concern was to discover how industrial societies maintain social solidarity and how this condition had developed historically out of traditional or preindustrial cultures. Moral codes were understood as the "glue" holding social systems together, producing configurations that Durkheim referred to as forms of social solidarity.

Classifying moral codes through systems of legal rules inevitably requires the sorting of the latter into different categories. This Durkheim did according to the kinds of sanctions employed in law. He identified two important types of sanctions, repressive and restitutive:

> "Repressive sanctions" are those associated with penal law: these consist in the inflicting of some form of suffering, such as loss of liberty or even loss of life . . . "Restitutive sanctions" . . . involve the restoration of the state of affairs which existed prior to the transgression of the law. The object of restitutive law is readjustment, or parity, rather than punishment. (Giddens 1978:29)

Legal codes could be classified as either repressive or restitutive according to the quantitative predominance of one type of sanction over the other.

Durkheim argued that these two forms of law were associated with specific social conditions: mechanical and organic solidarity (see Figure 1.1). Indeed, it is the existence of the forms of solidarity (which are themselves products of the division of labor or its absence) that gives rise to legal codes.

Durkheim's model of "mechanical" societies differs little from Maine's view of primitive society. Individuals are entirely subordinate to the social group. Political and economic organization revolves around kinship, and the division of labor is virtually absent.

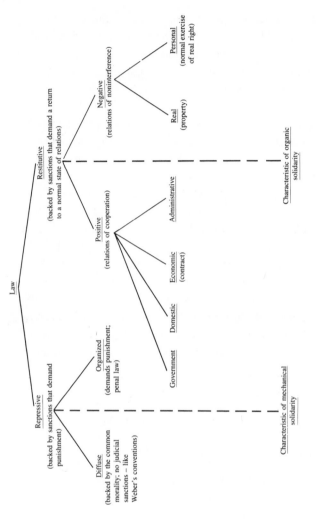

Figure 1.1 A Schematic Representation of Durkheim's Typology of Law

Individuals all resemble each other, both physically and mentally.[5] Because everyone in a mechanical society performs essentially the same tasks and because there is little in the way of status differentiation, the members share a common world view, "the collective conscience."[6]

All societies share a collective conscience, since all individuals within them share at least some experiences and some aspects of a common world view. Under conditions of mechanical solidarity, the experiential worlds of society's members overlap completely. Yet, at the same time, individuals are economically (though not politically) independent of each other. As self-sufficient producers, they have little need to rely upon each other. The significance and strength of the common conscience grows with the lack of interdependence. There is little else holding a mechanical society together.

Any threat to the collective sentiments of the community thus constitutes a challenge to the very fabric of society. Repressive law protects the primitive society from breakdowns in mechanical solidarity by the threat of punishment. Repressive law represents the collective vengeance of undifferentiated social orders. The process of punishment as it is manifest in penal law reinforces the sentiments and values of mechanical solidarity, thus bolstering the collective conscience.

As populations grow, and "moral density" increases, mechanical solidarity gives way to a more complex and differentiated form of society characterized by a well-developed division of labor. The repetitive and unitary nature of existence in mechanical society is replaced by functional interdependence or organic solidarity, where specialization characterizes an individual's occupation as well as

---

[5] Durkheim's discussion of the physical resemblances among primitive peoples causes consternation among modern social scientists and accusations of nineteenth-century racism. However, as Harris (1968) has pointed out, Durkheim insisted that sociocultural realities could not be explained as expressions of racial similarities since diverse organizational forms could be found among peoples of the same race and similarities obtained between peoples of different races.

[6] Durkheim defined the collective conscience as follows: "The totality of beliefs and sentiment common to average citizens of the same society forms a determinant system which has its own life; one may call it the collective or common conscience. . . . It is . . . independent of the particular conditions in which individuals are placed; they pass on and it remains. . .it connects successive generations with one another. It is, thus, an entirely different thing from particular consciences, although it can be realized only through them" (Durkheim 1933:78–9).

his or her social existence and moral experience. The collective conscience becomes more general and abstract and no longer pervades every corner of life, since the common activity that underlies mechanical solidarity has diminished.

Interdependence takes its place as the guarantor of social stability in a differentiated society. The division of labor renders individuals non-self-sufficient; they become reliant upon each other for the fulfillment of basic needs (Durkheim 1933:173).

How is this transition in social organization expressed in law? No longer the guardian of the common conscience, the law loses its punitive aspects, becoming restitutive instead, the facilitator of cooperative relations. The central characteristic of law under the division of labor is that it seeks to return conflictual relations to their former, normal states. It does so by specifying either the way in which certain spheres (e.g., domestic, economic) are to be coordinated, thus eliminating as much disruption as possible from the outset, or by specifying relations of noninterference. Restitutive law is required in order to keep organic solidarity functioning smoothly (Lukes 1972:155).

Having laid out the fundamental connection between the two forms of law and the two types of solidarity, Durkheim turned to the empirical evidence (as he knew it) and discovered that traditional, preindustrial societies indeed had laws that were predominantly penal. As the evolution of society progresses toward a more highly developed division of labor, the proportion of restitutive laws overtakes those of a repressive character. This he took as scientific evidence for his theory of moral evolution as measured or indexed by legal change.

The significance of Durkheim's theory of legal development is that he grounded it in "the conditions of social existence." Law is viewed as both reflective of underlying forms of social organization (and morality) *and* as an institution that caters to the specific requirements of these social structures, thus perpetuating them. Durkheim's analysis linked structural features of society (principally the division of labor) to moral forms via law. Where others, for example, Maine, were content to outline a scientifically grounded *history* of law, Durkheim sought a sociological (causal) explanation of its form and content.

Unfortunately, as Lukes (1972:159–60) has pointed out, Durkheim's theory of legal evolution suffered from the poor quality of the available data on preindustrial law and social organization (a point I will reconsider in Chapter 5). As such, his thesis is generally rejected today. Nevertheless, the effort to link law to socioeconomic structure remains a primary concern.

Karl Marx and Friedrich Engels shared this orientation and Durkheim's concern with the division of labor. However, their theory of historical materialism assigns a very different role to law and provides a distinct analysis of social change.

Karl Marx and Friedrich Engels: law and historical materialism

There is a long and varied tradition of Marxist writings on law and legal development. Marx and Engels themselves never provided a complete theory of law, but rather expressed their views on law in the process of discussing larger philosophical and historical themes. As a result, writers in the Marxian tradition have been confronted with numerous fragmentary passages on law in Marx's and Engels's writings, which they have synthesized in an attempt to build a Marxist theory of law. However, since the fragments themselves are not entirely consistent, room has been left open for divergent interpretations, all of which may legitimately claim the imprimatur of Marx and Engels.

One of the more heated controversies to emerge from the recent literature concerns the extent to which Marx and Engels argued for a "determinist" view of law in relation to economic forces. This problematic has traditionally been addressed by quoting passages that stress the dependence of superstructural institutions upon the system of material production, as in the following well-known excerpt:

> The sum total of [the] relations of production constitutes the economic structure of society, the real foundation, on which rises a legal and political superstructure and to which correspond definite forms of social consciousness. (Marx in Tucker 1972:4)

An extreme determinist reading of this statement would suggest that the agenda, form, and content of law are directly derived from the economic relations of production, with no reciprocal causation admitted. The metaphor of "reflection" characterizes this position.

Although it seems reasonable to interpret Marx as believing that economic relations between classes determine the nature of property in any given society, and that this in turn defines the core areas of law, one can also find statements that indicate an understanding of the reciprocal effect, whereby law molds social development:

> According to the materialist conception of history, the *ultimately* determining factor in history is the production and reproduction of real life. . . . If somebody twists this into saying that the economic factor is the *only* determining one, he transforms that proposition into a meaningless, abstract, absurd phrase. The economic situation is the basis, but the various elements of the superstructure . . . such as constitutions . . . juridical forms . . . political, legal, philosophical theories . . . also exercise their influence . . . There is an interaction of all these elements in which . . . the economic movement is finally bound to assert itself. (Engels to Bloch, in Cain and Hunt 1979:56)

Whichever reading was actually intended by Marx and Engels, contemporary Marxist scholars have advanced the view that superstructural institutions exist in reciprocal interaction. Each has a certain causal influence on the others, but retains a degree of independence.

The most influential proponent of this position is Louis Althusser (1969), who identifies three levels of social structure (or "instances," as he terms them): the economic, the political, and the ideological. In different modes of production, different "instances" will be dominant, that is, will play the major causal role. Nevertheless, each instance is "relatively autonomous." We take this to mean that each develops its own idiom and institutional form. Similarly, according to Althusser, each instance has its own history, that is, its own logic of development.

Although Althusser admits that the economy is "determinant in the last instance," he has clearly diverged from the more traditional reading of Marx and Engels, which lays much greater emphasis on economic causation. The Althusserian image seems to be one whereby each area of social structure *sets limits* for the others, but the content and form of each remains at least partially autonomous.

In discussing law, Althusserian or Structural Marxists argue that:

> Law is always under the control of the ruling class in the broad sense but it does not *always* originate in economic class conflict, function well for the ruling class, reflect the full range of ruling class opinion,

remain immune from the lawyers and bureaucrats who administer it, or serve economic ends. (Sumner 1979:255)

The actors who shape the law are not necessarily economic classes, nor is the agenda of law limited to the regulation of economic relations. However, whatever the degree of relative autonomy between law and economy, it is nevertheless clear that the Marxian paradigm as it was originally articulated posits a strong relation between the two realms. These relations are perhaps best understood in terms of the functions of law from the perspective of historical materialism.

Marx and Engels discussed three principal functions of law: ideological, political, and economic. These realms are always intertwined in the texts themselves; I separate them here for the purposes of analytic clarity.

Ideologies are sets of concepts and beliefs that describe and explain the world. Within the Marxian framework, ideologies are typically viewed as representing the position of a particular class in society and as such tend to be incomplete or biased systems of knowledge. Law may be seen as a form of ideology that describes social relationships and expresses a social morality. (See Sumner 1979 for a thorough treatment of this issue.)

As an ideological system, law performs in two ways. On the one hand, it legitimates the social order by presenting existing social relationships as normal, desirable, and just. On the other hand, according to Marx and Engels, law also fulfills an ideological function by obscuring and mystifying the true nature of social relations. Through doctrinal language, it presents an image of "legal man" detached from his foundations and stripped of his reality as "economic man." Law describes and guarantees a social realm of equality and liberty for all, which is *false* insofar as it ignores underlying socioeconomic inequalities. For example, the law regards an employment contract as an agreement freely concluded by two equal parties (employer and employee), whereas Marx argued that the propertyless laborer is *coerced* into selling his labor, given his inability to subsist any other way. The employer is *not* equal to the worker; in practice the former sets his own terms. Engels made a similar point with respect to the marriage contract: It obscures and disguises the subordination of wives. Law hides these realities behind the seemingly universal language of contract and as such is performing an ideological function.

Law is also ideological insofar as it represents people as isolated individuals – the citizen – rather than as members of classes. It is precisely one's inclusion in such groups that Marx argued determines one's social existence. Law therefore obscures relationships or conflicts between classes by presenting them as connections between individuals.

The second function of law in the Marxian tradition concerns its political role. Law is viewed as an instrument by which classes struggle to improve their lot vis-à-vis others. In most cases, the ruling classes will have the greatest access to law as a tool for furthering their interests. Marx described the Enclosure Acts, the Vagrancy Statutes, wage-reduction legislation, and the like as instances whereby property owners utilized the legal process to confiscate land, force the idle to work, and push down wages. Analyzing a series of statutes from the thirteenth century on, Marx showed that their cumulative effect was the creation of a landless proletariat (Marx 1970:672–93).

However, those in power are not the only actors seeking to use the law for their own ends. The role of law in the political arena is also seen in the struggle of nondominant classes to improve their living conditions by placing legal limitations on their opponents. Marx's discussion in *Capital* of the workers' struggle to enforce a maximum workday is an example of this latter type.

It is important to note that this "instrumentalist" reading of the political functions of law has been subject to considerable criticism by subsequent Marxist theorists, including Pashukanis (1978), Cain and Hunt (1979), and Sumner (1979). As Greenburg and Anderson (1981:295) put it, "instrumentalism exaggerates the extent of direct ruling class control over law." These objections are addressed to a position that overstates the influence of *one group* over the legal apparatus. However, most adherents to the Marxist tradition would agree that the law is an arena of struggle between groups and that particular laws can be read in many cases (though not all) as expressing the outcome of such conflicts. In this sense, law fulfills a political function.

Law also plays a crucial role or function in the economic realm. For Marx and Engels, social inequality flows from unequal access to basic resources, which are expressed in terms of property law. By defining and guaranteeing the rights of property owners, law regulates basic relationships between individuals. Another aspect of this involves the legal regulation of labor, either by contract or by traditional rules regarding pay, hours, and the mutual obligations obtaining between employers and employees.

All important economic relationships from the factory to the family find their expression in legal doctrine, which in turn guarantees a stable basis for economic production. As Engels put it:

> At a certain, very primitive stage of the development of society, the need arises to bring under a common rule the daily recurring acts of production, distribution and exchange of products, to see to it that the individual subordinates himself to the common conditions of production and exchange. This rule, which at first is custom, soon becomes *law*. (Quoted in Cain and Hunt 1979:55)

As this sketch indicates, Marx and Engels believed that law cross-cuts the ideological, political, and economic realms. Particular laws may address any or all three of these.

We will now turn to the theory of legal development they proposed. From their general perspective of historical materialism, Marx and Engels argued that in any given society legal change follows on the heels of developments in the economic mode of production. The best-known statement to this view is found in the preface to *A Contribution to the Critique of Political Economy*:

> At a certain stage of their development, the material productive forces of society come in conflict with the existing relations of production, or – what is but a legal expression of the same thing – with the property relations within which they have been at work hitherto . . . With the change of the economic foundation the entire immense superstructure is more or less rapidly transformed. (Marx in Tucker 1972:4)

As the forces of production develop, Marx and Engels suggested that the legal and political superstructure would eventually fetter the productive forces. Revolution would follow, which would overhaul the legal relations in society, once again bringing about a correspondence between the material foundation and the superstructure.

Marx and Engels did not elaborate this theory of legal change beyond this general formulation. It was left to later theorists, such as Karl Renner, to apply this framework. Renner was a Marxist scholar writing in the early 1900s. His book, *The Institutions of Private Law and Their Social Functions* (1949), is a classic work in the Marxist theory of legal development, although it is much criticized (cf. Sumner 1979:248–9, Cain and Hunt 1979:65). In it, Renner argued that an adequate understanding of the relationship between law and economy *cannot* be based on static studies of one historical period. Only by considering the connections between these two realms in the context of historical change can an adequate understanding be developed (Renner 1949:58). Renner's theory of legal evolution is based upon an examination of the transformations in law and society that took place between two important historical epochs: independent commodity production and early capitalism.

Renner's theory of legal change is explicitly analogous to one of the central tenets of Marx's theory of social change; namely, that the forces of production develop faster and therefore "out-distance" the social relations of production, finally coming into contradiction with them. Renner argued that:

> The historical development of the law, and the growth of individual laws and their decay, flow from the disparate development of the legal and economic institutions . . . The change in the social functions of legal institutions takes place in a sphere beyond the reach of the law and eventually necessitates a transformation of the norms of the law. (Renner 1949:52)

Renner presented a three-stage developmental model of legal change. The first stage consists of a point in time when law "matches" the social and economic circumstances from which it originates. During the second stage, transformations take place in the economic sphere (particularly in the organization of production), while the content of legal norms *does not* undergo any noticeable transformation. However, though the law itself has not altered, its social *functions* have undergone a drastic transformation: Preexisting legal doctrines combine to fulfill the social functions required by the new economic situation. The third stage of Renner's theory is the least explicated. He suggested that, over the long run, legal norms undergo a transformation in content such that they again correspond to the economic circumstances of their time.

Renner's discussion of transitions in property law provides an example of this thesis. In the age of simple commodity production, people owned their own means of production, sold their products directly to consumers, and were the owners of their homes and land. It was at this stage that the Roman law of *dominium* was adopted, which specified that individuals had the right "to free and unfettered control over tangible things." At the same time, a companion law emerged that allowed independent producers to purchase raw materials and sell finished products: the norm of free contract. Renner suggested that, at this point "the world of norms was . . . fully adapted to the substratum, the world of facts."

Gradually, however, simple commodity production gave way to classical capitalism. The independent producer became a wage laborer. He no longer owned the means of production: it owned him. He occupied his house as a tenant rather than as an owner. Despite these socioeconomic changes, the content of the law remained unchanged. How were these structural transformations dealt with by the law? Renner answered that the laws of property and contract were combined to accommodate the new arrangement. Workers themselves became "property" in the sense that the capitalists could now own their labor power.

> But what is control of property in law, becomes in fact man's control of human beings, of the wage laborers . . . We see that the right of ownership thus assumes a new social function. Without any change in the norm, . . . a *de facto* right is added to the personal absolute domination over a corporeal thing. This right is not based upon a special legal provision. It is the power of control, the power to issue commands and to enforce them. (Renner 1949:107)

One reading of Marx would lead the researcher to look for transformations in the institutional structures or substantive content of law as one economic epoch gives way to the next. In contrast, Renner suggested that an analysis of changing *functions* of legal doctrines rather than institutional structures will provide a better understanding of the transformation of law.

The Marxist theories outlined in this section derived from studies of law under capitalism (or from the transition between feudalism and capitalism). Hobsbawm (1965:20) has pointed out that Marx's interest in preindustrial epochs was directed more toward understanding them as crucibles of emerging bourgeois society than analyzing them for their own sake. What light, if any, does the Marxist theory of legal development then shed on the evolution of legal institutions in precapitalist or preindustrial cultures? I would argue that by using the general approach of historical materialism, one can anticipate what a Marxist anthropology of law would look like. Marx and Engels argued that each mode of production contained within itself a distinctive set of superstructural institutions (including law), which were an integral part of the reproduction of that mode of production. Thus, if we examine the successive epochs of human history as distinct modes of production, we should expect to find particular forms of political and juridical systems associated with them. Although this observation is not made explicit in the two works that deal with precapitalist societies (*The Origin of the Family, Private Property, and the State* [Engels 1942] and *Pre-Capitalist Economic Formations* [Marx 1965]), shadows of the theory are visible therein.

In the Preface to the first edition of *The Origin of the Family*, Engels (1942:5) noted that the "materialistic conception" of history posits the production and reproduction of life's immediate essentials as the determining factor shaping social life in any given period. The production of food and clothing, dwellings, and tools constitutes one part of this, whereas the reproduction of human beings themselves composes the other. Thus the "stage of development of labor on the one hand and of the family on the other" determines "the social organization under which the people of a particular historical epoch live" (Engels 1942:5).

According to Engels, societies characterized by low levels of labor organization (i.e., hunters and gatherers) are able to produce nothing more than what they require for subsistence. Wealth distinctions are unknown, for accumulation of any kind is unknown. The social order of such societies is "dominated by kinship groups" (Engels 1942:6). Engels took Morgan's (1912) description of American Indians as a case in point: With an economy based on the sexual division of labor and hunting technology, individuals own their means of production and households are communally organized.

Blood revenge and war constitute the only means for settling conflict in these societies. There is "no place for ruler or ruled" (Engels 1942:144). Participation in public affairs is required of all. To modern ears, the equation of blood revenge with participatory democracy is curious. Nevertheless, Engels's larger point is that where individuals control their means of production, they also have equal access to juridical life, such as it is. They confront public life unmediated by separate, specialized institutions of law and government.

At a subsequent stage of social development, the productivity of labor increases and "private property and exchange, differences of wealth [and] the possibility of utilizing the labor power of others," follows. Engels (1942:6) traced this transformation through pastoral, horticultural, and agrarian forms of production. He connected the emergence of slavery to the increased demands for labor wrought by these new technologies and argued that classes begin to emerge as property rights to land and control over slave labor develop. Hereditary military leaders arise to defend the privileges of the rich from the demands of the poor, and their existence lays the foundation for a hereditary nobility and monarchy (Engels 1942:150).

Amid these class-based cleavages, the old society based on kinship dissolves and "in its place appears a new society, with its control centered in the State" (Engels 1942:6), organized on the basis of territoriality rather than blood ties. Taxation is instituted to support a "public force" that bolsters state power. Class antagonisms bring forth "armed men, . . . prisons and coercive institutions of all kinds" (Engels 1942:156). The state arises "in the thick of the fight between the classes," but it is dominated by the economically powerful, who cultivate political control through the exercise of state authority.

Although Engels refrained from discussing law per se within this framework, legal institutions are clearly meant to be associated with the emergence of the state. Equally clear, I would argue, is the thrust of his argument: Such superstructural institutions as law that stand between the disadvantaged many and the privileged few grow and become elaborated as a result of improvements in the productive capacity of a society, the consequent growth in economic surplus, and the resulting class antagonisms. The state, and the legal apparatus that supports it, is necessary to control these internal conflicts and to regulate property and labor relations.

The theory of legal development sketched in this section is far less elaborated than Marx and Engels's general theory of precapitalist society. Both theories are weakened by the poor quality of the data that formed the basis of their original arguments. However, an approach similar to theirs will be taken up with modern techniques and more reliable data sources in Chapter 3.

Max Weber: rationalization and the law

Max Weber, the German polymath, was familiar with socialism as
a political movement and with historical materialism as a social
theory. Neither suited him. In particular, he took exception to (the
traditional reading of) the materialist view of law as servant to the
economic requirements of capitalism. He preferred to see a larger
variety of forces (economic, organizational, political, and ideological) acting to shape and constrain law. Moreover, he argued that
law evolves at least in part from the momentum of its own internal
logic. (In this regard, Weber's views have much in common with
Althusserian Marxism.)

The factors molding law were subsumed under a theory of increasing "rationalization," which Weber viewed as the master trend
in world history. The term "rationalization" encompasses several
elements: (1) increasing predictability of outcomes of action, (2)
increasing explicitness of principles of action and decision, (3) increasing internal logical coherence in administrative and legal rules,
(4) the conscious molding of institutions to achieve decided-upon
ends, and (5) the use of scientific rather than religious explanations
of causality.

In *Economy and Society*, Weber (1954) traced the origin of rationalization back to primitive law. In the section on Maine, I
discussed his description of the inspirational, or magical, basis of
legal decisions in the era of primitive law. Weber noted that this
magical basis "tended to more rational norm-formation, because
it required that the question to be asked [of the deity] had to be
precisely formulated" (Weber 1954:74). Appeal to a divine authority provides the distinctive break between custom (the earliest
stage of primitive law) and enacted law. Whereas under customary
law, timeless tradition formed the source of legal principles, the
advent of "oracles" opened the way for legislating social rules.[7]
Primitive law reveals indications of incipient formal procedure and
legislative enactment.

These early forms of rational procedure developed further under
the impetus of changes in political organization. Here, Weber followed Maine in suggesting that early law was derived from relations
between kin groups. In the absence of an administrative "umbrella"

---

[7] Weber argued that "revealed" law was the "parent of all types of legal rules" in
that it undermined tradition as the only source of decision (Weber 1954:76).

regulating intercourse between kin groups, law was developed to serve as a common authority for dispute settlement. Weber found that there were

> arbitration proceedings, originating in arrangements made between kinship groups and relating to the proof and composition of alleged injury. . . . Only in relations between kinship groups do we find established formalities, limitations as to time, rules of evidence, etc., that is, the beginnings of "judicial" procedure. (Weber 1954:46)

In short, customary law existed within families where authority was basically patriarchal, but the dawn of judicial procedure is found in intergroup relations.

As we move toward state societies, we find that changes in political organization continue to act as catalysts for legal rationalization. In state societies, administrative bureaucracies developed gradually as a means through which political rulers controlled their realms. Weber argued that organizational rationality was first forged in these "crude" bureaucracies. As these agencies grew larger and more rational themselves, legal institutions followed suit.

Legal rationalization in early state societies did not result from deliberate planning by political rulers. The "needs of their own administrative machinery" provided part of the impetus (Weber 1954:224). Where these pressures were absent, "the secularization of the law" and the development of codified law "either remained in an incipient stage or was even positively counteracted" (Weber 1954:225).

The emergence of a distinct legal profession has an ambiguous impact upon rationalization of the law, according to Weber. Where legal education is in the hands of practitioners (e.g., attorneys) there is a strong incentive *not* to rationalize the law. Practitioners prefer arcane language and nonsystematic legal doctrine, for this guarantees their privileged position as interpreters of otherwise unintelligible laws (Weber 1954:201–3). In contrast, where legal education is placed in the hands of legal scholars who are not practitioners (e.g., in universities), an interest develops in systematizing law. Hence legal rationalization increases with the rise of law schools (Weber 1954:204).[8]

---

[8] See Weber's (1954) essay on "The Legal Honoratoires and the Types of Legal Thought."

One final source of legal rationalization in Weber's scheme is the requirements of the economic order. As Rheinstein (1954) notes, Weber's discussion of the influence of economics is, in part, a response to the work of Karl Marx. In contrast to Marx as he read him, Weber stressed the multidimensionality of the relationship between law and the economy. He argued that economic influence in legal rationalization derives from the demands of market systems for calculable outcomes:

> To be sure, economic influences have played their part, but only to this extent: that certain rationalizations of economic behavior based upon such phenomena as a market economy or freedom of contract . . . have influenced the systematization of the law. (Weber 1954:61)

A second way Weber treated economic forces was as an articulation of class interests (and here, of course, he came closer to Marx's perspective). The movement from status contracts to "free" contracts occurred largely because of the political clout of property owners "who are economically privileged in the formally free competitive struggle of the market" and who therefore stood to benefit as a class from the introduction of free contract.

Summarizing Weber's views on the driving force in legal evolution, four distinct sources of rationalization are at work: (1) procedural needs, (2) demands of political organization, (3) the interests of legal professions, and (4) the requirements of the economic order.

The trend toward rationalization is manifested in the substance of particular laws and in forms of legal legitimacy, by which Weber meant the sources of validity that support the law. He identified an evolutionary trend in the kinds of legitimacy observable in legal history: They evolve from the earliest form, validity based on the sacredness of tradition; to legitimacy drawn from the authority of prophet or oracles; to validity based on a belief in Natural Law. They culminate in the modern form of legitimacy: the rule of law, a belief in the validity of a legal order for its own sake. In Weber's view, this sequence represents a decline in irrational or religiously inspired belief systems and a rise in rationality.

The same trend is identified in forms of legal "logic," which refers to the basis for rendering legal judgments. Here again, Weber saw a progressive development away from unsystematic decision making in the law and toward fully formal and rule-governed forms of legal logic. As Figure 1.2 illustrates, the earliest form of law is described as substantive and irrational: Decisions are made particularistically on the basis of reactions to individual cases. When oracles appear, a formal irrational law, an appeal to a higher authority, replaces reaction to particular cases, though a general rule structure for rendering judgment is still lacking.

The next stage involves the development of rules of procedure and substantive codes (rational law). Initially, these codes are closely tied to ideological principles (e.g., religious or other values). As rationalization reaches its zenith, we arrive at the final stage. Here legal systems become internally elaborated: The law formulates its own concepts, doctrines, and procedures and thereby grows autonomous from the world of religious and secular values. Law and morality become separate realms.

Although Weber would have balked at being identified as an evolutionist, he saw the thrust of rationalization as a constant force that transformed the law. As I have pointed out, he thought that this trend had a number of sources, each of which was "activated" during particular historical periods. There can be little doubt that he thought of legal history as consisting of a developmental sequence:

> The formal qualities of the law emerge as follows: arising in primitive legal procedure from a combination of magically conditioned formalism and irrationality conditioned by revelation, they proceed to increasingly specialized juridical and logical rationality and systematization, passing through a stage of theocratically or patrimonially conditioned substantive and informal expediency. Finally, they assume . . . an increasingly logical sublimation and deductive rigor and develop an increasingly rational technique in procedure. (Weber 1954:304)

Certainly Weber abhorred unicausal models and overgeneralization. His own explanation for the master trend of rationalization is therefore multicausal and grounded in historical examples. Yet Weber clearly argued that progressive changes could be observed in the form and logic of legal institutions.

Conclusion

Certain common themes emerge from the theories of legal evolution proposed by Maine, Durkheim, Marx and Engels, and Weber. For

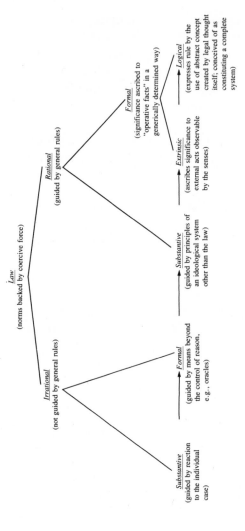

Figure 1.2 A Taxonomic Classification of Forms of Legal Logic

Law
(norms backed by coercive force)

Irrational
(not guided by general rules)

Rational
(guided by general rules)

Substantive
(guided by reaction
to the individual
case)

Formal
(guided by means beyond
the control of reason,
e.g., oracles)

Substantive
(guided by principles of
an ideological system
other than the law)

Formal
(significance ascribed to
"operative facts" in a
generically determined way)

Extrinsic
(ascribes significance to
external acts observable
by the senses)

Logical
(expresses rule by the
use of abstract concept
created by legal thought
itself; conceived of as
constituting a complete
system)

→ indicates developmental sequence

these scholars, the original human society consisted of the patriarchal family. The division of labor was completely absent. Consequently, each family constituted an independent entity. There was nothing in the way of a systematic legal code; the commands of the patriarch were not guaranteed by an external legitimizing force, nor were they subject to demands for internal consistency.

The first signs of an appeal to external authority were to be found among those customary societies that vested faith in revelation. Divine oracles received direction from a mystical source, and it is here that we find the beginning of legal procedure. For there is now the notion that judgments must exhibit some sort of consistency.

When commerce, marriage, and other forms of social intercourse began to bind independent families together (even in the most tenuous fashion), some suprafamilial administrative or legal institutions were created. The position of the patriarch may have remained strong within each family, but interfamily relations were now under the legal jurisdiction of an "independent" body. This occurred concomitantly with the beginnings of the division of labor. As the complexity of labor organization increased, kin-based authority declined and independent institutions grew progressively stronger. With the demise of kinship as the primary legal foundation of the social order came the end of the status-based concept of the legal "person" and the rise of free contractual relations. From Marx and Engels's viewpoint, this signaled the birth of class relations, which are expressed in law as property rights.

The development of legal institutions from this point forward was determined by the expansion of the social system. For Maine, this expansion was demonstrated by the inclusion of more and more diverse social groups under the rubric of one political authority (the Roman Empire). For Durkheim, the expansion was a by-product of the increasing division of labor, which brought about increasing social and economic interdependence, paving the way for restitutive law and organic solidarity. Marx and Engels's dialectical approach viewed legal expansion as an expression of increased stratification and unequal access to the means of production. As property systems developed and grew more elaborate, and as systems of labor exploitation expanded, so did the role of law. For Weber, the biggest break occurred with the advent of a market economy. Whichever analysis of socioeconomic change one chooses, for these theorists the law responds to (and in some cases paves the way for) these material realities.

As law became more complex, its content also changed, reflecting the requirements and benefits of rationalization. In addition, specialized legal practitioners emerged. Well-versed in the intricacies of the law, they wielded independent power by virtue of their monopoly over legal knowledge and practice and thereby became an important force for legal change.

What are The underlying forces moving this developmental scheme along this path? The classical theorists differ on this point. However, this much they hold in common: The prime mover of legal evolution is the increase in socioeconomic differentiation and stratification that can be observed throughout history. With each additional stage of complexity, larger and more varied groups of individuals fall under one legal-administrative umbrella. This pattern of inclusion is registered within the legal framework by the advent of definitive codes, the expansion of authority beyond that derived from status-based systems, the rise of contractual relations, and the efforts of dominant classes to gain control over the legal apparatus.

The accuracy of these various claims has been criticized by contemporary writers, who have access to a data base far superior for the study of legal development. In the next section, I examine what new perspectives have emerged from these more recent efforts.

Part two: contemporary theories of legal development

In constructing a summary of modern analyses of legal change, one is struck by the lack of a coherent "program" in the literature, especially when compared with the emphasis on evolutionism in the studies of the classical genre. With a few exceptions, modern theorists eschew the evolutionary paradigm; little in the way of a uniform theoretical approach has been put in its place.

A caveat must be entered here. The contemporary literature on legal development consists of contributions from scholars in many disciplines. By right, members of the "sociological jurisprudence" school (including Pound [1930] and more recent writers, e.g., Nonet and Selznick [1978]) should be included in any general discussion of this topic. However, I have limited myself primarily to contemporary anthropological perspectives on legal development because they focus most explicitly on preindustrial societies.

Only a few anthropologists have embraced an evolutionary perspective on law. Hoebel, Fried, and Black come closest to such an approach; the bulk of our attention is thus focused on them. More limited consideration will be given to several others (e.g., Gluckman, Nader) who have made important contributions to legal ethnography, but who have not focused on the theoretical topic of legal evolution.

E. Adamson Hoebel and The Law of Primitive Man

The Law of Primitive Man is one of the most important contemporary evolutionary treatments of preindustrial legal systems. Hoebel himself objects to such a characterization because he equates evolutionism with a unilinear view of social development: an inevitable progression of "stages" through which societies must pass. Like many other anthropologists, Hoebel is unwilling to commit to such a position.[9] At most, he is inclined to recognize a general increase in the complexity of legal institutions understood as a synchronic range of variation:

> Viewed synchronically, it is possible and wholly proper to treat the several law systems that are analyzed in [*The Law of Primitive Man*] as representing no more than a range of variation arranged on a scale of lesser to greater complexity with no inference as to growth sequence. (Hoebel 1968:290)

Although one may hold in abeyance a concern for the "growth sequence," most evolutionists would recognize Hoebel's methods as the first step in the formulation of any reasonable developmental paradigm. Maine, Durkheim, Weber, and others all organized synchronic data in terms of increasing complexity.

Drawing diachronic inferences from a synchronic "slice" can be justified if one is willing to grant that similar material conditions give rise to similar social institutions. By comparing the material cultures of extant societies with the archaeological record, one can make reasonable assumptions regarding the kinds of legal institutions that probably prevailed before recorded history. One can do

---

[9] Hoebel argued against unilinear theories of legal development on the grounds that "there has been no straight line of development in the growth of law" (Hoebel 1968:288). He believed that legal variation could be explained as local adaptations to socioecological conditions, rather than as a unilineal pattern of stages, one following the next.

so on the assumption that the primitive societies one can observe
or for which written records exist are similar to those in prehistory
with the same level of technological sophistication. If one sees legal
systems of a particular kind recur among various hunting-and-gathering groups, one can assume that extinct foraging cultures of the
same type practiced similar kinds of law. Utilizing what archaeology
can tell us about the evolution of technological systems (hunting-
and-gathering, horticulture, etc.), one can construct sequences of
legal forms as well. Hoebel recognized the validity of such a
procedure:

> What we can do by comparative study and causal association with
> known material remnants of early cultures is to generalize the broad
> characteristics of social institutions that probably were present, and
> we can negatively assert their absence if such institutions and forms
> are not found in directly observed hunting and collecting cultures.
>
> Thus can some of the main lines in the trend of legal forms from
> primal times to the present be sketched as they have unfolded through
> divergent evolution. (Hoebel 1968:291)

One must begin by determining the rough outline of the evolution
of technological systems. Hoebel's view of this evolution is shown
in the following diagram.

Hoebel's view of technological evolution

Hunting &	Hoe gardening	Plow agriculture
gathering→	Pastoralism →	Higher pastoralism
→	Modern industry	

Hoebel argues that if one examines the legal institutions of cultures
at the levels of technology given in the diagram, a trend is visible.
In the simplest of human societies, law is scarce. He is quick to
note that this does *not* mean primitive societies are more chaotic.
Quite the opposite, they are more orderly than complex societies
because "they are more homogeneous; relations are more direct
and there are fewer things to quarrel about" (Hoebel 1968:293).

Close relations increase the efficacy of informal means of social
control, rendering adjudication less necessary. Images of mechanical
solidarity abound here, though Hoebel draws conclusions clearly
at odds with Durkheim's. Where Durkheim saw punitive law emerging from undifferentiated societies, Hoebel sees more harmonious

methods at work. Law can be scarce only because social structure is simple and individuals exist in "face to face" communities.

As social structures differentiate, the homogeneous characteristics of simple societies give way to diversity, common interests are replaced by special interests, and close-knit (generally kin-based) relations no longer obtain between all members of a society. Stratification rears its head as inequalities in access rights to basic resources develop. With it comes the potential for conflict over goods. Hoebel echoes Engels in arguing that the consequence of these developments is that legal power intensifies as conflict accelerates (1968:293).

Complex societies embody inequalities of status and economics not present in simple cultures. Once groups of individuals control access to fundamental requirements of existence, both the potential for conflict and the need for more rigid means of controlling it develop. Hoebel's theory again departs from Durkheim's in claiming that social differentiation gives way to stratification and increased conflict rather than organic solidarity and restitutive law. Where Durkheim saw law as concerned with cooperative relations in societies with a high division of labor, Hoebel sees an emphasis on control and argues that the conditions of conciliation are undermined in complex cultures.

Hoebel is able to fill in the intervening steps in Durkheim's polar model of law. Hoebel traces the development of legal systems through a succession of technological stages. Thus, in hunting-and-gathering societies, where economic goods are shared by all, some rather basic mechanisms of social control operate. In general, adult males reach a consensus in situations that require dispute settlement. "The simplest societies are democratic to the point of near anarchy" (1968:294). The patriarchal authority that figures so prominently in the primitive legal systems of Weber and Maine were simply "figments of 19th century speculation." Pointing to ethnographic evidence from the Andamanese, the Shoshone, the Barama River Caribs, and the central Australian aboriginals, Hoebel suggests that the legal institutions of primitive societies are fundamentally egalitarian, emerging spontaneously in conflict situations.

Hunting-and-gathering societies in more abundant environments live in larger residential groups than those just discussed. Local populations may consolidate into a higher unit of organization, possibly into a tribal state. Although local (village) headmen will have some authority, the political heads of the largest unit will be chiefs:

> They possess attributes of authority that to some degree set them aside and above the usual run of men. A tendency to hereditary succession to chieftainship tends to be felt, but it is not yet ordinarily established as a fixed principle. (Hoebel 1968:309)

These "higher hunters" are exemplified by many of the Plains Indian societies with which Hoebel is eminently familiar. The Cheyenne, Comanche, and Kiowa cultures all exhibited this pattern of leadership. Some of the Northwest Coast societies could be included in this category as well. Legal process is not greatly modified from what it was in the simplest of hunting-and-gathering cultures, according to Hoebel. It is still largely a matter of adversaries facing each other or consensual decision making among male members of the social group. The difference is mainly one of an emergent quasi-hereditary political authority. At this level, chieftainship is not an all-powerful position: Authorities could be displaced. Incumbency remained contingent on popular support.

The "real elaboration" of the law, in Hoebel's view, begins with the growth of horticultural tribes:

> With gardening an economic base is established that permits the maintenance of larger populations within a single community. More important, more communities can be maintained within a given geographical area. The pressures to maintain peaceful equilibrium between the numerous closely interacting communities become intensified. A further growth of law and a more effective law is demanded. (Hoebel 1968:316)

The impetus for the development of law at this stage is one identified by Weber: Sustained interaction between distinct groups calls forth a regulating authority that can control intergroup grievances. What binds the groups together is an environmental base capable of supporting a larger, denser population than hunting-and-gathering technology can sustain. Horticultural production has implications for substantive law as well. Land "becomes a matter of primary interest for families and individuals." The concept of land ownership alters accordingly. Access to the means of production (to use Marx's phrase) is no longer equal and open to all; instead, land is controlled by corporate groups and individual-use rights flow from membership therein. Secondly, "chattel goods become (though still in relatively limited degree) issues of interest." An entirely new area of substantive law is thereby created, the "law of things" (as contrasted to the "law of persons").

The political and juridical expression of this intensified, land-based economy is found in a strengthened clan organization.[10] Clan organization figures prominently in substantive law, especially as the landholding unit. There is a tendency toward recognizing the clan as an exclusive unit, with collective responsibilities and rights, and collective reactions to infringements. The organizational expression of this corporate strength is usually found in the person of a clan chief and his accompanying council. Here chieftainship takes on definite attributes of power and is generally hereditary. Hoebel points to both the Ashanti and the Trobrianders as archetypal representatives of this sort of system.

Even at this stage, however, the legal authority of the chief does not entirely eclipse that of the kin groups. His role is not always central to a legal dispute. If called upon, he may render a decision; but he may not always be called upon. Therein lies the "residual" power of the kin groups.

This is essentially as far as Hoebel's scheme goes. He does not develop his theory of legal evolution beyond the horticultural level in any systematic fashion. He summarizes his basic findings as follows:

> What emerges from the data is this: within loosely organized tribes in which the local group is autonomous, trouble involving members of different local groups frequently brews physical violence which often leads to feuding; feud marks an absence of law...; yet it appears that every society has some set procedure for avoiding feud or bringing it to a halt; among the more organized tribes on the higher levels of economic and cultural growth feud is frequently prohibited by the action of a central authority representing the total social interest; this never happens on the lower levels of culture.
>
> As the scope of commonality expands, as community of interest reaches out beyond the local group, beyond the clan and self-conscious kindred, men find the means to create and implement judicial and executive power in such a way that internecine strife within the

---

[10] Hoebel regarded the clan structure as particularly well adapted to horticultural societies because "of its usefulness as an administrative unit in the allocation of land rights. In virtually every horticultural society it holds *de facto* control of the land..." (Hoebel 1968:317).

bounds of the larger society is checked and ultimately suppressed. (Hoebel 1968:330)

Hoebel is one of the very few anthropologists who attempts to build a comparative–evolutionary theory on the basis of post-nineteenth-century ethnographic data. He is among an even smaller minority who advocate something approaching a materialist perspective of legal development. He argues that the driving force behind the evolution of law is the development of resource bases capable of sustaining ever larger populations, organized in increasingly more complex forms. Legal institutions develop in response to the need to regulate conflicts emerging from these more complicated social structures; legal principles (e.g., concepts of property) become more prominent as the economic system provides for the possibility of group and individual control over resources.

There are three essential problems with Hoebel's work in this regard: (1) He does not explore the legal systems of a number of the technological bases shown in the diagram above; thus, he leaves us with an incomplete theory. (2) He does not subject his theory to any kind of systematic test. He illustrates his insights by reference to particular ethnographies. Yet without some form of hypothesis testing there is no way of knowing whether Hoebel's theory could account for the variation in legal institutions recorded in the ethnographic literature. (3) Within the technological systems he does discuss, his theory of the relationship between resource base, stratification, social organization, and law is not well specified. He appears to be arguing for a form of technological determinism, which would explain his lumping two gardening societies, the Trobriands and the Ashanti, into one category. Yet even a cursory examination of the ethnographic sources indicates considerable differences in economic scale and legal organization between the two, however much they may have in common with respect to technology. This suggests that a technological approach alone is insufficient for understanding legal development, though it is clearly one critical element. (These points will be reconsidered in Chapter 3.)

Clearly a central theme in Hoebel's work is the impact of stratification on legal development, though *The Law of Primitive Man* does not offer a theory of inequality as such. For that we turn to another significant figure in contemporary anthropology, Morton Fried.

Fried on the emergence of stratification

The Evolution of Political Society (Fried 1967) is one of the most important comparative studies in contemporary anthropology. Its central concern is the origin and development of social stratification:

> Some students continue to ask how the ordering of social relations became so complex, how invidious distinctions arose among the inhabitants of a single society, how exploitation developed, and how the political state came to be. (Fried 1967:x)

Just as Hoebel views law as developing in response to pressures created by inequality, Fried believes that political organization was molded around emerging patterns of stratification. An understanding of political evolution must therefore be based on a theory of social stratification and its development.

Fried divides societies into three types: egalitarian, ranked, and stratified. Each is characterized by a distinct kind of economy, property system, kinship system, labor organization, and a legal and political system. Emergent inequalities based upon differential access to status and/or material resources shape the nature of conflict and its legal-political control in egalitarian, ranked, and stratified societies.

The notion of an egalitarian society conjures up a vision of a utopian society where differences between individuals are unknown. However, Fried reminds us that there are no societies in which all individuals are exactly equal. Instead, egalitarian societies are those in which there are no absolute limits to the number of individuals who can achieve positions of high status:

> An egalitarian society is one in which there are as many positions of prestige in any given age-sex grade as there are persons capable of filling them. Putting that another way, an egalitarian society is characterized by the adjustment of the number of valued statuses to the number of persons with abilities to fill them. (Fried 1967:33)

Status positions tend to be based upon valued skills (e.g., in hunting). Recent research suggests that sex and age distinctions play a critical role in the distribution of status as well (see especially Blumberg 1978). Whatever its basis, prestige is an ephemeral commodity in such cultures. Misfortunes of an ordinary variety can bring down the "mighty." More importantly, most egalitarian societies "have powerful leveling mechanisms that prevent the appearance of overly wide gaps in ability among members." Among these mechanisms are value systems that frown upon individual accumulation of high-status goods, and group claims to individually procured items.

The kind of economy that generates an egalitarian society "approximates very well the type of economic integration that Karl Polanyi . . . epitomized as 'reciprocal' " (Fried 1967:34). Individuals are linked together in complex chains of exchange and mutual obligation. Reciprocal relations are therefore both social and economic in nature and the emphasis in both spheres is on the maintenance of balanced transactions (see Rosman and Rubel 1971; Rubel and Rosman 1978).

Fried suggests that two basic kinds of social structure develop in reciprocal or egalitarian economies: the nuclear family and the band. Leadership is held by high-status individuals, but they are able to exercise only a limited amount of authority. Their power to command obedience is minimal.

The definition of law adopted in *The Evolution of Political Society* leads Fried to reject the notion that egalitarian societies exhibit legal systems. Insofar as law depends upon the existence of organized coercion, egalitarian societies lack the institutional basis for law as Fried (and for that matter Radcliffe-Brown) understands the term. This does not mean they lack means of settling conflicts. As those conflicts tend to revolve around the failure to fulfill reciprocal obligations, social sanctions are applied either in the form of individual retaliation or through attempts to publicly humiliate the offending party, possibly culminating in an outburst of violence (Fried 1967:72–3). The invocation of any of these devices is likely to threaten the culprit's ability to continue with the reciprocal exchanges basic to economic life in an egalitarian society.

The defining characteristic of a ranked society is an apparent limitation on the number of prestige positions that may be filled. The limitations may or may not involve restricted access to basic resources. Prestige, for example, does not "convey any privileged claim to the strategic resources on which a society is based" (Fried 1967:110).

Ranked societies are generally found where an abundance of food permits population growth beyond the low levels characteristic of egalitarian societies. As Hoebel pointed out, under these environmental circumstances communities become larger and less mobile.

Corporate kin groups as well as lineages emerge as "a typical form of grouping at this level," according to Fried.

If egalitarian societies are based upon reciprocity, the economic systems of ranked societies rest on principles of redistribution. Goods flow from the bottom of the social pyramid toward the top and are dispersed again in the reverse direction. Northwest Coast societies that practiced the potlatch ceremonies are the best-known examples of this process (see Rosman and Rubel 1971). Potlatches are the more flamboyant ceremonial version of a mundane and regular process of redistribution that has its locus at the village level of ranked societies. At the head of these economic networks are the highest-status individuals, who also tend to be clan leaders or chiefs (representing their followers).

Leadership within ranked societies tends to be better defined than it is within egalitarian cultures. Yet, despite popular conceptions of chiefs, the leaders of ranked societies do not hold absolute sway over their followers. Their ability to command depends entirely on the followers' willingness to follow. A high-status individual can only exert pressure over his subordinates; he cannot force his will.

The limitations on leadership apply to the legal realm as well. Fried hesitates once again to claim that ranked societies have law, because there is an absence of power to enforce decisions in cases of dispute. However, unlike egalitarian societies, ranked ones do exhibit some more permanent structures of authority. Although they do not have law, in Fried's view they have means of coping with conflict that are "law-like" (Fried 1967:145). These methods generally involve some form of arbitration by third parties, who have no opportunity to render a decision, but who may be vested with enough authority to urge disputants to come to an agreement between themselves. Alternatively, such authorities may render a decision but be unable to *force* compliance.

Whereas ranked societies have status differences without differential access to basic resources, stratified societies exhibit both. For the first time "the exploitation of human labor in the conventional Marxist sense" becomes a reality, precisely because control over resources has become the exclusive province of the few. The many must seek food either by laboring for others or by paying for it with a portion of their produce (Fried 1967:188–9).

Every institution of the social order must respond to these "pressures unknown in egalitarian and ranked societies." In the political realm, the state emerges as a set of institutions and agencies whose raison d'être is the maintenance of the order of stratification. Law is but one part of this apparatus. State power lends both a legitimacy and a force to agencies of social control such that fully developed legal institutions emerge. Customary procedures of handling disputes do not completely recede, but they are "reinforced by formal iteration and application." Situational arbitration is replaced by explicit rules; ad-hoc procedure is replaced by formal institutions; and "officers of adjudication, officers of punishment, record keepers and communicators" develop. The state exists to protect the privileges of the elite; the law legitimizes differential access and tends to have a punitive orientation, because it is based not on consensus and participation but on naked control.

The relevance of Fried's three-stage model of social stratification to the development of legal systems is clear. Distinct forms of inequality emerge from patterns of differential access to resources in egalitarian, ranked, and stratified societies. In turn, these forms of differentiation give rise to conflict to which legal institutions (or their equivalents in egalitarian and ranked societies) respond.

Several points should be made about Fried's model. It is not always clear from the model whether stratification is an independent or a dependent variable (i.e., a cause or an effect). Taking the typology at face value, Fried sometimes seems to be suggesting that stratification is the independent variable, whereas the various features of economy, polity, and legal structure are dependent. Yet no argument for this kind of directionality is included. In fact, elsewhere he seems to be suggesting the more classic materialist thesis that economic organization (forms of property ownership, labor, technology) "determines" stratification.

The second issue concerns the breadth of a three-part typology. Although the categories egalitarian, ranked, and stratified are useful for abstracting certain properties of social systems, they are also broad enough to obscure some important features. The categories of egalitarian society and stratified society do find clear support from among certain of the hunting-and-gathering and state-level cultures, respectively. There is a great deal in between, however, that remains in the catchall category of ranked society. Although we can discover associations between certain types of legal insti-

tutions and the endpoints of Fried's continuum, it is the middle
range that exhibits the most variation. One needs to be able to make
predictive statements about the variation in legal systems within
the "ranked" category.

Fried's model provides a very helpful paradigm from which to
approach the question of how stratification molds the demands
placed on legal institutions in preindustrial society. *The Evolution
of Political Society* does not, however, take law as its primary focus.
Recently, several scholars have attempted to apply a general evolutionary model specifically to the problem of legal variation. We
will now turn our attention to one of them, Donald Black.

Donald Black and The Behavior of Law

> It is possible to formulate propositions that explain the quantity and
> style of law in every setting. Each of these propositions states a
> relationship between law and another aspect of social life – strati-
> fication, morphology, culture, organization, or social control. Each
> explains the behavior of law across time and space, in all societies
> for all time, wherever it is possible to measure law and other aspects
> of social life. Each explains known facts about law and implies
> countless other predictions as well. Given trends in the evolution of
> social life, each even forecasts the future of law. (Black 1976:6)

With this ambitious goal in mind, Donald Black offers what he
takes to be the most comprehensive theory of legal evolution. It
will become evident that I do not share an enthusiasm for *The
Behavior of Law* (Black 1976). Nevertheless, his work represents
another attempt to find regularities in the data on legal systems and
to express them as testable propositions.

Black defines law as "governmental social control" and as such
believes it to be absent in cultures that lack distinct political institutions. Where law is absent, anarchy prevails.[11] To this observation
Black adds another that distinguishes his work from that of other
theorists, namely that both the content and style of law are quantitative variables:

---

[11] Black equates law with "governmental social control" and therefore argues that
it is one among many forms of social control. Having adopted this definition,
he notes that "many societies have been anarchic, that is, without law." Indeed,
he points out that according to this definition "much social life in every society
is anarchic" (Black 1976:2).

> [Law] increases and decreases, and one society has more than an-
> other. The quantity of law is known by the number or scope of
> prohibitions, obligations, and other standards to which people are
> subject, and by the rate of legislation, litigation, and adjudication.
> (Black 1976:3)

Black's theory pivots on the "quantifiability" of law. For he believes
that the "amount" of law may be correlated with the "amount" of
other social phenomena (stratification, culture, and social differentiation) that are also amenable to quantification. Thus, for example, he argues that the "more culture" one finds, the "more law"
one finds. The more a society is differentiated, the more law it will
have. The bulk of *The Behavior of Law* is dedicated to formulating
a series of propositions such as these. For the most part, Black's
findings may be summarized by saying that as any of these factors
increases or becomes more complex, so too does law increase or
become more complex. Conversely, when these variables grow
smaller, law decreases and other forms of social control increase.

Multiple objections to Black's theory may be raised. At the outset,
one is hard pressed to accept the proposition that law is quantifiable
in the sense that Black uses the concept. The sheer number of
obligations and the absolute rate of legislation that might be calculated for a given society reveal very little about the ways in which
legal institutions are constituted, however much they may indicate
about the volume of legal "work" in a given setting. It is even
harder to see the validity of quantifying the other predictor variables
in Black's model. There is little sense in his statement that "culture
varies in its quantity from one setting to another." In fact, it runs
contrary to the anthropological tradition to which it is meant to
contribute. Such a perspective leads Black to formulate relationships
that most anthropologists would simply reject out of hand, for
example:

> In some places [culture] is so rich that a newcomer needs months or
> years to learn its many features . . . others have only a few shreds of
> culture . . . Some societies have more culture than others, some groups,
> situations or individuals more than others . . . When culture is sparse,
> so is law; where it is rich, law flourishes . . . The more culture the
> more law. (Black 1976:63)

Since Black never actually operationalizes such statements, it is hard
to tell how such a proposition would be put to a test. No empirical

test of the various hypotheses he formulates is included in *The Behavior of Law*.

Even if one were to grant the possibility of quantification for these variables, Black's work falls considerably short of an explanatory theory. At best, we are left with a series of hypothesized quasi-correlations: The more culture, the more law; the more differentiation, the more law; etc. There is nothing in the way of an argument that explains the hypothesized correlation between these variables and law, which surely ought to be a central issue for any theorist.[12]

This is not to suggest that such a relationship is, in principle, impossible to specify along the lines Black suggests. One more successful attempt to do so is contained in William Felsteiner's (1974) article, "Influences of Social Organization on Dispute Processing." Felsteiner delineates three different forms of dispute processing: adjudication, mediation, and avoidance. He argues that the predominance of each type is a function of social structure. Each system of dispute management requires different resources for compelling compliance as well as different degrees of intimacy between disputants. Social structures can be analyzed in terms of the extent to which they can marshal such resources:

> Within any society on an institutional basis, we should expect to find less adjudication where groups are infrequent and the coercive power which can be marshalled is weak, less mediation where shared experience is rare and less avoidance where avoidance costs are high. (Felsteiner 1974:77)

[12] The following example epitomizes this difficulty: "Over history, across the world, law has been increasing . . . It is possible to explain the evolution of law with other trends in social life. Beginning with the earliest and simplest societies, these trends have included the following: stratification, or inequality of wealth has generally increased. Differentiation has increased. The quantity and diversity of culture have increased, and yet at the same time the extreme diversity once seen across societies has been decreasing. The organization of social life has increased, but members of groups have become more autonomous as well. On the other hand, intimacy has decreased . . . Finally, social control other than law has decreased. Since the evolution of law obeys the same principles as any other kind of legal variation, these trends explain the increase of law over the centuries" (Black 1976:131).

Causal analysis is scarce in this paragraph. Black provides some observations about transformations in various social spheres (without citing any evidence) that appear to have accompanied changes in legal systems over time. The causal relationship between the independent and dependent variables is unspecified.

Felsteiner's basic concern is the size of the primary social group in a society. Within small groups (e.g., the nuclear family), individuals know each other well, an intimacy that implies both that group members are knowledgeable about each other's affairs (such that mediation is feasible) and that the costs of a rupture in relations is high (such that avoidance is costly since it is tantamount to a permanent rupture). Felsteiner applies the same argument to societies in which individuals are not linked to integrated groups, reaching the opposite conclusion. Where intimacy is lacking, avoidance is feasible and may well be the procedure of choice for many disputes. However, concomitant with the demise of the close-knit, kin-based society is the rise of the supra-kin-based institutions that bring to bear the coercive power of the state; the way is thus cleared for the use of adjudicative strategies for the solution of conflict. Felsteiner thus presents an explanatory hypothesis that can be tested empirically (though he refrains from doing so).

The contributions of legal ethnography
Recent studies of legal evolution would not have been possible without the field research of a large number of ethnographers working in particular societies. Indeed, it is precisely the desire to account for this corpus of data that distinguishes contemporary theoretical efforts from the classical studies discussed in part one of this chapter. The field of legal anthropology as it is known today consists mainly of the work of such individuals as Paul Bohannan, Lloyd Fallers, Phillip Gulliver, Max Gluckman, Sally Falk Moore, Laura Nader, Leopold Pospisil, and their many students. Though the legal ethnographers are generally not concerned with questions of legal evolution per se, they have contributed some important observations on the growth and development of law.

The classical theorists evinced a belief in the superiority of the modern-day legal system: Weber applied the term "rational" to the legal institutions of the modern market economies. Durkheim wrote of the facilitative qualities of law in organic societies. Implicit in these views is the notion that "primitive" law was crude, only marginally better than the rule of force.

Contemporary legal ethnographers have insisted that the classical perspective was poorly informed. Where modern legal institutions depend upon punishment and adversary relations, the law-ways of less complex societies embody conciliation and cooperation. Contemporary legal systems are prisoners of formal procedure; preindustrial legal systems seek substantive justice and deemphasize legal formalism. The ordinary individual in an industrial society finds it difficult to gain access to the legal process; simpler societies provide for direct access to the mechanisms of dispute settlement. In short, legal ethnographers reverse the nineteenth-century perspective of the progressive nature of modern law by suggesting that traditional cultures had found far better ways of settling conflicts.

These contrasts are indicative of two general concerns that have dominated the ethnographic study of dispute settlement: the *processes* of dispute settlement and the *substantive values* that underlie conflict resolution in preindustrial cultures. Some effort has been directed at an evolutionary perspective on these issues, particularly in the latter realm.

Max Gluckman (1955, 1965) has analyzed the legal values of Barotse society in terms of the "Reasonable Man," the ideal standard of conduct that Barotse judges use to evaluate the behavior of social actors. He has argued that this complex of normative ideas is adapted to the requirements of tribal social organization, where overlapping social, ritual, and economic ties form a web around each individual. A rupture in such a system of "multiplex" relations would have serious ramifications; there is thus an emphasis on conciliation. The normative world of the Barotse works to preempt such a breakdown by specifying the obligations and behavioral expectations of individuals as represented by the reasonable man. Laura Nader (1969) has followed Gluckman's lead in her analysis of the normative system embodied in legal decisions among the Zapotec (of the Oaxaca region of Mexico). Nader argues that the "master norm" in this culture is one that emphasizes balance.[13] The ultimate goal of dispute settlement is to return social relationships to their normal state. Compromise is emphasized (as opposed to the assignment of fault to one party) because it is the most effective way to ensure that the social order will return to a harmonious state.

---

[13] Nader explains that the Zapotec officials are supposed to find solutions to cases which will "make the balance between the *demandante* and the *demandado*. . ." She notes that such an ideal is common to many cultures, though the definition of balance may vary. "The Zapotec ideal is not 'an eye for an eye' but rather what restores personal relations to equilibrium" (Nader 1969:73).

I have already noted that this emphasis on compromise, cooperation, and peaceful settlement stands in marked contrast to the innocent/guilt judgments, adversarial relations, and punitive orientation characteristic of Western judicial systems. Gluckman and Nader have both argued that a systematic explanation for this contrast lies in the multiplex character of Barotse and Zapotec societies as opposed to the "simplex" (single-stranded and largely instrumental) nature of social organization in industrial societies. The rupture of an economic tie in a simplex society does not necessarily have implications in the domain of kinship. Should a political relationship disintegrate as the result of a dispute, it is unlikely that ritual relations will be affected. The differentiation of simplex society lessens the pressure to mend broken relations through compromise and thus encourages "winner-take-all" judicial decisions.

To the extent that a developmental trend from multiplex to simplex forms of social structure may be discerned in human societies, Gluckman and Nader's thesis would suggest an evolutionary movement from compromise orientations to adversarial, "zero-sum" juridical processes. Such a shift is not merely procedural in nature. Indeed, Barotse judges deliver verdicts via adjudication, but these verdicts aim at compromise in Gluckman's view. The developmental trend is mirrored not so much in procedure, though it may be there as well, as in the value systems upon which legal processes are based.

This is, of course, a fairly broad-scale thesis, one that leaves much unexplained variation between the two poles. It does not help us understand questions concerning the distribution of organizational forms in law across the spectrum of societies, nor can it be of assistance in explaining why substantive law (the topics to which law addresses itself as opposed to the procedures it utilizes), varies in content cross-culturally.

Conclusion

There are three basic reasons for the lack of progress on these questions since the days of the classical theorists. First, the notion of evolutionism fell into disrepute among anthropologists shortly after the turn of the century. With a few exceptions (e.g., Hoebel, Fried), comparative–evolutionary studies of legal systems virtually ceased.

The second reason is that the few comparative studies that have been conducted proceeded without the benefit of a theoretical paradigm other than the traditional functionalism of the Radcliffe-Brownian variety: Dispute settlement takes the form it does because it is necessary to sustain a social order that is undifferentiated, multiplex, and integrated on the basis of a kinship structure. This approach has been applied in many subfields in anthropology. It is problematic because it assumes that extant features of a society exist in order to perpetuate the status quo, a circular argument for which much of functionalist analysis has been duly criticized.

Much of legal anthropology has proceeded without reliance on any particular theoretical paradigm at all. This leaves us with a wealth of descriptive data but little synthetic understanding of the patterns they may display.

The third reason is that those studies that have utilized and developed other theoretical approaches for understanding the growth and variation in legal systems have tended to stop short of systematic testing of the hypotheses they develop. Consequently, we find some very useful models that are in need of empirical substantiation beyond illustrative use of ethnographic materials.

There is clearly a substantial body of data with which to approach the problem of legal development, and the injunction against comparative–evolutionary analysis no longer holds. We are in a far better position to examine the problem than were the classical theorists, because so much more of the preindustrial world has been described in the ethnographic literature and contemporary social scientists have developed a variety of sophisticated methodological techniques for testing hypotheses on a cross-cultural basis. In the following chapters I will therefore develop several hypotheses designed to explain the variation of legal institutions cross-culturally and test them on a worldwide sample of societies.

2

A typology of legal institutions

If one were to classify the intellectual pursuits of legal anthropologists, two fundamental concerns would emerge. On the one hand, one would find scholars interested in the substantive aspects of legal systems: the foundations of legal rules, the relationship between normative principles and legal principles, and the social process whereby legal culture is created and sustained. On the other hand, one would find anthropologists interested in the formal aspects of legal institutions: the structure of legal "bodies," the distribution of power in the legal sphere, and the existence or recruitment of legal authorities. Although there is a definite link between these two approaches, they do represent different analytic problems.

This chapter springs from the latter domain, the study of legal institutions. In particular, I will provide a typology of the legal institutions characteristically found in preindustrial societies[1] as the first step in understanding the distribution of these institutions across particular economic systems.

Constructing a typology

The construction of a typology requires the arrangement of a collection of unique items into a relatively small number of mutually exclusive categories. Any given case should fall into one and only one "type," and the types should be chosen to maximize both the contrasts *between* categories and the degree of homogeneity *within*

---

[1] The data base for these typifications consists of a sample of sixty preindustrial societies, which is described in detail in Chapter 3. It will not be necessary to discuss the nature of the sample at this point, beyond noting that the ethnographic materials cited in this chapter are drawn primarily from the societies included in it. Each of the typifications outlined in Chapter 2 represents a theoretical summation of the evidence in the data base.

them. In addition, we require a typology of legal institutions whose constituents can be ranked in order of increasing legal complexity. This raises two issues: the identification of several dimensions for differentiating legal institutions that can be used to construct a typology and a discussion of what constitutes "complexity" in the legal arena.

Perhaps the most basic dimension that differentiates dispute-settlement institutions is the presence or absence of a third (non-disputant) party or parties in the settlement process. This is the first basis of differentiation underlying a typology.

A second, though related, differentia concerns the extent to which disputing parties are socially *required* to turn to this third party for dispute settlement. In some societies, disputants retain the option not to involve a third party or "hearing body"; in others, normative behavior requires such involvement. The issue here is *not* whether disputants ever "take the law into their own hands." In both industrial and preindustrial societies, individuals occasionally wreak personal vengeance upon their enemies. The point is that in some societies self-redress is socially approved, whereas in others a disputant is expected to utilize the third party (at least as a first step in resolving disputes). Thus the presence or absence of a normative requirement to involve a third party is the second differentia underlying our typology.

A third dimension is the most complex and concerns the intended authoritativeness of third-party decisions. To understand this, one must first distinguish between authoritativeness and the power of enforcement. People have been known not to accept the verdict of courts, judges, or councils in all societies. Agents of enforcement are empowered to compel submission in some societies. Elsewhere, such a mechanism is totally lacking. But it is not the issue of enforcement that is of concern here. Instead, I wish to focus on the *social definition* of authoritativeness. In some cultures, a third party issues a decision or "verdict" that is *supposed* to be binding on disputants, whether they approve of it or not. That is an authoritative decision. In other cultures, the third party proffers what is socially defined as nonbinding "advice," a nonauthoritative decision.

A fourth aspect of the typology concerns the degree of centralization or concentration of legal decision-making power in the third party. Here I prefer to conceive of a continuum. At one extreme, disputants face a hearing body consisting of the whole community. Elsewhere, the hearing body consists of representatives from all sectors of society. In yet another case, the decision makers may be members of some ruling caste, or a single figure such as a paramount chief. This fourth dimension, then, indexes the degree to which legal decision making is taken away from society-at-large and concentrated in some distinct group or person.

A fifth dimension of the typology concerns the issue of levels of appeal or levels of jurisdiction. In some systems of dispute settlement, one institution acts as the first and only hearing body. At the other extreme, one finds layers of appeal organized hierarchically above the local level, possibly providing different jurisdictions for different offenses or categories of persons. The existence of multiple levels or areas of jurisdiction above the local level provides an additional basis for differentiating dispute-settlement institutions.

In summary, the five dimensions or differentiae that provide the underlying structure of a typology of legal institutions are:

> The existence of a third party or "hearing body"
> A social requirement to use the third party
> The authoritativeness of third-party "decisions"
> The centralization of decision making
> Multiple levels of jurisdiction or appeal

These are obviously a subset of all conceivable dimensions. But they have been selected because, taken in concert, they form the boundaries between distinct types of legal institutions.

Before proceeding to fill in the typology, the issue of legal complexity must be examined, for my goal is to identify a ranked order of the institutional forms. Of course, each of the five defining dimensions of legal systems tells something about the complexity of a legal system. For example, a society with a third-party hearing body exhibits a more complex legal system than one lacking such an institution. A multiple-level (or multiple-jurisdiction) structure is more complex than a single-level structure, and so on.

However, the argument becomes much stronger when we look at the five dimensions simultaneously. Instead of finding all possible combinations of the five differentiae, one discovers that the various dimensions are interrelated, and only certain combinations occur. In fact, they form a Guttman-like scale. Systems that lack third parties also lack authoritative decision making and multiple legal levels. At the other extreme, societies with highly centralized forms of legal decision making also have authoritative decisions and require third-party involvement. Intermediary steps are similarly structured. The fact that these various dimensions "stack up" in this fashion justifies my use of the concept of legal complexity. This is represented schematically in Figure 2.1, which ranks eight institutional types in terms of increasing complexity using the five dimensions.

The remainder of this chapter gives the details of these eight types of legal systems. It may be useful, however, to give a brief outline of each at the outset:

Type 1 represents the simplest form of legal institution, which lacks any involvement of third parties in dispute resolution. It corresponds to societies that only have self- or kin-based redress mechanisms for resolving conflicts; these mechanisms are labeled "self-redress systems."

Type 2 describes societies in which third-party involvement is available, but is *not* normatively defined as necessary. Third parties give "advice" rather than authoritative decisions; as such, these systems are labeled "advisor systems."

Type 3 describes a situation when self-redress has become socially unacceptable as a solution of first resort. Disputants are supposed to approach certain third parties for a solution to a dispute. However, these third parties lack authoritativeness; that is, they cannot make decisions that are socially binding upon the disputants. Instead, they can only aim at a compromise, which may either be accepted or rejected by the disputants (though social pressure may be brought to bear upon litigants to accept). Into this category fall various types of mediators and go-betweens, hence the label "mediator systems."

Type 4 requires disputants to turn to a third party and, for the first time, the third party may render decisions or verdicts that are socially defined as binding upon the disputants (whether or not they agree). Adopting a terminology used by Gluckman (1965:206) and elaborated by Gulliver (1979), this system involved *adjudication* rather than mediation.[2] The simplest form of adjudication institution may be termed an "elders' council."

---

[2] The distinction between adjudication and mediation is discussed in detail in the section on council systems.

Figure 2.1 A Typology of Legal Institutions

Differentiae	1	2	3	4	5	6	7	8
Third party available	–	+	+	+	+	+	+	+
Third party required	–	–	+	+	+	+	+	+
Authoritativeness expected	–	–	–	+	+	+	+	+
Multiple legal levels	–	–	–	±	±	–	+	+
Centralization of decisions	None	None	None	Low	Medium	High	High	Highest

Increasing legal complexity

– means a feature is absent
+ means a feature is present
± means a feature is sometimes present

Type 5 is another type of authoritative council that has a more restricted membership than elders' councils. As such, decision-making power is more centralized than in type 4. This second type of council system is labeled "restricted councils."

Type 6 describes systems where authoritative decision making has become further centralized and is in the hands of one person. This type is labeled a "chieftainship," but the term requires qualification. Only a subset of the leaders whom individual ethnographies label chiefs have centralized power and can adjudicate disputes. My use of the term "chieftainship" is limited to contexts where the ethnographic evidence confirms that the chief can give authoritative verdicts. Societies where the "headman" or "chief" can play only a *non*authoritative role will be categorized as "mediator" or "advisor" as appropriate.

Type 7 describes authoritative chieftainships with multiple levels of jurisdiction and/or appeal. Such societies are often referred to as "paramount chieftainships" and are so labeled here.

Type 8, the most complex institution I will consider, is that known as a "state-level" legal system. It is distinguished from paramount chieftainships by a higher concentration of legal authority, as will be explained in detail in the appropriate section of this chapter.

Two general points should be made about this typology before we turn to a detailed discussion of each type. First, when categorizing a society in terms of this typology, its most complex legal institution serves as the reference point. Thus, for example, a society that has a paramount chief judging disputes on appeal in the capital city and a headman adjudicating in each village is classified as a paramount chieftainship. Second, whenever possible, the legal institutions discussed here are the indigenous ones, rather than those subsequently imposed by colonial administrations. In many societies, native dispute-settlement institutions were supplanted or transformed by foreign governments. Legal ethnographers are usually sensitive to this issue and discuss which institutions are indigenous and which imposed. I have always sought to characterize a society in terms of its traditional institutions.[3]

---

[3] It is sometimes difficult to determine what the "pristine" legal institution in a society was like, particularly given the variable quality of ethnographic data. Wherever possible, I have relied on the earliest accounts of disputing practices for any given society. I am, however, mindful of the fact that nineteenth-century

Finally, there is the issue of mixed types. In particular, one sometimes finds chiefs with advisory councils or councils whose spokesman is the village headman. These cases have been categorized
according to the locus of power. If the ethnography describes a
council as advisory to a paramount chief, the society is categorized
as a paramount chieftainship because it is the chief who has the
final say. Where a chief is described as the spokesman or convener
of an elders' council and the data suggest that the council as a whole
makes decisions, then I categorize this as an elders' council. Let us
now turn to a more detailed look at each of the eight kinds of legal
systems.

Self- or kin-based redress

In thinking of a legal system, one tends naturally to imagine a body
of individuals who respond to transgressions of rules in a systematic
and orderly fashion. Although this image is drawn from the experience of social scientists versed in Western legal traditions, it is
not completely culture-bound. Most anthropologists would concede
that one need not find a judge, jury, and set of attorneys in order
to recognize behavior that is distinctively legal in nature. It would
be enough to locate any individual or group of individuals whose
responsibilities include (but are not necessarily restricted to) the
hearing of disputes. This might be considered the necessary and
sufficient condition required to identify legal institutions within any
given social order.

However, anthropologists have identified many societies in which
no such hearing body can be found. Yet it is clear that even in

ethnographers were less concerned about ethnocentric bias than contemporary
anthropologists. Consequently, the early sources are often tainted with the particular perspectives of their authors, who often worked at the behest of colonial
authorities.

Secondary sources based on travelers' reports or early ethnographies often
repeat the mistakes of the primary materials and must therefore be treated with
caution as well.

To correct for misrepresentation, I have utilized multiple sources and cross-
checked one account against another. This appears to be the only practical means
of coping with uneven quality in the data.

Finally, I assume that inaccuracies that remain undetected would make it more
difficult to find systematic patterns of the kind reported in Chapter 3. Random
error is generally assumed to lower the strength of correlations and their levels
of statistical significance, which happily did not develop in the data analysis
presented here.

cultures bereft of recognizable legal bodies, disputes are resolved in regular, socially sanctioned ways.

Confounding the absence of hearing bodies in many simple societies is the presence of a high degree of violence. The incidence of feuding and warfare as a reaction to conflict has provoked comment from scholars interested in primitive law (especially Bohannan 1967). In Western cultures, violence is often equated with lawlessness; thus it comes as no surprise that simple societies where violence appears endemic have been characterized as lawless and anarchic.

Before examining the characteristics of "self-redress" systems of dispute management, the issue of violence and warfare must be addressed. Three points are relevant: First, the actual level of violence in primitive societies is difficult to document adequately. Assertions of constant warfare within simple societies have been challenged by scholars (e.g., Fried 1967) who argue that, appearances notwithstanding, warfare is not an especially prominent feature of life in small-scale societies. Second, several individuals have argued that warfare is not endemic to "pristine" cultures, but results from intensive and destructive contact between traditional cultures and exploitative nation-states (Davis and Mathews 1976). The Yanomamo Indians of the Brazilian rain forest are a case in point. Napoleon Chagnon (1968) has described Yanomamo culture as riddled with violence, infanticide, and warfare. Shelton Davis, a prominent critic of Chagnon, has argued that Chagnon has both failed to document these claims and ignored the ramifications of Brazil's economic-development activities in the Amazon Basin for the Yanomamo (Davis 1977). Davis suggests that warfare among the indigenous peoples in the basin is a response to the increasing encroachment of mining interests into native lands in Amazonia, rather than an aboriginal pattern of behavior.

To these points, a third should be added. The description of preliterate societies as violent and therefore lawless often results from unexamined assumptions regarding the boundaries of social systems. If one assumes that a common language, common cultural traditions, and similarities of social structure constitute the minimal condition for identifying a "society," one may well view simple societies as prone to violent internal conflict. However, a different perspective may emerge if the focus is on the level of social communities.

A community consists of a group of individuals linked together in demonstrable ways, perhaps the most important of which is subsistence production. Individuals who "earn their bread" together constitute a fundamental face-to-face unit. When one looks at the level of violence *within* these primary groups or communities, one sees a very different picture than that which obtains *between* them, even where the groups share a common cultural configuration. Internal primary-group relations are generally characterized by a great deal less violence and a strong emphasis on harmonious dispute settlement than are external relations, where the incidence of warfare may be much higher. The violence reported in the literature may well be a feature of intergroup conflict rather than intragroup dispute settlement.

Jules Henry's (1964) ethnography of the Kaingang, *Jungle People*, provides an apt illustration of this distinction. He notes that the Kaingang maintained warm interpersonal relations within "their own circle of relatives and companions," avoiding internal conflict at all cost. However, quite the opposite sentiment prevails between social groups:

> The most striking single feature of Kaingang disintegration is the contrast between the warm, highly affective relationships within the "families" and the uninhibited ferocity of the behavior of the members toward all outsiders. Within their own circle of relatives and companions the Kaingang will endure a high degree of personal discomfort to avoid a quarrel, but toward "other" groups of their "own people" their overwhelming desire is to shed blood. (Henry 1964:60)

The "families" to which Henry refers were not necessarily kinship units, though this may be the core. Kinship ties were often tenuous in Kaingang society; much stronger were the "bonds that grow up between men and their hunting companions" and the women associated with them. Within these "production groups," social relations were marked both by an absence of conflict and a desire to downplay disputes that do occur. Between these groups, however, murderous vengeance was the dominant mode of interaction. Nevertheless, all these individuals were Kaingang: They spoke the same language, shared the same cultural traditions, and referred to each other as "my own people."

In sum, the differences in patterns of dispute management described here suggest the existence of important social boundaries: Prolonged violence is indicative of intergroup or intercommunity conflict, whereas the avoidance and calm management of conflict often characterizes intragroup dispute resolution. Having dealt with these preliminary problems, we can now turn to intracommunity systems of dispute management based on self-redress.

Defining self-redress

> Since there is no formal political or kin organization, the Jivaro apply sanctions against alleged violators of the norms purely by means of informal partisan action. The aggrieved party, together with those relatives willing to support him, takes upon himself the responsibility for punishing the person or persons he believes to be guilty of an offense against him or a close member of his family. (Harner 1972:171)

Several kinds of dispute-management systems can be classified as resting upon self-redress. However, the description given by Harner of Jivaro conflict management is an example of the classic form. In the absence of any institutional means of adjudication or mediation, self-redress systems rely entirely upon the actions of the disputants and those individuals prepared to lend support.

Why should self-redress be described as a "lawlike" system of dispute settlement rather than an instance of spontaneous and unrestrained conflict? The ethnographic record suggests two features of self-redress systems that justify the former characterization: (1) Self-redress does not occur in response to just any negative social behavior. Rather, "actionable" transgressions are defined by cultural norms. Although codified law is surely absent, there are behaviors that are understood to be unacceptable and deserving of response. (2) The same rule system prescribes appropriate reactions to such violations. Self-redress systems are therefore *rule governed.*[4]

---

[4] Though I have argued that self-redress operates on the basis of shared normative rules defining crimes and prescribing responses, Harner notes that unanimity is often problematic: "On an abstract level, there is near unanimity among the interior Jivaro as to what is correct, normative social behavior. In any specific case, however, there is usually radical disagreement as to whether a particular anti-social act was justified as a punitive sanction in reprisal for some past offense, or whether it was, in fact, an unjustified act which itself deserves the application of retaliatory punitive sanctions" (Harner 1972:170). The disagreement Harner discusses would appear to be more a matter of determining the *application* of normative rules than a dispute over the rules themselves. This, after all, is a problem in state societies as well.

A range of variation is present in the form these rules take, the degree to which control can be exercised over the application of sanctions, and the size and composition of the "response group." Three basic forms of self- or kin-based redress may be identified: "classic" reprisal systems; shaming rituals; and illness belief/supernatural sanction systems.

The most common form of self-redress involves physical retaliation on the part of the aggrieved party and his or her kinsmen. Schapera's description of the !Kung Bushmen system of redress is a good example of this type of dispute settlement:

> In general when disputes arise between members of the band . . . there is not appeal to any supreme authority, for . . . there is no such authority, nor are cases of wrongdoing or quarrels referred to the chiefs where these exist. The only remedy is self-help. But insofar as self-help is the recognized mode of reaction, it must be regarded as a legal institution. Blood vengeance is the principal, if not the only, recognized way of dealing with serious offenses committed against a person even by members of the same band. (Schapera 1930:152)

Cultures practicing self-redress have a keen sense of balance regarding the seriousness of an offense and the appropriate degree of response. Reactions are "tailored" to the severity with which the society in question views a transgression.

Some cultures view illicit sexual relations with extreme tolerance. Adultery is likely to provoke only the mildest forms of rebuke, if it is noticed at all. Many other societies take a dim view of it and react strongly. In both cases, there are shared norms that fit the punishment to the crime. If the norms governing response patterns are breached, secondary mechanisms of social control come into play. Thus, for example, among the Mataco, infidelity was "punishable" in certain defined ways; that is, the adulterer had to vacate the home. When the response to adultery escalated beyond that which the Mataco regard as appropriate, "last resort" reactions ensued:

> We have seen how infidelity normally entails the imposition of sanctions by the injured party, in that the offender must leave home and children. However, when infidelity leads to homicide as a result of jealousy this is regarded as too stern a sanction, and is immediately countered by another: a blood-feud or some other form of compensation. In case of homicide resulting from jealousy, the lesser offense

is completely expunged by the greater, and the adulterer's family become justified avengers. (Fock 1974:224)

There is a normal response to a transgression that would evoke no counterresponse because it was understood by the Mataco as justified (as "legal"). If that normality is exceeded, the "crime" became that of overreaction and the original offender's kinfolk had the right to strike back.

Similarly, among the Aranda there were socially defined punishments for adultery that included "cuts around the shoulder blades of the offending man, inflicted by the offended husband in hot pursuit." However, if the husband cut too deeply, and therefore exceeded the standard of acceptable punishment, he stood to forfeit his wife (Chewings 1936).

These examples indicate that self-redress systems relying upon retaliation entail clearly defined notions of right and wrong, despite the absence of third-party authority figures. Legitimate retaliation will not engender further reaction. When an individual violates a cultural rule, he or she suffers the consequences; his or her kin will not come to his or her aid. Their lack of support confirms the social definition of both a wrong and its punishment. Conversely, when punishment is unfairly exacted or is too extreme, a counteroffensive will be launched. Eventually, a homeostasis is achieved whereby both sides are satisfied with the resolution of the situation. This state is often signaled by the exchange of gifts, symbolizing an end to hostilities.

Reprisal mechanisms are generally activated when spontaneous trouble erupts, as distinct from situations of chronic conflict. An individual whose behavior marks him or her as a troublemaker is often treated differently from the person who occasionally oversteps the bounds of propriety. Public ostracism and exclusion is the more likely response where the hardened recidivist is concerned. This is not a routine method of dealing with occasional disputes. Expulsion represents the final blow of the frustrated community against the incorrigible offender.

Although some forms of self-redress require physical action on the part of the disputants, other types entail the public voicing of complaints coupled with derogatory characterizations of an offender's persona. The term "shaming ritual" seems appropriate here for two reasons: The goal of this form of redress is to obtain satisfaction for having been wronged by reducing the social status[5] of the offender via shaming; and the method used to shame usually involves formulaic speech, stylized gestures, and other forms of ritualistic communication associated exclusively with dispute management.

The most important structural feature of shaming rituals is the existence of a public forum. Shaming has no effect unless it is publicly recognized. The actors in the "degradation ceremony"[6] are still restricted to the disputants and their kin, but the general public plays a key role, if only to acknowledge the resolution of the conflict.

The ethnographic literature contains three different kinds of shaming rituals. The first is the basic public insult: The aggrieved party engages in name calling in an open area. The accused may or may not respond in kind. (Malinowski [1926:78] describes an incident where public insults provoke a suicide, but this is rare.) In some cultures, eloquence in formulating insults is a praiseworthy skill in and of itself. These word fights usually conclude when a consensus emerges as to which party was most successful in making the insults "stick."

A second form of shaming consists of highly ritualized "song duels," a variation on the theme of public insults. Hoebel describes such a system in his discussion of the law-ways of the Greenlandic Eskimo:

> Song duels are used to work off grudges and disputes of all orders, save murder. An East Greenlander, however, may seek his satisfaction for the murder of a relative through a song contest if he is physically too weak to gain his end, or if he is so skilled in singing as to feel certain of victory. . .
>
> The singing style is highly conventionalized. The successful singer uses the traditional patterns of composition which he attempts to deliver with such finesse as to delight the audience to enthusiastic applause. He who is most heartily applauded is "winner." To win a song contest brings no restitution in its train. The sole advantage is in prestige. (Hoebel 1968:93)

[5] I use the term social "status" in the sense that sociologists employ it. I refer to the socially recognized degree of prestige that attaches to individuals by virtue of their roles within a community.

[6] Harold Garfinkle (1956) coined the term "degradation ceremony" to refer to public occasions where the status of an individual is readjusted in a downward direction.

The third type of shaming ritual involves stylized physical aggression between disputants. These "duels" are often fought in front of the community at large and the outcome is predetermined. In fact, it is a misnomer to refer to these forms of redress as "duels" because there is seldom any question as to the identity of the blameworthy party. The aggrieved is allowed to inflict a wound in a preordained location on the body of the transgressor with a preordained degree of force. The guilty party is allowed a ritualized response, but never enough to prevent a well-earned injury. Both the Tiwi and Aranda practiced this form of shaming (Hart and Pilling 1970, Chewings 1936).

These public contests are accompanied by an open harangue on the history of the relationship between the disputants and their families. The dispute at hand is thus put in context as part of an ongoing and therefore socially significant set of relationships.

Running through the three forms of shaming rituals identified here is a common appeal to a moral code that must be publicly validated during the dispute. Occasions that call for shaming rituals often serve as opportunities for the articulation of cultural ideals of right conduct. Conflict is resolved by the reiteration of social rules and moral obligations, with bouts of status degradation and minor physical harm.

Shaming rituals rest upon what Nonet and Selznick (1978) term "legal moralism," the attempt to utilize legal mechanisms to enforce communal morality.[7] This is accomplished via the use of public forums for the manipulation of personal prestige rather than (as in a more complex legal system) the imposition of a formal code.

Illness beliefs and supernatural sanctions

In the case of the Salteaux, there were no chiefs nor any kind of political organization in aboriginal days. Nor were there any institutionalized juridical procedures or jails. . . . A close examination of

---

[7] The term "legal moralism" has a negative connotation for Nonet and Selznick (1979). When applied to shaming ceremonies, these negative connotations seem unwarranted. Anthropologists have been attracted to these methods of conflict management precisely because they display certain positive characteristics: They are highly poetic and imaginative methods of expressing cultural values. More importantly, shaming rituals are comparatively nonpunitive (when contrasted, for example, with incarceration), even as they are effective.

> the dynamics of Salteaux society reveals the fact that fear of disease is the major social sanction among the Indians. (Hallowell 1942:268)

> Each Manus household is governed by a ghost of a recently dead male relative. In conception this ghost is a father, but a son may actually be raised to this position after death. The skull of the ghost is kept in the house and presides over the moral and economic life of the household. He punishes sex offenses, scandal-mongering, obscenity, failure to pay debts, failure to help relatives, and failure to keep one's house in repair. For derelictions in these duties, he sends illness and misfortune. (Mead 1937:220)

"Illness belief systems" or "supernatural sanction systems" have a peculiar status in the ethnographic literature on preindustrial legal institutions. Dispute settlement is ordinarily considered a process activated after a socially recognized infraction has occurred. Yet there are societies that operate on the basis of preexistent fears of the harm likely to befall those who violate cultural rules. The Salteaux and Manus material excerpted above suggests that these belief systems emphasize the power of supernatural forces or illness to strike down those who transgress. The inference often drawn from these cases is that fear alone acts as a powerful social-control device. Either transgressions never occur because individuals fear the deadly consequences, or illnesses and misfortunes actually do strike those who offend community standards. Both alternatives seem implausible. As Malinowski (1926) pointed out long ago, there are no societies where misconduct is unheard of regardless of potential consequences. The notion that bad luck or sickness is directional and can be "turned upon" malefactors seems problematic.

These concerns warrant a closer examination of how these belief systems operate in the context of disputes. Two kinds of cultural strategies surface in the ethnographic literature. The first, represented by the practices of the Jivaro, involves poisoning, a direct means of inflicting illness upon an offender. The use of sorcery or poisoning is part of a retaliatory system of self-redress:

> Most poisoning is done at the large *tsantsa* victory feasts, where a dozen or more women of different households are continually circulating among the guests serving manioc beer. The poisoner, under such circumstances, is very difficult to detect. The family of the victim, however, invariably accepts the opinion of the dying victim as to the identity of the guilty party, and her brother is marked for death. (Harner 1972:174)

The rationale behind Jivaroan beliefs in the inevitability of illness following transgressions is not hard to comprehend.

Another version of this kind of sanction system involves the reliance upon a conjurer (among the Ojibwa) or a shaman (among the Jivaro) to interpret the significance of an illness. Such specialists are asked to explain the meaning of a certain symptom and to determine the identity of the person responsible for causing it. Alternatively, diviners may pinpoint a violation of customary law that the sick person has committed, thereby bringing misfortune upon him- or herself. The Manus believed that the ghost of the household sent illnesses to family members who default on obligations. Determining which action has angered the ghost was the task of a male or a female medium (Mead 1937).

These mechanisms can be read metaphorically, in the sense that illness provides an opportunity for a social conflict to be openly articulated. Conjuring, shamanistic curing, and ghostly divination (whatever else they may signify) involve the exposure of problematic conduct. Among the Jivaro, this interpretive work might have led to poisoning as a retaliation for sending sickness. Among the Ojibwa, however, public exposure of wrongful behavior might have been sufficient to correct the situation and avoid all-out conflict (Hallowell 1942:86).

The role of the diviner is clearly central to the process of settling disputes in this fashion. Individuals who perform this role tend to have similar characteristics across unrelated cultures. They are said to be wise persons, knowledgeable about the customs of the people. They are almost always male, though women are occasionally involved. They are generally old: Young men are thought "insufficiently mature" to be good conjurers. Men of high character, these individuals are expected to be intimately familiar with community life. Such knowledge is essential to the task of an interpreter because he or she is acting in a legal role: defining the nature of a transgression, identifying the actors involved, and (in some sense) urging a response to the situation. Conjurers do not actively intervene in the settlement of a dispute. They do not act as judges, yet there is an element of legal process involved. The intervention of third parties in dispute settlement does not really occur until one considers our second type of legal institution.

Advisor systems

Advisor systems can be considered extensions of self-redress in that the enforcement of "punishment" remains in the hands of the aggrieved or his or her kinsmen. However, here we see evidence of third-party intervention in the processing of disputes, albeit in a rather passive form. Yet it is enough to warrant distinguishing this form of conflict management from self-redress.

The popular image of the Indian chief as a minor monarch commanding at will is scattered throughout the records of pioneers, missionaries, militia men, and others who left behind some of the earliest records we have of the pristine cultures of the Great Plains. Ethnographers did not completely escape this romantic legacy.

Societies with advisor systems of dispute settlement do not exhibit this kind of authority structure. Within them are individuals who have been called chiefs and who fall into the category of "advisor" in the typology. They tended to be men; often they were distinguished in battle or known for hunting prowess; they were invariably mature, though by no means the eldest men of the community; and they were regarded as public repositories of wisdom about customs and rituals. Advisors were known for oratory, and the ethnographic record suggests that they were often called upon to discourse on problems of local concern, including disputes. In short, advisors are respected individuals by virtue of personal attributes (rather than hereditary birthright), as the following excerpts from the Ona and the Andamanese suggest:

> Each of these localized families of kinship groups recognized the moral leadership of one of the elder men. He could hardly be called a chief. He had no real authority. The office was in no sense hereditary. He would not have to be a shaman. He was well versed in tribal traditions and [Ona] customary law, and spoke often of them. His influence was persuasive, not coercive. For acceptance of his counsels he counted on the general respect for elders and for established customs. (Cooper 1946: 117)

> A man possessing [skills in hunting and warfare, who is known for generosity and good temper] inevitably acquires a position of influence in the community. His opinion on any subject carries more weight than that of another even older man . . . In each local group [of Andamanese] there was usually to be found one man who thus by his influence could control and direct others . . . . Such men might be spoken of as "chiefs," but the term is somewhat misleading, as

> it makes us think of the organized chieftainships of other savage races. (Radcliffe-Brown 1948:45)

These descriptions point up a number of important aspects of this social role. First, recruitment for advisorships is neither hereditary nor enduring. The vicissitudes of age and good fortune can effect one's skills and therefore one's respect. The ability to command a following waxes and wanes; leadership is therefore unstable. Second, advisors have no "Austinian" authority. Their power is a function of the respect with which their opinions are treated. Third, the advisory system endows its central figures with moral authority. To use Weber's term, the legitimacy of advisors derives from a belief in the moral leadership that skilled men are seen to possess. As such, they are expected to be exemplary in their own social conduct.

Moral authority does not, however, guarantee obedience. As Cooper and Radcliffe-Brown point out, these influential men could not impose their views. Indeed, ethnographies frequently note that an advisor's opinions were solicited and their advice subsequently sidestepped.

The process of dispute settlement is activated when one or both parties to a dispute seek out one of these high-status figures. They are not obliged to do so, yet the evidence indicates that this is the normative procedure. Having secured the ear of an advisor, the parties present their sides of a dispute. This hearing often takes place under informal conditions with none of the ceremonial trappings of a public event. (Indeed, the public is not a particularly important part of this process, a point that distinguishes this system from the shaming rituals described in the section on self-redress.) In some cases, the hearing consists of one disputant "cornering" the third party and attempting to persuade him of the righteousness of his or her cause; this is followed by a similar approach by his or her opponent.

The advisor then typically considers the case and speaks his mind, invoking his views on the significance of the normative rules in question, as the following description of Ona *kemals* indicates:

> The head influences others more by cautioning and admonishing them, rather than by threatening and upbraiding them. To be sure he had no means of punishment at his disposal, but much more effectively he awakens the sense of honor and points out the danger

for the good name of the individual himself as well as of the whole kin group.. . . Everyone submits when the *kemal* gives good advice, when he settles disputes, when he mediates between hostile groups . . . His decision is never legally binding, but it has strong moral force. (Gusinde 1975:476)

It falls to the advisor to protect the social group's conceptions of appropriate behavior, though his ability to do so is constrained by the lack of enforcement resources. However, he can put pressure on litigants by shaming them, suggesting that refusal to follow his advice is tantamount to disrespect for the customs and codes of the people. Among the Trukese and the Marquesans, an advisor could take more coercive steps by indicating which side his own kin group would back in the event of a reprisal, a sanction that may have proven sufficient to convince litigants of the worth of his opinion. As Goodenough points out, however, this sanction is rarely invoked because it signals weakness in the advisor's moral authority:

> The chief's lineage may aid another lineage in revenge if he thinks the latter is in the right. Thus, there is always the threat of the chief's kinsmen taking sides in a fight. However, on the whole, the chief is meant to keep the peace and thus will rarely give his blessing to revenge. (Goodenough 1951:143)

Linton describes a similar situation among the Marquesans:

> In case of dispute the chief did not administer justice. All that he could do was to intervene through his messengers, announcing which side he would back. When the chief gave backing to one side, the other usually withdrew and the dispute died down. (Linton 1939:162)

Though this might be considered a limited form of coercive authority, it should be understood as an extension of the general coercive nature of self-redress, rather than incipient "state" power. Marquesan and Trukese advisors did not and could not order their kinsmen to go out and punish offenders. The most they could do was link up with one side in the course of a reprisal.

This threat was taken seriously because, as most ethnographies suggest, advisors tend to come from the more powerful families. Although positions of prestige are by no means hereditary in the strict sense, there is evidence to suggest that certain families produce more than their "fair share" of advisors. Among the Marquesans, there was clear rivalry between advisors belonging to powerful kinship groups. This may have represented incipient features of stratification or concentration of power. In any case, one would not take lightly the threat of involvement of an advisor's kinsmen if indeed they constitute a power to be reckoned with.

Resolution of a dispute is reached when a consensus emerges regarding the satisfaction of the aggrieved, which can be achieved either by accepting the advisor's counsel or the initiation of retaliatory action by those immediately concerned.

The constraints placed on advisors in dispute processing are both structural and normative. Advisors have only limited enforcement resources at their disposal, and most societies organized in this fashion express extreme distaste for anything approaching autocratic leadership:

> No social structure is weaker and more fragile than the Nambicuara band. If the chief's authority appears too exacting . . . , discontent will very likely appear. The individuals or families, will separate from the group and join another band believed to better managed. (Levi-Strauss 1948:23)

– or with reference to the Marquesans –

> The chiefs, in spite of their power, were never oppressive, for there was the constant threat of other strong households, and if the chief became unpopular, allegiance would be shifted to another powerful household head. (Linton 1939:162)

An advisor's vulnerability to the loss of his position either through the waning of the hunting or warfare skills that brought him prestige or by overstepping the bounds of his authority inclines this system toward democratic politics. Consent of one's followers is required in order to effect any decision whatsoever:

> Consent is at the origin of leadership, and consent too, furnishes the only measure of legitimacy . . . The chief has no coercive powers at his disposal. The eviction of the bad people can take place only in so far as the chief is able to make public feeling coincide with his own opinion. Thus, he must continuously display a skill belonging more to the politician trying to keep hold of his fluctuating majority than to an over-powering ruler. (Levi-Strauss 1948:23)

Although personality may well be a factor contributing to the effectiveness of an advisor (a point raised in many ethnographies), cultural constraints on the exercise of authority clearly limit the scope of decision (or verdict) making. At the same time, the concentration of advisors in certain families suggests that there are emergent aspects of stratification at play here that bolster somewhat the position of the advisor.

When we consider the differences between this system and self-redress modes of conflict management, the most striking is the appearance of distinct third parties in the legal process. Disputants choose to approach the advisor, for there is no requirement that they do so, and there is typically a prohibition against an advisor interfering unless invited to do so. The "advice" given is not a "verdict." The parties may ignore what they have been told. Instead the opinion of the advisor tends to confer social legitimacy upon a particular settlement in what is basically a self-redress system.

Mediator systems

Roy F. Barton's classic ethnography, *Ifugao Law*, is one of the earliest studies devoted entirely to the legal institutions of a small-scale society. Written in 1919, it describes a systematic body of substantive law governing the family, property, contracts, and the like. These categories were the backbone of Ifugao ethno-legal doctrine. To the delight of universalists, Ifugao law appears to be remarkably similar to English common-law traditions.

The same cannot be said of Ifugao legal procedures. They had no courts of law and no formal judges. Yet there were individuals among them specifically charged with the responsibility of mediating disputes between opposing parties in the light of an elaborate legal "code" and according to a set of known procedures. This form of dispute management is referred to as *mediation* in view of the mission of the third party: to negotiate a settlement between two disputants (Gulliver 1979:6). The mediator cannot impose a judgment or verdict to conclude a dispute; instead he must seek a mutually acceptable compromise, a joint agreement by the litigants (Gulliver 1979:5).

Mediator systems differ from advisor systems in several important respects: Disputants are under a much stronger normative obligation to submit to the mediation process. It is not considered socially acceptable to seek self-redress unless and until mediation has failed. Mediators *are* allowed to behave in a more authoritarian fashion in an effort to gain a settlement, unlike advisors who must be careful not to exceed their circumscribed authority. Nevertheless, the two systems have in common the constraint that third parties cannot impose verdicts; they can only suggest compromises.

There are two variants of mediator systems in the literature. The more common type requires that disputants stay away from one another, while the mediators act as go-betweens engaged in shuttle diplomacy. The Goajiro, Ifugao, and Yurok (to name a few) handled their grievances this way. In the other type, the disputants and their mediators meet and the negotiations proceed with the mediators taking the principal role. The Arusha are the best-known example of this version.

Legal proceedings in the former case were activated by the commission of a socially recognized delict. Among the Ifugao and the Yurok, this occurred via a public argument or, where property was involved, by the failure to return an object or the withholding of an expected payment. The Goajiro identified conflicts by using "informers," individuals on the lookout for violations of social norms that affected interested parties with whom the informer was in contact. Gutierrez de Pineda describes the procedure as follows:

> In La Guajira the informer acquires the character of an institution which helps to maintain ... social stability in the peninsula. This individual – man or woman – busies himself bringing to members of family groups news of an infraction of any legal precept which affects them and which has not been done in their presence. For instance, if the name of a dead man was spoken ... the informer carries the news to the interested parties, so that when the indemnity is paid for the aggressive act, he as informer will get his share. (1950:197)

The "crime" having been determined, the next step in the mediation process was to call upon those individuals who (by virtue of certain characteristics identified later) had the right to act as mediators. The Yurok *wego*, Ifugao *monkalun*, and Goajiro *palabras* were supposed to be impartial individuals, unrelated to the disputants:

> [Wego] were ... supposed to be impartial enough to be able to reach a fair agreement with the representatives of the other side. It is specifically stated that they could not be kinsmen, who would be partial, but were men of restraint, wisdom and knowledge of the law. (Kroeber 1926:514)

> The *monkalun* should not be closely related to either party in a
> controversy. He may be a distant relative of either one of them.
> (Barton 1969:87)

Once the mediators were selected, contact between the litigants
was completely suspended; all transactions were conducted through
the intermediaries. This was said to prevent the violence that might
attend face-to-face meetings of adversaries.

Each side presented its view of the dispute and its demands for
satisfaction to the mediator. Exaggerated expectations were voiced
along with protestations of innocence and virulent denunciations
of the opposing side. The responsibilities of the go-between were
multiple. He had to attempt to "poke holes" in the disputants'
renditions of the conflict, pointing out the fault that lay on either
side. Cajoling, teasing, admonishing, and even threatening were
tools of the trade as the mediator tried to soften the stances of the
adversaries.

Among the Ifugao this was accomplished after repeated visits
with the parties. The *monkalun* spoke with one side, arguing against
their version of the dispute by invoking the words of the other side
as if they were his own. He then returned to the opposing litigant
and repeated the exercise. In so doing, he was creating an atmosphere of compromise by inducing the litigants to recognize their
contributions to the conflict. He was also hammering out an agreement involving concessions from both parties. If he could secure
an agreement to this compromise, he could bring the dispute process
to a successful close.

Yurok *wego* utilized a different procedure. Like the Ifugao, the
Yurok chose their own mediators when disputes arose:

> Mediators or go-betweens . . . called *wego* (crossers) . . . were cho-
> sen by the parties at issue: two or three, possibly four, to a side.
> There was always expected to be more than one, since a single man
> could not properly maintain his case against several opponents.
> (Kroeber 1926:514)

The crossers examined the litigants and then argued amongst
themselves until a compromise settlement was reached. Once again
the litigants were segregated from each other during negotiation.
The *wego* had to find a settlement acceptable to both sides. Much
the same process was followed among the Goajiro.

The pressures to achieve a peaceful compromise were very strong.

Among the Ifugao, in particular, failure to make an amicable settlement brought shame upon the litigants and the *monkalun*. The mediator stood to lose both material rewards and prestige:

> It is greatly to the interest of the *monkalun* to arrange a peaceful settlement, not only because he usually receives a somewhat larger fee in such case, but because the peaceful settlement of cases in which he is a mediator builds up a reputation for him, so that he is frequently called and so can earn many fees. (Barton 1969:89)

Yurok crossers received compensation in the form of "a standard fee of one detalium shell" (Kroeber 1925:89). Goajiro informants and go-betweens also received fees for concluding a dispute.

Neither the normative values of compromise nor the personal interests of concerned parties could ensure a peaceful resolution to a dispute. As with self-redress and advisor systems, private force remained the final resort if mediation failed. Ifugao *monkalun* imposed a fourteen-day truce in the event of a failure. Immediately following this period, fighting commenced between litigants and their respective kinsmen. The ban on face-to-face contact expired as they met to battle out their differences.[8]

The social characteristics of mediators differ considerably from those of advisors, whose tenure of office was based on fluctuating conditions (of skill). In contrast, the prerequisites for appointment as a *monkalun* were fixed:

> The Ifugao, when wealthy, acts occasionally as a go-between in controversies between kinship groups and profits from the fees he gains in this way. But only a rich man or sometimes a very forceful character with probably a headhunting reputation can become a go-between, because only he can command the cooperation of his kinship group to enable him to speak with the threat and authority requisite for dealing with people so stiffnecked as the Ifugaos are in a controversy. (Barton 1969:15)

Most Ifugao *monkalun* were wealthy men because, according to Barton, only a rich person could speak with authority backed by the threat of force. The mediator's kinsmen were, in fact, never involved. Their presence in the background, combined with the

---

[8] Mindful of the damage retaliation practices would do to his claim that the Ifugao "have law," Barton argued that, even in Western society, the state has the power to retaliate with force against those who transgress.

monkalun's wealth, conveyed sufficiently high social status for him
to command an authoritative air. There was actually little the mediator could do if the litigants themselves failed to agree to his
suggestions for compromise.

The type of shuttle diplomacy described above is the most typical
form of mediation. However, Gulliver (1963) describes another
used by the Arusha of Tanzania. It shares with the Ifugao, Yurok,
and Goajiro the basic features of mediation: Disputants were obliged
to eschew self-redress (Gulliver 1963:220–1) and had to submit to
the mediation process. The settlement was in the form of a compromise that took effect only if both disputants found it acceptable.
Authoritative or binding verdicts had no place here. Like the *monkalun*, the Arusha "counsellor" might try to cajole and bully his
party into accepting a compromise, but the final decision remained
the litigants' (Gulliver 1963:105–8).

Beyond these resemblances, the two versions of mediation diverge. If an Arusha tribesman found himself embroiled in a dispute,
his first action was to consult with his lineage counsellor, who was
an individual selected by the adult males of his maximal lineage as
their spokesman and public representative. This man approached
the counsellor of the opposing party's lineage and arranged one of
two kinds of meetings, a conclave or a moot. The former involved
the two disputants, each with his closest associates and his counsellor. A moot was a more "public" event. The litigants, their counsellors, and as many close kin and associates as each side could
muster were invited. However, participation was limited to disputants and their supporters (Gulliver 1963:232). Persons having
no connection to either side were not allowed.

Unlike the go-between situations just described, here the disputants
confronted each other. In fact, the moot split into two factions, seated
on opposite sides. The procedures differed also in that mediators were
expected to be partisan on behalf of their kinsmen (Gulliver 1963:228),
rather than impartial as in the Ifugao or Yurok cases. A process of
negotiation began in which the counsellors were major spokesmen
and behind-the-scenes negotiators. Though they were clearly opposed
to one another, they were simultaneously allied to steer the proceedings
toward a decision (Gulliver 1963:229).

The nature of this decision was a compromise:

> The process of establishing a settlement consists of discussion and

negotiation, argument and counter-argument, offer and counter-offer, between the disputants' parties in an endeavor to find an area of mutual agreement . . . For [the Arusha], the emphasis lies in the joint participation of the conflicting parties so that the settlement of their dispute emerges from within – that is, together. It is not an imposed decision, a judgment, on the disputants from outside. (Gulliver 1963:232)

Each of the three social subsystems in which an Arusha was involved (lineage, age-set, parish) provided a different forum or cast of characters for these conclaves and moots. Individuals therefore calculated the relative advantages and disadvantages of appearing before each in selecting a site for dispute settlement.

Despite the complexity of Arusha social structure, legal process remained entirely within the domain of mediation. Counsellors could not force litigants to accept a proposal, though they would work hard to persuade their parties to do so. This lack of authoritative decisions, combined with the obligatory use of third parties, is a hallmark of mediator systems.

Elders' and restricted councils

One of the most common political and juridical institutions described in the ethnography of preindustrial societies is termed a council. The meaning of the term is so broad as to encompass any meeting of limited membership typically held in one place, in which behavior is constrained by certain conventions (Richards 1971:1–2). Councils may have a variety of functions – legal, political, economic, administrative – or may simply operate as forums for discussion.

Because the term has been used to describe virtually any assembly, it is used to describe quite disparate legal systems: The Arusha moot has been called a council, as has the Barotse *kuta* (where judges pronounce binding verdicts). The small group of notables who advised the Ashanti king has been called a council, as have the sovereign decision-making assemblies of the Santal. These bodies clearly differ in their capacities to issue verdicts; in the extent to which disputants may be members of the assembly or outsiders who appear before it; and in the degree to which the council represents society as a whole, some group of elites, or simply the disputants themselves.

Given the heterogeneity of institutions labeled councils, one is tempted to avoid the term altogether. Instead, I will draw from this variety two distinct and limited categories, "elders' councils" and "restricted councils." These types do not exhaust the range of possibilities, but they do provide homogeneous categories that are systematically related to the dimensions of legal complexity discussed in the beginning of this chapter.

The classification system used here requires that a council possess the final authority to render judgment, rather than simply advise another judicial figure. The literature is replete with examples where a king or chief rules aided by a council of kin or close advisors. The Ashanti (Rattray 1929) and the Barotse (Gluckman 1955) are cases in point. There is no doubt in such cases that the ruler rather than the "council" retained final power:

> [The *kuta's* decision] is . . . referred to the ruler of the capital, who confirms, rejects, or alters it, or refers it back to the *kuta* for further investigation and discussion. (Gluckman 1967:63)

The categories used here distinguish between such advisory situations and cases where councils are "sovereign" bodies. Elders' and restricted councils encompass the latter. My scheme would classify the former as an instance of a paramount chieftainship.

Within councils as defined here, there may be figures who take special roles (e.g., the presiding elder in a Kikuyu *kiama*). These individuals often recite the verdict or carry out ritual functions, yet the locus of decision making remains with the council as a whole. Adam Kuper discusses such a case for the Kgalagari of southeastern Botswana. A council called a *lekgota* met to adjudicate decisions. The headman summarized the consensus of the *lekgota* and issued a verdict. However, the headman followed the council's opinion, not his own:

> In passing judgment the headman indicated that he thought all four accused were guilty. However, he could sentence only two of them, for he said, "The *lekgota* has refused. The *lekgota* has said that only two men are guilty. . ." In this case, as often, the headman accepted a decision with which he disagreed in part. (Kuper 1971:93)

Determining whether a body is a sovereign or advisory council is sometimes empirically difficult, even though the analytic forms express different degrees of centralization of authority and often occur in distinct economic and political contexts.

My typology requires that a particular body render *authoritative verdicts* in order to be considered a council. This excludes systems like the Arusha moot, where no one was able to impose a judgment. Councils, as I have defined them, must be empowered to adjudicate, that is, make authoritative decisions binding the disputants, with or without their agreement.

The mediation–adjudication distinction is a crucial one for legal anthropology. Gluckman (1965:206) stressed its importance, and Gulliver (1979) devoted a book to it. The distinction has not been without critics. Some have argued that a single legal institution may utilize both strategies; consequently, it is inappropriate as a means of distinguishing between institutions (Epstein 1974). Gulliver's response (1979:22–34) is that even though third parties may first attempt to negotiate a compromise between disputants (mediation), the fact that the third party may subsequently impose a binding decision is critical. The orientation of the disputants and the social role of the adjudicator are qualitatively different where verdicts can be issued without the agreement of disputants. I concur with Gulliver and have therefore used the mediation–adjudication distinction as a basic boundary in my typology.

The two categories of councils identified here represent more complex legal institutions than the self-redress, advisor, and mediator systems described in the preceding sections because disputants are socially required to submit to them *and* they are empowered to render judgments. Restricted councils are, in turn, more complex than elders' councils because the former are constituted on a more exclusive basis than the latter. Having dispensed with these preliminary analytic issues, the two types of council systems can be described in more detail.

Elders' councils
Elders' councils operate at various levels of jurisdiction, depending on the relationship between the litigants and/or the existence of appeals mechanisms. There is often a two- or three-tiered structure, with a local or village-level council at the bottom; a secondary "regional" council, which stands above a certain number of village councils; and (in some rare cases) a "tribal" council, which links the various subordinate regions into one political unit.

The membership of an elders' council represents all the socially significant sections of a given society. This may include nuclear families, lineages, clans, residential groups, and other building blocks of social structure. Because these units often have overlapping membership, one often finds that one of them serves as the organizing principle of council membership at each level.

There are, of course, different ways to achieve this democratic representation. It may be that all individuals who meet certain criteria in a community (e.g., married men or older men) are included. Alternatively, each section may select an individual to represent their interests in the council, as was the case among some Finnish Lapps:

> The administration of the *siida* was done by a council, composed of one man from each family . . . The council had judicial authority and undertook hearings, imposed penalties and executed judgement on those who had offended either against individuals or the community. (Vorren and Manker 1962:144)

Selection was generally governed by a sex-biased seniority principle: The oldest male of the family (or lineage) claimed a seat on the council. There are instances where elections determined council membership, as Smith and Roberts (1954) report for the Zuni and Nachtigall (1955) notes for the Paez *cabildo*.

In many societies, official representatives are accompanied to council meetings by "eligible" kinsmen who can participate in some fashion, though their influence is less than that of a council member. Thus, among the Somali,

> in the smallest structural unit, the *rer*, . . . which is also a minimal lineage, the council regulating and controlling the affairs of the group is. . .open to all adult free-born males who are entitled to carry spear and shield. . .Any adult can speak at the deliberations of the council, but the views of the family heads carry the greatest weight. (Lewis 1955:97)

Whatever the criteria for membership, elders' councils are basically democratic.[9] Participation is not contingent upon wealth, for example. All men who survive into adulthood can, in most cases, eventually become eligible for membership. Village councils com-

---

[9] This democratic spirit did not often extend to the inclusion of women on councils. With some exceptions (e.g., Samoan women's *fonos*, described by Margaret Mead), most councils were male provinces.

posed of household heads will eventually see most adult males join their rosters because each will eventually establish his own household or become the eldest male within an extended family. Councils composed via election are similar in the sense that those who are voted onto the council do not differ in systematic ways from nonmembers. There is no indication that those who serve are wealthier or more powerful than those they represent. This is not the case with restricted councils, which will be described in the following section.

At the village level, the elders' council is the most authoritative legal body. However, many societies have local councils and secondary councils at some more inclusive territorial level. The latter tend to parallel the composition of the local council; for example, where village councils are constituted by all adult males, secondary councils will include the adult males of a geographical region of linked villages, and so forth.

Louis Leakey points out that the Kikuyu recognized a political unit above the village, which he called the "fire-linked unit" (*mwaki*). Each *mwaki* had a council that considered disputes involving members of different villages within the fire-linked unit:

> The councils of each "fire-linked unit" were appointed by the lesser councils of nine which controlled the affairs of each *itura* or village group within a given fire-linked unit. In any affair or dispute or religious ceremony that affected only the members of a given village, the council of that village acted. In affairs which affected persons of more than one village, but all of the same fire-linked unit, it was that council that was responsible. (Leakey 1952:36)

Each village was represented on a fire-linked council, though in the event of a complex case all the elders of all the village councils in the *mwaki* could be convened.

The Todas, a pastoral people of India, had a clan-based social structure. Each Toda clan had a council that adjudicated disputes arising among clan members. However, the tribal *noim*, a body composed of members from only four of the clans, served as a hearing body for the tribe as a whole. This supreme council's major responsibility consisted of settling disputes between "individuals, families, and clans" (Rivers 1906).

Secondary or regional councils were also found among the Nama Hottentots, whose social organization was similarly clan-based:

> The council . . . acts as a court of law. The clan elders try petty
> disputes and minor offenses, but serious crimes and disputes involv-
> ing different clans or their members come within the jurisdiction of
> the tribal council. (Murdock 1934:492)

Finally, the Santal (of India) recognized a regional council that resolved disputes within a political unit composed of approximately twenty villages:

> The second court of appeal in Santal tribal law is presided over by
> a *Desh-Prodhan* having jurisdiction over about twenty villages. The
> unwritten Santal procedure code requires that the president of the
> tribunal should be assisted by a *"Monren hor"* (village elders) rep-
> resenting the villages under him, as well as the Headman of the village
> from whom the case came by way of reference or from the appeal
> of the party aggrieved by the decision of the village court. (Mukherjea
> 1962:157)

These regional councils tend to be the highest level of judicial authority, although there are some societies that have one higher, all-inclusive council that stands above all others. These "councils of the whole" tend to encompass all the adult males of the polity. They are rarely reported in the literature, but those that do appear tended to convene infrequently, usually during important festivals. The Santal "hunt council" is an example of this phenomenon:

> According to immemorial custom, the Santals join together in an
> annual hunt (*Lo bir sendra*) on the conclusion of the spring flower-
> festival, when the opportunity is taken to discuss various questions
> affecting the social and religious problems of the tribe, and to decide
> the reference cases of the *Desh-Prodhans* [regional councils].
>   Here grave social offences necessitating social excommunication
> and ostracism. . . , constitute subjects of grave deliberation by the
> tribe. . . . All our enquiries revealed that the *Desh-Prodhans* of the
> tribe assisted by the elders . . . jointly deliberate together before de-
> claring their verdict.
>   This parliament of the *Desh-Prodhans* is held at some halting
> place. Here it is that the people aggrieved by the decision of the
> *Desh-Prodhans* appear to the assembly of elders to reopen their cases
> and try them according to law. (Mukherjea 1962:158–9)

The hunt council apparently disappeared due to restrictions on wild-game hunting by the state. Informants knowledgeable about customary legal procedures maintained that it had been the "highest court in the land," which could overturn decisions of village and regional councils (Culshaw 1949, Datta-Majumder 1956, Kochar 1970, Orans 1965).

The Kikuyu had a similar supreme council:

> All full elders of the whole ridge or *rungongo*, the widest political unit would not assemble very often; yet on this level the highest authority in the tribe is to be found in the *kiama kinene* . . . the senior council of nine of each ridge. (Prins 1953:111)

> If there is any matter which affected persons of more than one fire-linked unit within the ridge, but all of the same ridge, then the ridge council took the matter in hand. (Leakey 1952:37)

The Kikuyu *kiama kinene* was composed of all the elders of the ridge, with primary authority vested in the oldest members (Lambert 1956).

Although the Zuni handled most legal issues via the elected council discussed previously in this section, special cases sometimes required the judgment of the "Great Council":

> Meetings of the Great Council were formerly held for the purpose of providing a public hearing of cases of extraordinary interest . . . such meetings could be convened by the tribal council on its own authority or on the request of an individual. . . . The subject matter of these hearings was usually of a nature important to all the people, and something that could not satisfactorily be settled privately or before the Council alone. The hearings were conducted and controlled by the Council, but every older male was permitted to discuss the matter and to express his opinion with a view to arriving at a general agreement. (Smith and Roberts 1954:114)

This council was said to have met some twenty times per year to hear important cases.

The jurisdictions of these various councils were determined according to different principles in each society, though some commonalities can be abstracted. Perhaps the most prevalent rule was based upon the relationship between the litigants, determined with reference to both kinship and residence. For example, among the Kikuyu

> disputes within a family are settled by the father. . . . If the two families immediately concerned cannot settle a dispute, it is the business of the family heads of all the kin to do so.
>
> When, in Kikuyu, the two disputants are so remote in kinship that they are not members of one clan the matter may be settled by the

elders of the clans, or if they live in one *itura* (village) by the *kiama kia itura* (village council), or if they live in two *matura* (villages), by the elders of the two or by the *kiama kia mwaki* (council of the fire-linked unit, . . . the smallest territorial jurisdiction not based on kinship territoriality). (Lambert 1956:108)

A second jurisdictional principle involves the concept of appeals. Supra-village-level councils may consider cases that emanate from the village councils. These "lower" decisions may be reviewed by the regional councils at the request of the litigants themselves if they are not satisfied by their treatment at the local level. In most instances, the review process involved a rehearing of the entire dispute and a decision without prejudice vis-à-vis the opinions of the council "of first instance."

Finally, regional councils may be the court of first instance for unusually complex or serious disputes, even if the litigants are closely related and could therefore seek a solution closer to home in less serious matters. The same jurisdictional rule applied to the councils of the whole among the Zuni, Kikuyu, and Santal. However, among the Santal (for example), each time a case was heard litigants had to pay fees to their judges, often in the form of reconciliation feasts. As such, the number of times a review hearing could be requested was largely contingent on the fiscal resources of the plaintiff (David Mandlebaum, personal communication).

Council procedures are, in all cases, marked by a degree of formality not characteristic of the other legal institutions considered thus far. Indeed, council procedure is not unlike that of Western courts. Typically, they entertain statements from both sides. Litigants usually arrive with supporters and kinsmen in tow. Council hearings often require the use of special linguistic forms to denote the seriousness of the occasion and rules of conduct that specify the appropriate behavior of litigants, elders, or supporters. Finally, judgments are put forth that represent the council's verdict and the appropriate punishment or resolution.

Beyond this, there is variation in the procedures of different cultures. Tiv moots were often concerned with the "mystical causes behind facts," and as such opened with reports from diviners (Bohannan and Bohannan 1953). Lepcha disputes were conducted in the context of feasting and drinking of *chi*, a brew that required eight days to prepare. During this period, council members examined the litigants, threatened them with heavy fines, and ultimately drank the *chi*, symbolizing the conclusion of the dispute, as Gorer explains:

> The three adjudicators take a statement from each party and then . . . they call them together and threaten them that if they do not make peace, they will be heavily fined . . . The sum demanded is calculated to be beyond their reach, so that they beg the [council members] not to proceed further; whereupon the [headman] agrees to be contented with a much lesser sum . . . . After that the two quarrelers and the three adjudicators eat and drink *chi* together; at the end of the feast the two quarrelers are given a wordy and imposing sermon on the duty of laying amicably at peace. (Gorer 1938:140)

Fosbrooke (1948) describes a similar procedure preceding the processing of disputes among the Masai.

At this stage of legal complexity, rules of testimony and evidence come into play. It is not uncommon to read of ordeals or oaths, which are used to establish the credibility of those who give testimony. Among the Gheg of Albania, litigants had to call upon elders to take oaths as well, as a form of insurance against perjury:

> When trying a case, the judging elders might decide to make one of the disputants take an oath. Then, to guard against the man's forswearing himself they stipulated that a certain number of men must swear at the same time to his innocence. . . . They were called 'juror elders' for the period covered by the oath.
>
> A subsection of juror elders was known as 'murder elders.' Men of unusually high repute . . . were qualified by their character for swearing to this innocence of a man accused of murder. This crime being the most serious of all, 24 of them had to be found on each occasion. (Hasluck 1954:137)

It is clear from the foregoing accounts that councils represent a considerable step in the direction of legal power when compared with any of the other legal systems that I have described. They adjudicate disputes and conclude the process by issuing a binding verdict. What force can they bring to bear to support their judgment in the face of a recalcitrant litigant? The ethnographic record is of little assistance in settling this issue. In some instances, councils turn to the aggrieved party's kinsmen and essentially order a reprisal with the council's blessing. (Self-redress without official permission is not allowed.) Among the Gheg, village elders could ask all the local men to compel an obdurate defendant to capitulate to their judgment by "threatening to destroy his house and property" (Hasluck 1954:135).

However, the major locus of legal authority is found in the high regard in which the opinions of the elders are held. They are viewed as legitimate authorities, exercising their rightful responsibilities to determine the community's best interest in a dispute. Community morality generally dictates an obligation to accept this judgment. Audrey Richards (1971b:8) has suggested that the presence of a large body of community members ensures that council verdicts are publicly witnessed, thus serving as "record-keepers" in these typically preliterate societies. Such an assemblage further reinforces the moral stature of the council, the primary source of its legal authority.

Restricted councils

I now shift attention to councils whose principles of composition are more exclusive than those of elders' councils. I will not detail the procedural or jurisdictional aspects of restricted councils, for these are much the same as those of elders' councils. Instead, I will concentrate on the limitations on council membership.

As Bailey (1965) and Kuper (1971) have put it, restricted or "elite" councils conceive of themselves (and may, in some cases, actually be) "ruling oligarchies." Several criteria serve to demark potential council members from the "common man." The most common device is the use of hereditary titles, whereby the right to sit on the adjudicating body is passed down through the generations within particular lineages. Margaret Mead's research in Samoa uncovered a legal-political body that was composed along these lines, called a *"Fono"* ("formal gathering"). In theory, the (Great) *Fono* ties the Samoan Islands together. It is composed of "names [titles] held in certain families in particular villages throughout the Samoan archipelago" (Mead 1930:10). However, the Great *Fono* "has not met in historical times" (1930:11) and its status as a functioning body is therefore questionable.

Mead writes that the village-level *fonos* were operative during her fieldwork. Membership was contingent upon possession of one of the hereditary titles, rather than on any consideration of representation.

Another means of restricting council membership is to limit participation to the wealthy and/or prominent members of the community, as was the case in the Tanala council of "notables" (a term conferred by French colonial administrators):

> The affairs of the village were controlled by a group of important men, comparable to the "key men" of American communities. The position was unofficial and the natives seem to have had no generic term for such leaders. They are now referred to by the French word *notables*. The Notables were heads of lineages or large families, rich men. . . . They were usually middle aged or old, but age in itself brought little prestige and no authority. (Linton 1933:148)

In contrast to elders' councils, Tanala restricted councils were composed of representatives of *certain* families, those with wealth or those that were large (often one and the same thing).

A final device for limiting membership is found in those societies where concepts of private landownership exist. Among the Fellahin of Egypt, in addition to criteria such as age and sex (old and male), one's position as a landowner carried with it the right to sit on the village council:

> The Arab council is the traditional agent for maintaining law and order in the village, and its composition and functioning reflect the traditional concept of authority. Prestige derived from age, experience and sobriety combined with power attached to landowners and heads of large families who are well known for their hospitality are the main qualifications for selection in these councils. (Ammar 1954:60)

It should be clear that, whatever the rule of restriction, these councils represent an elite, whether that elite is defined by hereditary titles, wealth, landownership, or the size of family groups.

The concentration of legal power in the hands of an elite council entails the development of stronger enforcement sanctions than those available to elders' councils. There are references to the "dispensing of punishment" on the part of Menabe Tanala councils, who dealt with thieves as follows:

> Fines were rarely levied, thieves being punished by a severe beating and repeated offense by formal disownment and expulsion from the village. (Linton 1933:157)

Moreover, because council members are by definition members of the wealthiest and most prominent families, the threat of their intervention or the severance of reciprocal ties has important implications in the context of unequal status relations. As will be shown in the next chapter, societies with restricted councils are more highly stratified than those with elders' councils. The emergent inequalities are expressed in the relative power of elites and reinforced by their control over the judicial process.

Chieftainships

In the section of this chapter on advisory systems, it was noted that some monographs tend to exaggerate the role of prominent men in simple societies in an effort to identify the locus of authority. There were, however, many cultures in which substantial power was formally vested in individuals; at the risk of minor confusion, I shall designate cultures with such authoritative figures as "chieftainships." A working definition of this form of dispute settlement might be stated as follows: A chieftainship exists where there is an individual who is formally recognized as the final authority in settling disputes at the highest level of political integration in a given society; his decisions are *not* advisory. Rather, they are understood to be binding, though he may require the support of others to enforce sanctions. Normative rules require that cases be submitted to his adjudication.[10] This working definition differentiates chieftainships from advisor and mediator systems along the following dimensions: (1) formality; (2) duration of office; (3) decision-making authority (adjudication); and (4) enforcement ability.

Chiefs usually share with their advisor counterparts a reputation for outstanding ability as orators, sagacity, and knowledge of customary ways. Unlike advisors, who "spring up" because they possess outstanding talents deserving of respect, chieftainships tend to be hereditary and often reside in the hands of the senior male of a prominent family, lineage, or clan:

> Great chiefs were the heads of the communities. Each community was composed of little settlements that taken collectively constituted a political unit. The great chief was a hereditary office among the Eastern Pomo. (Kroeber 1925:250)
>
> The chief [of the Yokut] as so often among the Pacific coast natives,

[10] Systems that include recourse from a chief to a higher authority are dealt with separately in sections on paramount chieftainships and state-level legal organization later in this chapter.

> was the rich man . . . chiefs were also expected to know more, especially regarding religion, than common men. The son succeeded the father. As women occasionally became chiefs, it is evident that inheritance was an important factor, and that chieftainship was a regulated and established institution. (Kroeber 1925:496)

> The real administrative officials of the Pawnees were the chiefs of the villages. All people within a village considered themselves kin, and the chiefs were conceived as heads of extended families, rather than as superimposed government officials. (Weltfish 1965:7)

Most hereditary chieftainships allow for the bypassing of individuals lacking the requisite abilities for the position, even if they have the appropriate bloodlines:

> Chieftainship is hereditary in the female line [among the Tuareg] but within fairly broad and seemingly rather indefinite limits of degree of relationship, and so an undesirable heir-apparent can easily be passed over in favor of a less direct heir who is considered acceptable. (Briggs 1958:86)

The inheritance of legal authority indicates that chiefs are drawn from the wealthier, more powerful families within a geographical area. The continuity of leadership within these bounds implies a centralization of legal authority.

At this point, several amendments are in order. I have discussed chieftainships as if one and only one individual in any given society exercised this power. This is often the case, though there are cultures in which several individuals vie for power, each having jurisdiction over his own political unit but seeking to expand beyond these borders.

> If the leading rivals live in the same village, its inhabitants form two semihostile groups of a new type. Each leader of such a group decides cases among his followers and tries to compete with his rival in adjudicating disputes on the village level. (Pospisil 1958:15)

Kapauku Papuan *tonowi* were lineage leaders who shared the characteristics of chiefs outlined above: They had the authority to determine the outcome of disputes, and they were deferred to as legitimate holders of power within their own domains (Pospisil 1958). The selection of the appropriate *tonowi* to hear a dispute depended in part on the kinship relations between the litigants and on the reputation of the man in question.

Powell (1967) observes a similar situation in the Trobriand islands, where "cluster leaders" attempted to draw several villages into their spheres of influence by competing with each other in economic generosity (the classic "big man" system). Rwala *arefa* were hereditary judges who lived several to every Bedouin group (Chelhod 1971).

The multiplicity of personnel is not inconsistent with the definition of a chieftainship advanced at the beginning of this section, for each official regards himself (and is regarded by his faction) as the last word in dispute resolution.

One more caution is in order. Although the predominant tendency is definitely in the direction of hereditary chieftainships, not all the societies falling into this category follow this trend. Szyliowicz's (1966) study of rural Turkish villages indicates that the selection of chiefs, although not strictly hereditary, was sensitive to the influence of local elites:

> Leadership resided in the few families who had always comprised the local elite. In neither community were leaders recruited either by heredity or election; rather a process of emergence occurred so that a person with the necessary social background and the appropriate qualities of integrity, wisdom, wealth and ability was recognized as chief. Should the [chief] decide to relinquish his post he would be replaced by another member of the ruling group. Sometimes the office was monopolozed by one clan. (Szyliowicz 1966:47)

Generally, wherever nonhereditary chieftainships are found, elite influence on the selection process will also be found.

Unlike advisors, chiefs usually serve on the basis of a permanent "appointment." Individuals hold the position for the duration of their productive days, relinquishing it voluntarily. The incumbent often has the prerogative of naming a successor within the bounds of specified rules and subject to the consent of the populace, for the community remains the final guarantor of an individual's position of power. Rebellions can and do take place in order to unseat unpopular executives. Nevertheless, the chief's duration of tenure, ability to name successors, and the hereditary tendencies of chieftainships are hallmarks of the increasing formalization and institutionalization that this kind of legal system represents.

The legal role of the chief resembles aspects of the other institutional configurations that have been considered. Chiefs often encourage disputants to settle amicably through mutually acceptable compromises before attempting further action. However, unlike an advisor, a chief *can* intervene in a situation that appears headed toward a confrontation. He has the right to step into the breach and take control of the ongoing dispute. Advisors have no such authority: They can only proffer an opinion when asked.

Leopold Pospisil's description of Kapauku disputes provides a clear example of this point:

> The Kapauku "process of law" starts usually as a quarrel. The "plaintiff" accuses the "defendant" of having performed an act which causes harm to the plaintiff's interests. The defendant denies this or brings forward justification for his actions. The arguments are usually accompanied by loud shouting which attracts other people, who gather around. The close relatives and friends of the parties take sides and present their opinions . . . by emotional speeches . . . As soon as the exchange of opinions reaches a point too close to an outbreak of violence, the rich headman steps in and starts his argumentation. He admonishes both parties to have patience and begins questioning the defendant and the witnesses. He looks for evidence that would incriminate the defendant . . . The native authority makes a long speech in which he sums up the evidence, appeals to a rule, and then tells the parties what should be done to terminate the dispute. (Pospisil 1974:35–6)

The *tonowi's* knowledge of customary "law" was important because he was expected to do more than simply settle a situational dispute. He was to do so in accordance with the "rules" and was meant to cite the principles that underlay his judgment.

Though the chief is often the first and last person to adjudicate a dispute, in some societies he is the source of appeals when all other informal means of dispute management have failed. This is particularly true in lineage-based societies, where informal negotiations are the first resort, followed by hearings before the chief. Tallensi dispute practices illustrate the role of the chief as an appellate "court":

> Settlement by negotiation between the lineage heads, conducted through a privileged intermediary like a *tendaana*, or a kinsman of both units, or the head of a lineage connected with both [parties], would be attempted to begin with, and often succeeded. . .But if [the dispute] is acute or involves two major segments, now as formerly it may be brought before the chief or *tendaana*, who with the elders threshes it out. (Fortes 1940:269)

My working definition of a chieftainship asserts that the chief's adjudication is considered binding and that he has the authority to order sanctions, even if he is dependent on others to help effect them. It is often difficult to analyze the empirical data on a particular society in order to know whether such a sanction system operates or not. Indeed, different sources on the same culture often conflict; the same source may be internally contradictory. Much of the confusion is due to the variance between an informant's idealized version of appropriate procedure and the behavior observed by the ethnographer, as the following description of Bambara chiefs illustrates:

> Theoretically, the *dugu-tigi* has no right to enforce the verdict because the communities are extremely jealous of their independence. As a consequence, they yield only to the extent that it is in their best interests.
> It may happen, however, that the *dugu-tigi* supported by his council does exert authority when he has the power and is seconded by notables who make common cause with him for various reasons. Thus, the *dugu-tigi* can invoke police powers to maintain order in the community . . . (Monteil 1924:252–3)

Monteil suggests that a Bambara chief could enforce his decisions only under certain circumstances, that is, when he had the backing of the senior members of his social group. He was still regarded as the author of legal opinions, even when enforcement was problematic.

Pospisil's detailed discussion of Kapauku sanctions may be helpful in understanding the problem. In the 132 cases he records, he discerns four kinds of punishments that *tonowi* could bring to bear on Kapauku Papuan miscreants: (1) *corporal punishment*, including execution, beating, and slapping; (2) *economic sanctions*, such as the payment of blood money, the payment of a sum stipulated in a contract, or the destruction or confiscation of a culprit's property; (3) *public reprimands*, "the most dreaded and feared of the psychological and social sanctions," which involved "intermittent public scolding, shouting of reproaches, and the dancing of a 'mad dance' in front of the squatting defendant"; and finally (4) *legalized self-redress*, which entailed the regaining of one's property or the plaintiff's punishing an offender *after* such actions have been approved by the authority (Pospisil 1967:92–4).

Pospisil points out that self-redress may be the end result of a Kapauku dispute; but unlike the systems described in the first part of this chapter, here it must be sanctioned by the authorities rather than invoked as a first resort. Gayton makes the same observation regarding Yokut law-ways:

> If a family wanted revenge upon a malicious shaman, poisoner, or murderer to the extent of taking his life, the case had to be laid before the chief before any overt action could be taken ... When the chief gave permission for a person who was regarded as a public enemy to be done away with, no retaliation could be taken by the victim's family. (Gayton 1930:381)

Yokut chiefs were careful to consult "respected elders" before rendering such a decision (Gayton 1930:411).

In common with council systems, chieftainships place authority into the hands of distinct individuals. In contrast to councils, this centralization of legal authority centers on one person (or several rivals) supported (to be sure) by followers. Chieftainships share with restricted councils a strong trend toward hereditary positions, with a similar tendency toward the representation of elites. Nevertheless, community members are often consulted before chiefly decisions are made; often their active participation is required to effect enforcement.

Paramount chieftainships

The form of legal governance considered in this section exhibits very little of the tendency toward participatory democracy common in the institutions discussed thus far. A paramount chieftainship resembles the image of a royal kingdom, though in practice it is more decentralized than this vision suggests. Paramount chieftainships tend to be based upon hereditary aristocràcies and draw together a larger number of villages or communities than the other legal-political systems. Yet despite this centralization, local autonomy is retained to some degree. In fact, the tension caused by the opposing organizational "principles" of centralization and local control runs throughout the ethnography of paramount chieftainships.

In *Politics, Law and Ritual in Tribal Society*, Max Gluckman (1965) grapples with the classification of African kingdoms and chieftainships. Noting that "chiefs in the tribal world range considerably in power. . .from the heads of small tribes to the kings of nations" (1965:155), he identifies one category of chiefs that could "demand the right to forbid internal fighting, . . . compel submission to their adjudication, and . . . command officials and bodies of troops to enforce their decisions" (1965:167).

I have designated such systems paramount chieftainships to emphasize that they are constructed out of complex legal-political hierarchies. The paramount chief typically stands at the apex of a multilevel structure surrounded by his royal lineage, who often aid him in judicial and administrative tasks.

Paramount chieftainships are often run by a "civil service," functionaries who handle the daily affairs (legal and otherwise) of the society. In this respect, these cultures resemble Weber's concept of the patrimonial bureaucracy, for the "civil service" tends to be recruited from the ranks of royalty. By virtue of his extended relations, a paramount chief is able to extend his administration over a wide geographical area. However, the exigencies of communication in these societies generally means that the "bureaucrats" control daily affairs out of the paramount's immediate range of surveillance. Hence a premium is placed on the loyalty of subordinates.

The "capital" village in which the paramount resides is usually the largest within his territory. Bemba villages, for example, normally numbered from 30 to 50 huts, but rose to 300 or 400 in the case of the paramount's village (Richards 1961:171). Within his own village, the paramount's court was the first and last hearing body. Local residents were under his immediate jurisdiction. Members of the immediate royal family typically lived in the paramount's village and often served as members of an advisory council.

The extent of council involvement in legal matters varies from culture to culture. Among the Bemba, the strength of the executive was such that this aristocratic council merely advised him against unpopular decisions (Richards 1971b:104). However, among the Ashanti the chief's royal council was intimately involved in the discussion of cases. The Ashanti high tribunal more closely resembled a multijudge court, though the paramount was considered the final authority in all cases (Rattray 1929:93).

Outside most capital villages, there is a secondary level of jurisdiction, which Gluckman refers to as "counties"; below this is a local or village-level unit. Each of these jurisdictions has its own leadership exercising primary legal control.

Ganda legal-political organization illustrates this pyramidal arrangement:

> For the purposes of government, the kingdom was divided into *szaza* (counties). In the early days, when the kingdom was very small, these appear to have been three in number; but with the gradual expansion of the kingdom by conquest, these had increased to ten by the time British overrule was established. Each county chief had under him a number of sub-county chiefs, each of whom governed a section of the county. Below these there were one or more further levels of chiefs, the lowest level being the chief of the *kyalo* (village). Each chief was responsible to the chief immediately above him in level of seniority, just as the area he governed was a segment of the area governed by the more senior chief. A hierarchy of authority was fitted over a segmentary pattern of local governmental units, as it is in most centralized states. (Southwold 1965:90)

The number of intermediate units between the regional and village levels varied from culture to culture, as did the methods of selecting leaders. Among the Ganda, there were competing hierarchies; one was appointed by the paramount chief and one was composed of preconquest clan leaders unrelated to the paramount, who were nevertheless technically subordinate to his authority. Those appointed by the supreme tribal authority were obviously loyal to the paramount and served as his regional watchdogs in legal and administrative matters.

Those who inherited positions by virtue of their clan positions were not necessarily loyal and, in Southwold's words, "were often somewhat resentful of [the paramount's] authority." This situation is particularly common where paramount chieftainships are conquest states. In such cases, local clan officials are actually hereditary leaders of subject peoples. Some paramount chieftainships operate on an indirect-rule principle, attempting to govern through these preexisting authorities. This relationship is always problematic, particularly where local leaders represent a threat to the stability of the paramount's regime. Gluckman put the matter succinctly:

> In many African tribes, each chief in succession found an existing distribution of power, in which counties were already headed by traditional, often hereditary leaders to whom their subjects recognized an allegiance independent of the allegiance which they granted

to the chief himself. A chief might reduce the power of these county chieftains by placing members of his own family among, or above them: this gave power against him not only to commoner chieftains, but now also to "princes" who had claims to the chiefship itself ... Though theoretically they were subordinate to the main heir, and in one way the latter's state officials, in other respects they became leaders of autonomous blocks of followers. (Gluckman 1965:168)

Paramount chiefs must rely upon others to maintain their administrations, even at the risk of creating independent power bases.

Theoretically, each subordinate level of jurisdiction is subject to the judicial review of the next highest level, up to the court of the paramount chief. In practice, the likelihood of appeal is a function of: the proximity of the court of first instance to the chief's court (which also indicates the relative independence of the "county" – those closest to the chief are also likely to be better integrated into a central political structure); the wealth of the litigants (since each appeal cost the disputants fees); and the political relationship between the litigants and officials serving as intermediate authorities – each appeal represents an unwillingness to accept the judgment of a political superior. Caution is exercised in mounting challenges to the chain of legal authority, particularly in societies with strong regional power bases.

The contradictory tendencies of regional autonomy and tribal centralization imply that the depth of a legal hierarchy is as much a matter of the distribution of political power as it is a question of "constitutional" provisions for judicial appeal. This, more than any other feature, has led to controversy over whether paramount chieftainships can be called "states." The difference between states and chieftainships is a matter of degree, particularly of the vertical integration of legal and political authority. The paramount's inability to completely subordinate the authority of regionally based (and opposition-oriented) power groups is often cited as an important feature distinguishing these systems from "true" states (Fried 1967:227–40, Balandier 1970:123–30).

Each legal level in a paramount chieftainship manifests its own institutional form. In most cases, one finds an appointed (or confirmed) official who is directly responsible to the next level above, often *aided* by a council. At the regional levels, these councils are usually composed of ranking members of an elite, whereas at the local (or village) level elders' councils often survive. Though paramount chieftainships are pyramidal in their legal organization, the closer one gets to the bottom the more egalitarian the institutional form and the greater the emphasis on reconciliation and compromise.

State-level legal systems

As a prelude to discussing legal institutions in state societies, it will be useful to remember precisely what the concept of a state consists of:

> A state is not simply a legislature, an executive body, a judiciary system, an administrative bureaucracy, or even a government . . . A state is better viewed as the complex of institutions by means of which the power of the society is organized on a basis superior to kinship . . .
>
> Of great importance is the claim of the state of paramountcy in the application of naked force to social problems . . . In the final analysis the power of a state can be manifested in a real physical force, an army, a militia, a police force . . . and other paraphernalia of structured control. It is the task of maintaining general social order that stands at the heart of the state. (Fried 1967:229–30)

Fried argues that the purpose of the state is social control, a requirement generated by the conflict inherent in the forms of social stratification common in state societies. No longer do we find diffuse or informal mechanisms of conflict management characteristic of nonstratified cultures. State-level institutions are fully differentiated and supported by coercion.

The consolidation of social-control agencies in the hands of the state has important implications for the process of dispute resolution:

> The state must deal with trouble cases. Quite clearly there appears some statement of norms associated with sanctions. Customary handling of disputes does not automatically disappear, but customary rules and procedures are reinforced by formal iteration and application. Rules that might have applied between kin groups are now applied within kin groups by an external force. With the state comes the possibility that members of a common kin group can accuse one another, use one another, and betray one another to a larger society that stands beyond kin. If the emergent state defines the limits of interpersonal injury and aggression, it also is soon required to handle disputes over things and over agreements. Beyond the growth of law in this sense, there is the necessary growth of procedure, of courts

or their equivalents, of officers of adjudication, officers of punishment, record keepers and communicators, and varieties of functionaries. (Fried 1967:237)

The legal institutions of state societies are constructed of multiple levels, hierarchically organized with an emphasis on control from the top.[11] The difficulties associated with centralizing authority in paramount chieftainships are greatly diminished in state societies, as each jurisdiction is defined according to increasingly narrow boundaries of power and discretion.

At least three mechanisms for increasing centralized control distinguish state systems from paramount chieftainships. First, in the former, uniform legal codes emerge that recognize as serious crimes those acts that threaten the stability of the state. The imperial code of the Inca Empire provides an example of this phenomenon:

> The imperial code concerned itself with acts which directly or indirectly threatened the established order such as treason, lese majesty, official misconduct, evasion or embezzlement of tribute, the violation of sumptuary and game laws, and attacks upon life, property, and morality. (Murdock 1934:432–3)

The existence of a uniform code does not necessarily imply the disappearance of local adjudication. It does indicate the state's intentions to secure its interests and perpetuate its domination in the legal sphere, especially where political stability and state finance are concerned.

The second feature of state centralization involves the development of improved communications between the seat of administration and outlying areas. This may be ensured by placing court emissaries in the regions in addition to permanent authorities. Allegiance to the state is bolstered by requiring these state representatives to return to the "capital" frequently. The ability of the state to "hire and fire" helps to ensure the accountability of local officials, who are subject to surveillance by state emissaries.

---

[11] Leopold Pospisil (1959, 1974) has revitalized the concept of legal levels. He suggests that within any society subgroups may be said to possess their own "legal systems." "Even a small grouping such as the American family has a legal system administered by the husband, or wife, or both. . ." (Pospisil 1971:112). Thus, within a society we often find multiple and possibly competing jurisdictions, each with its own rules. In Pospisil's view these rule systems exhibit the attributes needed to label them law.

Record keeping is also more advanced in state societies than in paramount chieftainships. These records sometimes contain notations on legal decisions. It has been suggested that Inca *quipu*, colored knots used principally to keep taxation, tribute, and census data, were also used to "record" legal cases:

> Each lunar month, the local judges reported on the cases they had handled to other judges of higher rank, and the latter to still others, up to the supreme judges, who were the governors or viceroys of the Empire. All these reports were thus transmitted to the Inca's court by means of colored cords, tied in a certain way. (de la Vega 1961:60)

It has been suggested (and disputed) that the Aztecs utilized written communications for the same purposes:

> Some early writers state that the cases were depicted on paper, and the case thus put on record for transmittal to a higher court, but Aztec hieroglyphic writing was so clumsy that one can't conceive of much detail being noted in such records. However, by the combined system of picture writing and glyphs it would be possible to record the prisoner's name, his crime, . . .the town where the crime was committed, the name of the victim, and the sentence, if it were a case of death or some fine. No records of this nature have survived, but there is no reason to doubt that they were used as aids to memory. (Thompson 1933:111)

The third device for increasing state control is to limit the jurisdiction of lower courts to disputes involving small amounts of money or goods or crimes of a less serious nature. Important offenses are reserved for the higher courts to consider, as was the case in the kingdoms of Korea (Heydrich 1931) and Burma (Aung 1962, 1967). Finally, the prohibitions against self-redress increase in state societies.

State-level legal systems generally develop specialized practitioners whose primary (if not sole) function is the operation of the judiciary. Under the Burmese kings, the legal profession flourished: Lawyers were officers of the court, wore special gowns, and "were entitled to a scale of fees based on the value of the suit " (Aung 1962:27). At the local level, hereditary headmen continued to serve as dispute settlers. At the regional level, judges appointed by the king handled cases on appeal from the villages as well as civil suits involving large amounts. Rather than simply members of the royal family, these regional officials were specialists, as were the judges of the *Hlutdaw*, the supreme court.

The great Islamic states of Africa, such as the Fulani Hausa kingdom of Zazzagawa, had elaborate legal systems maintained by
trained legal scholars functioning alongside an executive authority
composed of the king and his lesser chiefs (Smith 1960). Among
the responsibilities of judicial personnel was the adaptation of Islamic patterns of legal administration to the customary legal traditions of preexistent (now subject) societies.

The emergence of specialized practitioners is common but not
inevitable in state societies. In many of the early states, legal functions were performed by military mandarins appointed by the central government to oversee the interests of the state in outlying
regions. However, the construction of bureaucratic structures is a
hallmark of state legal systems, however they are staffed.

In state-level societies, there is a more developed monopoly of
legal authority than in any of the other systems we have considered.
Although we have discussed complex hierarchies of council systems
and paramount chieftainships, state-level institutions exhibit the
highest degree of vertical integration and a greater concern for
controlling sources of opposition.

Conclusion: a comparison with other typologies

I have now presented a complete typology of legal institutions commonly found in preindustrial societies. For each category, I have
identified the basic structure of the institution and discussed the
allocation of authority and the recruitment of personnel. Each of
the eight types of legal systems has been characterized by a particular arrangement of five underlying dimensions of legal complexity:
the presence or absence of a third party; a social requirement to
utilize this third party; the authoritativeness of third-party "decisions"; the degree to which legal authority is centralized in the
hands of the few; and the presence or absence of multiple levels of
jurisdiction or appeal.

I have argued that these five dimensions represent a parsimonious
and ethnographically accurate basis for distinguishing between the
various types of legal institutions in preindustrial societies. Other
scholars have conceived alternative typologies. In concluding this
chapter, I will consider briefly the merits and demerits of a few of
these alternative approaches.

Paul Bohannan

Bohannan is best known for his ethnographic research on dispute practices among the Tiv of Northern Nigeria (Bohannan 1957). He has, however, also made important contributions to debates on the status of "primitive" law *qua* law and to the classification of dispute-settlement systems.

Bohannan relies primarily upon the distinction between "administered rules" and "fighting" (Bohannan 1967:xiii), arguing that the two modes of disputing behavior are antithetical: Law versus war.

I have refrained from using this distinction because, as this chapter's section on self-redress makes clear, violent force is often utilized in a controlled or rule-governed fashion to settle disputes. Fighting is not necessarily synonymous with anarchy or with the absence of normative rules of conduct, definitions of delicts and appropriate responses, and symbols of conclusion. Indeed, contrasting administered rules and fighting is most appropriate where the two coexist and the latter is regarded as either a nonnormative response or a means of last resort where more peaceful means of dispute settlement have failed.

Bohannan's discussion of unicentric versus bicentric power systems is more helpful here. The former refers to social structures that have at their pinnacle a single source of authority standing above subordinate groups or individuals. State-level legal systems are clearly unicentric. Bicentric power structures, in contrast, exhibit no such superordinate authority. Bohannan sees stateless societies as typically bicentric; disputants and their supporters represent two centers of power:

> The mark of the stateless society is the absence of a unicentric power system. All situations of dispute that occur between people not within the same domestic unit *ipso facto* occur between two more or less equal power units. (Bohannan 1967:52)

Bohannan argues that the unicentric–bicentric dichotomy corresponds to a distinction between adjudication and compromise styles of dispute management. Where bicentric power prevails, no one is able to enforce a decision; thus compromise must be the dominant mode of settlement (1967:53).

Bohannan's attempt to link forms of legal systems with types of

sanctions and the predominance of either compromise or adjudication is important; however, my analysis differs from his in certain
respects. Bohannan suggests that adjudicative institutions are only
to be found in state-level societies, where the law stands above the
disputing parties. Yet the ethnographic record displays many societies in which "hearing bodies" make binding decisions (rather
than compromises), even though these cultures are far from states.
The elders' councils described in this chapter operate as third-party
adjudicators in many nonstate societies.

Bohannan also indicates that one does not find adjudication unless there are coercive enforcement agencies as well. This again leads
him to associate adjudication with state-level organization. The
empirical evidence I have reviewed suggests a more complex picture.
Judgments are rendered in societies that lack police or other enforcement bodies. For elders' councils and chieftainships, moral
authority (or what Weber called "legitimacy") forms the basis of
decision-making power. The absence of enforcement agencies does
not necessarily imply that compromise is the sole style of dispute
settlement, though it may indeed encourage such a tendency.

Bohannan's typology focuses on the extremes: adjudicative, unicentric, state systems on the one hand; compromise-based, bicentric, nonstate systems on the other. For the large number of societies
falling between these poles, these variables are found in various
combinations. The variables themselves are, of course, very
important.

F. G. Bailey and Adam Kuper

Bailey's (1965) efforts to provide a typology of council systems is
one of the more useful analyses for understanding the diversity of
functions this institution fulfills. His central concern was to understand why some councils strive for internal consensus while others
opt for majority-rule styles of decision making.

Bailey begins by building a two-part typology consisting of "elite"
and "arena" councils:

> Elite councils are those which are, or consider themselves to be . . . a
> ruling oligarchy. The dominant cleavage in such a group is between
> the elite council . . . and the public: that is to say, the dominant
> cleavage is horizontal. The opposite kind of council is the arena
> council. These exist in groups in which the dominant cleavages are

vertical. The council is not so much a corporate body with interests against its public, but an arena in which the representatives of segments in the public come into conflict with one another. (Bailey 1965:10)

Bailey argues that the two kinds of councils use different styles of decision making. Elite councils will tend toward consensus while arena councils tend toward majority vote, though these orientations may be influenced by the council's function or its concern with external versus internal relations (1965:13).

Adam Kuper (1971) suggests that Bailey's typology is applicable to political or administrative councils but requires qualification when applied to councils acting as legal bodies. He argues that "in many legal systems the court is structurally opposed to the litigants," which will push even arena councils in the direction of consensual rather than majoritarian decision processes. Kuper also points out that Bailey's model cannot accommodate councils in which "all full members of the political community have the right to attend and participate" (1971:14).

My typology makes use of the distinctions drawn by Bailey and Kuper with respect to the dimension of council membership. Hence elders' councils are composed either of all members of the political community (however that may be defined) or representatives of all segments included within that designated group, whereas restricted councils represent (or include) only members of elite classes or status groups.

However, rather than focus on *styles* of decision making I have emphasized the authoritative qualities of council decisions. Three kinds of councils have been distinguished on this basis. In an Arusha moot, only disputants and their partisan kin took part in an effort to reach an acceptable compromise. As such, I have classified the Arusha legal process as a mediator system.

Any arena council that represents all sectors of the community that can *adjudicate* cases has been categorized as an elders' council, for they tend to seek members from among the older men of the political community. Any elite council that similarly makes binding verdicts has been categorized as a restricted council. Thus the typology represents a modified version of those presented by Bailey and Kuper. The structural differences between systems like the Arusha moot and most elders' councils are too great to consign them to one category (i.e., arena councils).

Max Gluckman

Gluckman is known for his ethnographic research on the Barotse (then of Northern Rhodesia) and his theoretical and comparative work on preindustrial legal systems. Of particular interest here is his typology of "secular leadership," which he suggested could be ranked in terms of increasing authority. In ascending order of power, these institutions include: (1) *the patriarch*: the "most senior and able kinsman in an inter-related band"; (2) *elders of a number of kin groups*, who "may cooperate in giving joint leadership and direction"; (3) *big men*, who depend upon their industry, wealth, and prestige (in addition to kinship alliances) for their authority; (4) *village headmen*, who are generally drawn from a particular lineage or subclan; (5) *symbolic kings*, "who can exercise important influence in major disputes," though their main role is sacerdotal; and finally (6) *authoritative chiefs*, "who were considered to have the authority to demand the right to forbid internal fighting and to compel submissions to their adjudication, and who had at their command officials and bodies of troops to enforce their decisions" (Gluckman 1965:146–66).

Gluckman's typology is based upon one central dimension: increasing authority. I accept this as a crucial element that distinguishes different kinds of legal systems. However, I invoke a number of other principles of classification, including third-party presence, multiple levels of jurisdiction, and the like.

Richard Abel

Abel (1973) has identified various structural and processual dimensions of dispute settlement in face-to-face and complex societies. These include: specialization of roles, differentiation between interveners and disputants, and bureaucratization of dispute-settlement systems. For each of these general factors, Abel provides more detailed variables. For example, under specialization of roles, he distinguishes: (1) time devoted to performing the role, (2) role independence, (3) number of role occupants, and (4) specialization among interveners. These variables are further subdivided because Abel is aiming toward the measurement of these phenomena.

The purpose of his scheme is to predict processual variables from structural ones. For example, Abel is interested in demonstrating that structural differentiation will affect rules governing the attendance of disputants, standards of admissible evidence, standards of veracity, and so on. His analysis helps to answer questions that have long been central concerns for legal anthropology, namely, the ways in which structure determines aspects of legal process. He is not especially concerned with detailing the institutional formations into which these variables may be arranged. As such, I do not see in his work a *typology* of legal institutions. What I do find is a very detailed set of characteristics that could be used to differentiate institutional types.

If one wishes to build a typology of legal institutions, it becomes necessary to prioritize numerous potential distinctions and to select a subset that will account for empirical variation in the most economical fashion. The five dimensions of a typology outlined in this chapter all appear in some form in Abel's scheme. His formulation is a far more detailed and exhaustive list of potential differentiae than is necessary for our purposes. But his work remains a very useful study of the systematic dimensions of legal institutions.

Having discussed both my own typology of preindustrial legal institutions and parallel efforts by others, it remains for me to show that these systems of dispute settlement are systematically linked to particular modes of production. This problem is approached in the next chapter.

3

Modes of production and the distribution of legal institutions

Recent years have seen an upsurge of anthropological interest in the works of Marx and Engels. Nowhere has this been more evident than in the burgeoning literature of French anthropology, though British and American scholars have also drawn inspiration from the Marxian heritage.

On the whole, this resurgence of historical materialism has focused on reanalyzing particular ethnographies that derive originally from functionalist traditions; developing more appropriate theoretical constructs for understanding precapitalist economic formations and their economic and political relations with capitalist societies; and conducting ethnographic research in precapitalist cultures utilizing Marxian precepts as the analytic framework (e.g., Meillasoux's [1964] research on the Guoro). Relatively little attention has been paid to the use of the materialist paradigm for broadscale comparative efforts, for most anthropologists in this intellectual movement believe that an overhaul of the discipline's theoretical and methodological arsenal is the most important task at hand. Yet if the constructs of Marxism are useful in particular ethnographic contexts, they are also likely to prove helpful for dealing with comparative problems that have long been at the heart of anthropology, including the patterning of legal institutions across preindustrial economies.

Building an empirically grounded materialist theory of legal development requires the specification of theoretical constructs, an operationalization of these concepts, a test of their explanatory power, and finally an interpretation of the results. Unfortunately, this plan of action is anathema to many Marxists, who reject theory testing as "empiricism" and who are often hostile to most methodologies employed in contemporary social science. To explain the basis of this aversion, I must make a brief detour into the somewhat rarefied atmosphere of Marxist epistemology.

Historically, Marxism has opposed the epistemological theories of the orthodox social sciences. The Frankfurt School developed a trenchant critique of positivism – the belief that science should examine what is and not what ought to be and that objective knowledge exists, which is independent of the circumstances and/or position of the observer. In contrast, Critical Marxism insisted on an epistemology that used observation and experience but intertwined them with an intellectual critique based on critical reason and a view of what might be, not simply what was. One unsettling result of this *Methodenstreit* was a predilection to pursue Marxist theoretical studies rather then enter the positivistically infested waters of empirical research.

This tendency was reinforced, especially in Britain and France, by the extraordinary popularity of Louis Althusser's reinterpretations of Marxism. Although Althusser is justifiably renowned for his attacks on reductionism in Marxist theory and for his insistence on the relative autonomy of economic, political, and ideological levels of social structure, he is also known for his epistemological writings. I leave detailed criticism of these to those more familiar with his work in this field (see especially Sumner 1979). However, Althusser's criticism of "empiricism" does bear comment here.

At one level, Althusser's critique of empiricism is unobjectionable: He argues that those who believe that data organize themselves, that sense data provide the categories for their own interpretation, are mistaken. Theory must take primacy over observation; research questions must be articulated first as theoretical problems; and theory must inform empirical research. The tendency of some researchers to treat their projects as nontheoretical enterprises devoid of epistemological issues is both naive and intellectually indefensible. Thus far, I can agree with Althusser and with phenomenological critiques of empiricism, which make a similar case.

However, this critique has been extended much further, particularly by some of Althusser's followers. For them, theory becomes an enterprise that can only proceed internally: Theory cannot be disproven by data. All the techniques of systematic observation and/or measurement of the historical and social sciences are dismissed as irremediably positivist or empiricist, and so on (cf. Hindess and Hirst 1975). The result is an ethereal, theoretical Marxism that perceives an unbridgeable gulf between itself and the techniques of social science.

I reject this latter position because it is antithetical to the purposes and historical practice of materialist analysis. Any materialist epistemology is predicated upon an intimate relationship between theory and observation–experience. Of course, empirical research in the materialist tradition demands that methods and measurement be informed by one's theoretical agenda, as one would expect of any rigorous research. However, this does not imply a total rejection of the methodologies developed by historians, anthropologists, and others.

I remain sympathetic to John Moore's (1977) call for an empirical, diachronic, anthropological science that attempts to assess the validity of historical materialist approaches for problems of social evolution. This validity can only be established by subjecting a specific data base to a set of statistical or other tests, according to accepted canons of scientific research.

The concept of mode of production

Theory testing cannot proceed without first clarifying the central concepts that guide the analysis, the most important of which for our purposes is the mode of production.[1] In Chapter 1, I reviewed Marx and Engels's definitions of this term in the context of their more general theory of the relation between law and economy.

The original concept was developed in the course of Marx's analysis of nineteenth-century industrial England. It has been left to twentieth-century scholars to clarify its application to precapitalist societies. Many anthropologists have elaborated the concept for their special research concerns. I have chosen to discuss the renditions of only three: Emmanuel Terray and Maurice Godelier representing the French school, and Jonathan Friedman, whose work blends both American and British perspectives.

Terray's (1972) essay, "Historical Materialism and Segmentary

---

[1] Readers interested in more extended treatments of the "mode of production" debate are referred to Aiden Foster-Carter's (1978) article, "The Modes of Production Controversy," and Asad and Wolpe's (1976) paper, "Concepts of the Mode of Production."

Lineage-Based Societies," opens with some general remarks on the meaning of mode of production. He notes that the term is sometimes mistakenly equated with the notion of an economy.[2] Yet

> the concept of mode of production is far more precise. It [is] . . . a three part system: an economic base, a juridico-political superstructure, and an ideological superstructure. (1972:97)

Terray argues that the economic base exerts a determinant influence over the other institutional spheres and must therefore be further specified. It consists of a "combination of a system of productive forces and a system of relations of production," both integral elements of the economic organization of a society. The productive forces include raw materials, tools, machinery, and labor power combined in a particular fashion. In Marxist theory, the productive forces are related to the level of development of a society, there being an assumption that technology evolves through history to ever greater degrees of productive power. Thus one can speak of a series of stages in the development of the productive forces.

Jonathan Friedman (1974) has provided a useful account of the meaning of the term "social relations of production." He argues that they in fact "dominate the material process of production . . . at a given stage of the development of the forces of production" (1974:446). That is to say, within the constraints of what a given technological-ecological system can maximally produce, the *social relations* determine:

> (a) the use to be made of the environment . . . (b) the division of productive labor – who shall and shall not work, and the intensity of labor input . . . (c) the forms of appropriation and distribution of the social product and the utilization of surplus . . . (d) the "socially reckoned" value of the rate of surplus . . . and the rate of profit.[3] (1974:446)

---

[2] Friedman (1974:447) has raised the same criticism of cultural materialists and others who equate mode of production with technology.

[3] Friedman suggests here that "objectively" the forces in any given society have the potential for a set level of productivity. This does not mean that this level will always, in fact, be reached. On the contrary, "the social relations of production . . . impose a less than objective evaluation of the reproductive potential of the society" (Friedman 1974:446). Given two hypothetical societies with the same forces of production, it is the social relations that determine exactly what the rate of profit (extraction of surplus) will be.

The extent to which the two parts of the economic base (forces and relations) are shaped by their mutual interactions remains a subject of much debate. Some scholars argue that the technological organization of a society dictates, in some sense, the social relations of production by making possible a certain level of surplus production and therefore certain social formations of cooperation, exploitation, and surplus extraction. Friedman (1974:463), on the other hand, has argued that the forces and social relations should be understood as "relatively autonomous" domains – neither totally determined nor completely independent. I agree with his point; although the nature of technology, ecological conditions, and available labor input set certain *constraints* upon the total level of surplus that can be produced, variations in social relations will produce very different patterns of allocation, stratification, and the like.

This fact points up the importance of describing *both* the forces and social relations in analyzing a given mode of production. All too often, as Godelier has pointed out, writers mistakenly equate the economic base with the *forces alone*:

> The most common error, among Marxists, is to confuse the study of the production process in a society with that of the labor process, and to invent as many modes of production as there are labor processes. For this reason, one cannot speak of agricultural, pastoral, cynegetic, or other "modes of production". . . . A [mode of production] in fact, consists not only of one or more labor processes . . . but man's relationship to man, producers and non-producers, in the appropriation and control of the means of production . . . and the products of labor. (1977:24)

The traditional anthropological concept of subsistence economy therefore represents only one half of the equation: the forces of production. Describing a mode of production also entails the inclusion of the social relations between the individuals (or groups) who carry out the labor process and who are the beneficiaries (or losers) of the distribution of work and goods. Neglect of this second factor has been responsible for projecting an unfortunate but familiar image of historical materialism as mechanical, economic, or technological determinism.

For Marx, all the "historical" societies were characterized by considerable inequality in the social relations of production, whereby one group was able to gain enough control over the means of production to enable itself to live largely or exclusively upon the products of others' labor. Such highly stratified societies result in the formation of social classes. In its ultimate form, capitalism, there is a complete separation such that one class monopolizes ownership over the production resources while the other class becomes totally dependent upon the owners for access to livelihoods. The historical-materialist approach can be applied to less extreme situations, however.

Godelier has pointed out that hierarchical relations appear in *classless* societies where not all producers control the means of production equally:

> Modern ethnology has uncovered much information on economic and political inequalities to be found in classless societies – between older and younger siblings, men and women, "big men" and commoners, founder lineages and stranger lineages, etc. (1977:32)

Wherever inequalities are found in the production process (which appears to be true in some form in all societies), these distinctions will also be represented in ideological systems, which form the superstructure in any given mode of production. Political, legal, and cultural institutions both express and reproduce the property and labor relations that form the economic infrastructure. Godelier and Terray have both claimed that kinship systems must be understood in this vein: as ideational representations of relations of production, although they emphasize that kinship systems are clearly more than just this.

Ideological (or ideational) representations, including law, should not be understood as simple, passive reflections of economic organization. The historical-materialist position is that they are active (indeed, for Althusserians, semi-autonomous) realms that both justify and continuously re-create the economic base that gives rise to them.

Conflict, law, and the mode of production
The materialist paradigm posits a causal path between mode of production and legal institutions. The first step is that the degree of development of the forces of production both makes possible and places a limitation on the amount of surplus production in a given society. The materialist perspective emphasizes the centrality

of surplus in generating social conflict and strain; we would therefore expect that the more developed the technological capacities of
a society, the greater the surplus and hence the greater the potential
for conflict over surplus allocation.

The next step in the model is to recognize that the social relations
of production – the means whereby surplus is extracted from some
people by others (e.g., through rent, credit, labor obligations, taxes,
etc.) – are an important determinant of conflict as well. The more
elaborate the mechanisms for exploitation, the greater the potential
for conflict and the greater the need for legal sanctions and legitimation of these social relations of production.

Social stratification does not exist until one finds a certain degree
of development of both productive forces and social relations. In
this sense, surplus production is a prerequisite for stratification.
However, once inequalities in the relations of production begin to
create systematic wealth differentials between families, a new factor
contributes to social conflict. When these wealth distinctions crys-
tallize into social classes, which are often endogamous and hereditary in membership, conflict increases even further: Inequalities are
thrown into relief and redistribution systems either fade from prom-
inence or become the central focus of rebellion. In addition, once
there is a full-fledged class system, law begins to recognize the
differential rights and privileges of rank and to protect and legitimate these marks of status.

In sum, the materialist model suggests that *three variables* (forces,
social relations, and stratification), although interrelated, contribute
individually to conflict; thus, each exerts a force toward greater
legal complexity.

Having established the general framework of analysis, I shall now
consider the extent to which such a paradigm can explain an empirical problem: the distribution of the eight types of legal institutions identified in my typology across various preindustrial modes
of production. This is equivalent to asking whether mode of production is an effective predictor of this distribution. The analyses
presented in this chapter will show that this distribution is far from
random and *can* be predicted from the form of a mode of production. The validity of this proposition can be demonstrated by sub-

jecting a representative sample of preindustrial societies to a series of statistical tests outlined later in this section.

As a prelude, however, I must make clear how I have chosen to operationalize the abstract, theoretical constructs discussed above in the section on "the concept of mode of production." For the purposes of my analysis, the variable "forces of production" will be defined as the basic subsistence activities in a society, for example, the state of technology, tools, raw materials, and techniques of producing a society's livelihood. I have grouped preindustrial societies into seven basic categories according to the level of their forces of production: (1) hunting and gathering, (2) fishing, (3) pastoral, (4) incipient agriculture, (5) extensive agriculture, (6) intensive dry agriculture, and (7) intensive wet agriculture. This variable is based upon Murdock's (1967) coding scheme: He examines the relative dependence of each society in the *Ethnographic Atlas* upon these forms of food production, classifying them according to their *major* technique of subsistence.[4]

Hunters and gatherers gain the largest portion of their subsistence through hunting wild animals and collecting edible plants. *Fishers* obtain the largest portion of their food from fish or other aquatic sources (e.g., shellfish). *Pastoralists* depend upon animal husbandry for their livelihoods. *Extensive agriculturalists* are of two types. They may cultivate plants in a shifting fashion, whereby new fields are cleared annually, cultivated for a year or more, and then allowed to revert to forest or brush for a long fallow season. Or they may cultivate vegetable gardens or fruit groves (as distinct from cultivating field crops). This latter form of extensive agriculture is commonly called horticulture. In contrast, *intensive agriculturalists* grow crops on permanent fields, "utilizing fertilization by compost or animal manure, crop rotation, or other techniques so that fallowing is either unnecessary or is confined to relatively short periods" (Murdock 1967:159). This intensive-agriculture category has been

---

[4] To be placed in one of the categories outlined above, a society does not have to depend exclusively on the subsistence technology in question. Indeed, most historical materialists would argue that any given society (or, in Marxian parlance, "historical formation") may contain different modes of production. As such, a society's forces of production may be categorized according to which level of the forces (fishing, extensive agriculture, etc.) provides the largest proportion of its subsistence requirements and surplus production.

split into two subsistence systems, *irrigated intensive agriculture* and *dry intensive agriculture*.

Murdock posits a residual category of *incipient agriculture*, which describes societies that derive their subsistence from both agriculture and some mix of fishing, hunting, gathering, and pastoralism. The sum of the nonagricultural activities exceeds the society's dependence upon agriculture itself, yet agriculture is the single largest source of subsistence.

In sum, I use a seven-level variable to represent the forces of production, whereby societies are classified according to the predominant forces they employ.

At the core of the concept of social relations of production is the idea that, in some social systems, certain individuals or definable groups consume not only the products of their own labor, but also control (consume and/or distribute) the products of the surplus labor of others.[5]

In the preindustrial cultures that anthropologists have considered in most detail, the productive units tend to consist primarily of kin groups. Even the wealthiest families are confined mainly to the domestic economy, where they produce a large proportion of what they consume. However, in some societies mechanisms develop whereby some individuals or families garner a substantial addition to their income from the production of others. It is at this point that we can begin to identify what Marx referred to as the "exploitation" of labor, the appropriation of surplus product by persons other than the producers.[6]

What are these mechanisms of surplus appropriation? Tuden and Marshall (1972:442–3) have coded each of the societies in Murdock and White's "Standard Cross-Cultural Sample" (a subset of the *Ethnographic Atlas*) according to various sources of power, wealth, or influence available to individuals. Using their data, I have con-

---

[5] John Moore (1977:45) has argued that relations of exploitation are central to understanding the core of any society and in fact suggests that anthropology should abandon the notion of mode of production in favor of "mode of exploitation."

[6] This definition does not take into account the existence of surplus appropriation within the family unit (i.e., of males from females, or older members from younger members). These forms of "exploitation" (surplus extraction) are important but represent a more complex level of analysis than our statistical data sources permit. I do touch on this subject in various places in Chapter 4.

structed an index that represents the various ways in which individuals, families, or classes obtain the surplus product of others, including (1) controlling the labor or products of slaves or unfree dependents; (2) obtaining contributions, taxes, or labor of free citizens; (3) securing rents and/or other incomes from large landholdings; (4) levying tribute or taxes against a conquered or subject people; (5) gaining profits from investments in industry, business, or other capitalistic enterprises; and finally (6) extending loans or credit.

Each of these six mechanisms represents an important source of income that does not derive from domestic production within families. From a materialist's vantage point, they represent modes of surplus extraction from nonfamily members. Most of these devices are self-explanatory, with the possible exception of credit.

In simple societies, individuals often find themselves in need of financial support beyond their normal means. Throwing a feast on a ceremonial occasion, paying brideprice – these and other similar events often necessitate borrowing. Borrowers may enter into loan agreements, often at exorbitant interest rates (cf. Barton's [1969:40] discussion of Ifugao credit contracts), to fulfill their social obligations.[7] Repayment often takes the form of free labor for a long period of time. In any case, the lender derives additional income in the form of labor or payment in kind for having extended credit; as such, we can consider credit a form of surplus extraction.

From the six mechanisms, I have built an index that represents a simplified operationalization of social relations of production. At one extreme, a score of zero on this index indicates that a particular

---

[7] Margaret Mead's description of the debt cycle that obtains between younger men and older men (inside and outside of family relations) among the Manus of the Admiralty Islands provides a case in point: "There was one additional factor which welded the young men to the economic treadmill. This was the circumstance that, after a long and carefree childhood, their services were demanded by their financial backer in the name of the wife for whom not they but their backer had paid .... The dependent position of being paid for, above all else, having one's future sexual life, which was regarded with enormous shame, paid for by someone else, was intolerable. It struck at the centre of their sense of their own autonomy, which had been cultivated throughout all their upbringing. So young men worked for older men, their uncles and elders' cousins, hardly ever their fathers, in a sort of sullen, driven anger, working to get out from under, to take control of their own households ... " (Mead 1956:58–9).

society lacks all the forms of surplus extraction. Even the most
high-ranking individuals depend solely on domestic production. At
the other extreme, a score of six indicates that the society exhibits
all the mechanisms by which the exploitation of nonfamily labor
takes place.[8]

I have now operationalized two independent (predictor) variables: forces and social relations of production. I must next do the
same for the concept of stratification, for it plays a key role in the
materialist model of legal development.

Preindustrial societies vary considerably in the degree to which
status and/or wealth distinctions are present and the extent to which
these distinctions are hereditary. At one extreme are societies where
the only status differences between individuals are based upon sex
and age, or variations in personal abilities (Fried's "egalitarian society"). At the other end of the spectrum are social systems replete
with endogamous hereditary aristocracies.

My analysis utilizes a modified version of Murdock's "class stratification" variable, constructed for the *Ethnographic Atlas*. It encompasses the range of status inequalities parsimoniously in five
steps: (1) "*Absence of significant class distinctions* among freemen. . .ignoring variations in individual repute achieved through
skill, valor, piety, or wisdom." (2) "*Wealth distinctions*, based on
the possession or distribution of property are present and socially
important but not crystallized into distinct and hereditary social
classes." (3) "*Elite stratification*, in which an elite class derives its
superior status from, and perpetuates it through, control over scarce
resources, particularly land, and is thereby differentiated from a
propertyless proletariat or serf class." In contrast to category (2),
this form of stratification *does* entail hereditary social classes. (4)
Dual stratification into a "hereditary aristocracy and a lower class
of ordinary commoners or freemen, where traditionally ascribed
noble status is at least as decisive as control over scarce resources."
(5) "*Complex stratification* into social classes correlated in large

---

[8] Of the various sources of influence, power, or wealth coded by Tuden and Marshall (1972), I have utilized only those that meet the materialist notion of labor
expropriation for my index of social relations of production. Thus I have excluded
from my index certain codes, including: plunder, income from foreign commerce,
payments for shamanistic services, and perquisites derived from political office.

measure with extensive differentiation of occupational statuses" (Murdock 1967:165–6).

Murdock's variable collapses several important dimensions. On the one hand, he classifies societies on the basis of the extent to which their social groups are distinct (e.g., hereditary classes). On the other hand, he codes the sources upon which prestige differences between groups are based (e.g., forms of property or ascription). My analysis separates these two significant dimensions. The social-relations-of-production variable discussed in this section already describes sources of income. Therefore, I have modified Murdock's typology so that it refers *only* to the distinctiveness of social groupings. My stratification variable therefore includes three levels:

1. Societies that have neither significant wealth differences nor class distinctions among freemen
2. Societies that *do* have significant wealth differences between individuals, but where these have not "crystallized into distinct and hereditary social classes"
3. Societies with distinct and/or hereditary social classes

This is an ordinal variable that expresses increasing levels of stratification.

As explained in Chapter 2, legal complexity is represented as an eight-level ordinal variable consisting of the following categories:

1. Self- or kin-based redress
2. Advisor systems
3. Mediator systems
4. Elders' councils
5. Restricted councils
6. Chieftainships
7. Paramount chieftainships
8. State-level legal systems

Having defined the major concepts and operationalized them, it remains for me to formulate hypotheses that express the expected relations between the variables. The traditional materialist model argues that stratification in a society is a function of both the development of the forces of production *and* the extent to which the social relations of production enable some groups to extract surplus labor from others. This may expressed in the following hypotheses:

Hypothesis 1. The greater the degree of development of the forces of production, the greater the degree of social stratification.

Hypothesis 2. The greater the opportunities for some individuals to control the surplus labor of others, the greater the degree of social stratification in a society. (The larger our index of exploitive social relations, the greater the degree of stratification.)

I have argued (in agreement with Fried 1967) that there is a close relationship between legal complexity and social stratification, for the emergence of distinct and unequal social groups leads to heightened conflict, which law must manage. I therefore hypothesize that:

Hypothesis 3. The more stratified a society, the more complex its legal institutions.

To this I shall add two further hypotheses. The materialist model suggests that the forces of production exert an influence on the complexity of legal institutions *independent of and in addition to* that imposed by stratification. For if, as is detailed in Chapter 4, legal systems regulate surplus allocation, it follows that the more surplus produced, the greater the potential for conflict in a society and the more complex the institutions that regulate property rights and labor relations. Thus, for example, within a group of societies with the same level of stratification, one would expect to find that those with more developed forces of production (and therefore higher levels of surplus) will also exhibit more complex legal institutions. Phrased as a hypothesis, we expect that:

Hypothesis 4. Holding stratification constant (i.e., within each given level of stratification), the more developed the forces of production in a society, the more complex its legal institutions.

A parallel line of reasoning extends this framework somewhat further: If stratification is an independent predictor of legal complexity, then even when two societies have identical forces of production and hence (for the purposes of argument) equivalent amounts of surplus, the one that is more stratified will also have the more complex legal institutions. This follows from the notion that increased stratification implies increased conflict over surplus products. We express this idea as follows:

> Hypothesis 5. Holding the forces of production constant (i.e., within each subsistence type), the more stratified a society, the more complex its legal institutions.

Finally, the complete model can be given; it suggests that there are three independent causes of legal complexity: forces of production, social relations of production, and social stratification, which interact and complement one another in any concrete case but which can be separated statistically for purposes of causal analysis. This model can be expressed as a final hypothesis:

> Hypothesis 6. The greater the development of the forces of production, social relations of production, and social stratification, the more complex a society's legal institutions.

To test these hypotheses, it was necessary to examine a large body of cross-cultural data. I have chosen to use two samples of societies. The larger of the two, Murdock and White's (1969) Standard Cross-Cultural Sample (SCCS), was developed to provide a simple controlled solution to some sampling problems commonly encountered in cross-cultural survey research. SCCS consists of 186 carefully selected societies, coded for a large range of variables. The advantages of using the SCCS are twofold: First, it includes carefully precoded material, which enables the construction of variables representing mode of production and social stratification. Second, the sample was constructed bearing the following concerns in mind:

> "The universe from which a world sample should be drawn consists not of the totality of the world's culture bearing units, but of clusters of such characterized by close genetic relationships." (Murdock 1967:111)

The point here is to establish units of measurement that are sufficiently different to be treated as independent cases. There are 412 such clusters in the *Ethnographic Atlas*, the largest "data bank" available for cross-cultural analysis. These clusters were grouped into 200 sampling provinces from which 186 specific cases were chosen for the Standard Cross-Cultural Sample.

> "No world sample should include any two societies located geo-

graphically so close to one another that diffusion is likely to have jeopardized the essential independence of their cultures." (Murdock 1967:112)

This issue is commonly known as "Galton's problem," whereby contact between societies leads to diffusion and thus interferes with the independence of the cases. The SCCS was selected with Galton's problem in mind and thus provides some "insurance" against intercase contamination.

> The universe from which a world sample may appropriately be drawn consists, not of all the societies of clusters which are known to exist. . .but only of those whose clusters have been adequately described. (Murdock 1967:113)

One scholar's "adequate description" may be another's travesty. However, the cases in the SCCS have been selected according to the "superiority of ethnographic coverage" they evidence. This judgment is based on the reputation of the ethnographers whose works form the basis of each file, the conditions prevailing during the fieldwork, and the availability of corroborating sources.

The Standard Cross-Cultural Sample therefore provides a source of reliable information on 186 carefully selected societies, which represent the six major regions of the world as follows:

Sub-Saharan Africa	28
Circum-Mediterranean	28
East Eurasia	34
Insular Pacific	31
North America	33
South and Central America	32
	186

I will be using the SCCS to test Hypotheses 1 and 2 described above, those that speak to the relationship between the mode of production (forces and social relations) and social stratification.

The Standard Cross-Cultural Sample does not contain information on types of legal institutions.[9] I have therefore constructed a

---

[9] Variable 3 codes levels of political jurisdiction above the village. However, it does not capture the institutional form of legal systems, which is my primary concern; on this basis, I have elected not to use it. Instead, I have created a new coding system for identifying types of legal institutions.

second sample and have assembled data on legal institutions for each of its component societies.

This second sample was constructed in accordance with the cross-cultural theory-testing methodology developed by Reinhardt, Blumberg, and Winch (1975). These researchers utilized a subsample drawn from a triple-overlap of the *Ethnographic Atlas*, the Standard Cross-Cultural Sample, and the Human Relations Area Files. The subsample, which includes sixty cases, was constructed to ensure the correct representation of each of the six major regions of the world and all the major subsistence systems.

The reader should note one difference between the SCCS and my subsample as regards the representation of subsistence systems. The former includes a residual category, "incipient agriculture" (societies that use a mix of agriculture, hunting and gathering, and fishing, where none of these was clearly predominant). This category is more of a confusion than a help in my analysis because it cannot be used to test the linkage between forces of production and stratification. As such, where my data analysis relies on SCCS data alone, this category has been included. However, in selecting the subsample for which legal data were to be collected, I have sampled only from the six relatively "pure" subsistence categories (and as a result my subsample does not include any incipient agriculture societies).

The subsample of sixty societies is patterned after that used by Reinhardt et al., with some minor alterations based on the availability of legal data. Table 3.1 presents the breakdown of my subsample according to geographic regions and subsistence systems. (Appendix 1 presents the actual societies included, with their subsistence codes.)

Once this subsample had been selected, I carried out archival research on the legal institutions of each of the sixty societies. The data come from original ethnographic sources, each of which is listed by society in Appendix 2 (with full citations in the Bibliography). An average of six sources was consulted for each of the sixty societies.

All information pertinent to dispute processing was culled from these sources and a typology or coding scheme was developed to categorize the results. This was explored in detail in Chapter 2, where the eight types of legal institutions were discussed. Each of the sixty societies was coded according to the most complex legal

Table 3.1. *Sixty-society subsample by geographic region and subsistence type*

	Africa	Circum-Mediterranean	Asia	Pacific	North America	South America	Total
Hunting and gathering	1	0	1	2	2	4	10
Fishing	0	0	1	2	4	2	9
Herding	2	4	2	0	0	1	9
Extensive agriculture	5	1	1	4	1	1	13
Dry intensive agriculture	4	3	1	0	0	1	9
Irrigated intensive agriculture	1	2	3	1	2	1	10
Total	13	10	9	9	9	10	60

institution present by two individuals working independently and without reference to data other than the legal materials.[10]

To summarize this section on the use of cross-cultural samples, I will use these materials as follows:

1. To test Hypotheses 1 and 2, that stratification can be predicted by the forces and relations of production, I will use the Standard Cross-Cultural Sample of 186 societies.

2. To test Hypotheses 3, 4, and 5, that stratification and the forces of production *independently* predict legal complexity, I will use the subsample of 60 societies.

3. Finally, I will test the composite model (involving forces and social relations of production, stratification, and legal institutions) by examining 56 of the 60 societies for which we have complete data on all variables. To meet the criteria of a representative sample with adequate information on legal systems, it was necessary to include four societies that are not part of the SCCS, and which therefore lack data on the social relations of production. This 56-society subsample will be used to test Hypothesis 6 and to confirm steps 1 and 2 above.

The next section reports the results of these statistical analyses. Readers who are not concerned with the statistical details of this analysis may wish to move directly to the nonstatistical summary of the results in the concluding section of this chapter.

Data analysis and findings

Mode of production and social stratification

Table 3.2 presents 184 societies in the Standard Cross-Cultural Sample cross-tabulated to show the relationships between the forces of production (subsistence type) and social stratification.[11] Our hy-

---

[10] Although agreement between coders was high, there were a few cases where disagreement appeared. In these cases, files were reviewed by both coders and additional source materials were investigated until a consensus on the most appropriate score on the legal variable could be reached.

[11] The number of cases in the Standard Cross-Cultural Sample is 186. However, 2 of these have been coded as having "no information" on the variables I use for social relations of production. These cases had to be dropped from the sample as a result and my "working sample" therefore has only 184 cases.

Table 3.2. Cross-tabulation of forces of production (subsistence types) by social stratification for Standard Cross-Cultural Sample[a]

	Forces of production (subsistence types)							
Stratification	Hunting & gathering	Fishing	Pastoral	Incipient agriculture	Extensive agriculture	Dry intensive agriculture	Irrigated intensive agriculture	Row total
Absence	25	8	3	15	16	4	5	76
	32.9	10.5	3.9	19.7	21.1	5.3	6.6	41.3
	89.3	44.4	20.0	68.2	34.8	13.8	19.2	
Wealth distinctions	2	7	8	2	13	9	2	43
	4.7	16.3	18.6	4.7	30.2	20.9	4.7	23.4
	7.1	38.9	53.3	9.1	28.3	31.0	7.7	
Class stratification	1	3	4	5	17	16	19	65
	1.5	4.6	6.2	7.7	26.2	24.6	29.2	35.3
	3.6	16.7	26.7	22.7	37.0	55.2	73.1	
Column total	28	18	15	22	46	29	26	184
	15.2	9.8	8.2	12.0	25.0	15.8	14.1	100.0

[a]The top figure in each cell is the cell count, the middle the row percent, and the bottom the column percent.

pothesis regarding the relationship between these two variables is as follows:

> Hypothesis 1. The greater the degree of development of the forces of production, the greater the degree of social stratification.

Inspection of Table 3.2 shows a strong relationship between the two variables. For example, 89.3% of the hunters and gatherers have neither class stratification nor wealth distinctions, whereas only 3.6% have social classes. There is a trend across the table such that by the time we come to irrigated agricultural societies, only 19.2% lack wealth distinctions and social classes, whereas 73% exhibit class stratification.

The relationships embodied in Table 3.1 may be summarized by several alternative nonparametric measures of correlation, as follows:

Correlations between the forces of production and degree of stratification (zero-order correlations) for Standard Cross-Cultural Sample (184 societies)

	Correlation coefficient	Level of significance
Statistic		
Gamma	.53548	
Spearman's Rho	.4801	$< .001$
Kendall's Tau C	.45333	$< .0001$
Somer's D (asymmetric)	.36021	

The relative merits of these four measures of rank-order correlation are discussed in Appendix 3. However, the unanimity of these measures, and the very high levels of significance that accompany them, indicate that the patterns in Table 3.2 are unlikely to have occurred by chance. Moreover, the magnitudes of the correlations indicate that the relationship between the forces of production and social stratification is quite strong.

Table 3.2 represents the simple (or zero-order) correlation between the independent or predictor variable (forces of production) and the dependent or predicted variable (social stratification). However, for my theoretical purposes it is important to know the effect of the forces of production on stratification *independent of other contributing factors* (e.g., social relations of production). This can be determined in two different ways. One can look at the correlations between the forces of production and stratification for groups of societies that have equivalent social relations of production. In other words, one can examine the relationship between forces and stratification holding the social relations of production constant. Alternatively, this result can be achieved statistically using the technique of partial correlation.[12]

Conceptually, both techniques provide the same result; they measure the relationship between forces of production and stratification after factoring out any influence from the social relations of production. The results of the first method are given in the tables in Appendix 4. The results of the second method may be summarized as follows:

Partial correlations between forces of production and degree of stratification (first-order partial correlations, controlling for social relations of production)

	Correlation coefficient	Level of significance
Statistic		
Gamma	.29847	
Spearman's Rho	.1724	< .01
Kendall's Tau	.1812	< .007

The partial correlations above are much lower than the zero-order correlations. This means that part of the relationship between forces of production and stratification displayed in Table 3.2 was due to an underlying interaction between forces and social relations of production. However, even when one factors out the effect of social

---

[12] Partial correlation is a method of calculating a correlation coefficient that describes the relationship between two variables while simultaneously adjusting for the effect of one or more other variables. One of the difficulties in interpreting a simple (zero-order) correlation between two variables is that the observed relationship may be spurious. That is, the relationship may result from a third variable that is correlated with the other two. Partial correlation is a method of avoiding this problem. If the effect is spurious, controlling for the third variable will cause the original correlation measure to drop to zero. For a more detailed description of the mathematical basis of partial correlation, see Nie et al. (1975:302–5).

relations via partial correlation, a statistically significant, though more moderate, correlation between forces and stratification remains.

I therefore conclude that Hypothesis 1 is upheld and proceed to the second hypothesis, replicating this form of analysis.

> Hypothesis 2. The greater the opportunities for some individuals to control the surplus labor of others, the greater the degree of social stratification in a society.

Table 3.3 presents the 184 cases in the Standard Cross-Cultural Sample cross-tabulated to show the relationship between the social relations of production and the forms of social stratification. I have defined social relations of production as the degree of control over surplus labor of nonfamily members. Accordingly, the columns of Table 3.3 are arranged in the form of an additive index, with 0 representing societies that have none of these forms of surplus extraction and where domestic production is the sole source of income of all individuals and family groups. At the other extreme, a score of 6 represents a society that has all six of the possible mechanisms by which individuals benefit from the labor of nonfamily members.

Table 3.3 shows a striking trend toward the development of wealth distinctions and class stratification as the social-relations-of-production index increases. Thus, 89.5% of all the societies that have neither wealth distinctions nor social classes also have a zero score on the index of the social relations of production. The remaining 10.5% of the societies in the stratification "absent" category have only one source of labor appropriation. None of the societies in this nonstratified category has more than one source of surplus labor for income.

Within the next category, societies that have wealth distinctions but no classes, 60.5% have no sources of surplus expropriation, while 39.5% have between one and three sources. None of these societies has more than three sources of labor appropriation. Finally, turning to societies that have social classes, only 12.3% have no sources of surplus extraction other than domestic production, while 87.7% have between one and five sources; 58.8% of the class societies have two or more sources of income other than domestic production.

The following nonparametric measures of correlation assess the strength of the relationship between social relations of production and social stratification:

Table 3.3. *Cross-tabulation of social relations of production (additive index) by social stratification for Standard Cross-Cultural Sample*[a]

	Social relations of production (additive index)						Row total
	0	1	2	3	4	5	
Stratification							
Absence	68	8	0	0	0	0	76
	89.5	10.5	0	0	0	0	41.3
	66.7	19.5	0	0	0	0	
Wealth distinctions	26	11	5	1	0	0	43
	60.5	25.6	11.6	2.3	0	0	23.4
	25.5	26.8	18.5	9.1	0	0	
Class stratification	8	22	22	10	1	2	65
	12.3	33.8	33.8	15.4	1.5	3.1	35.3
	7.8	53.7	81.5	90.9	100.0	100.0	
Column total	102	41	27	11	1	2	184
	55.4	22.3	14.7	6.0	.5	1.1	100.0

[a]The top figure in each cell is the cell count, the middle the row percent, and the bottom the column percent.

Correlations between the social relations of production and degree of stratification (zero-order correlations) for Standard Cross-Cultural Sample (184 societies)

	Correlation coefficient	Level of significance
Statistic		
Gamma	.85694	
Spearman's Rho	.6995	< .001
Kendall's Tau C	.59662	< .0001
Somer's D (asymmetric)	.64381	

These statistics shows that there is a strong zero-order correlation between the social relations of production and the degree of social stratification. However, it will be important also to test for this relationship, controlling for the influence of the forces of production. Following the strategy adopted in the previous discussion, I have presented cross-tabulations between the social relations of production and stratification for societies with the same forces of production in Appendix 5. Partial correlations are another way of representing the same information:

Partial correlations between social relations of production and degree of stratification (first-order partial correlations, controlling for social relations of production)

	Correlation coefficient	Level of significance
Statistic		
Gamma	.80204	
Spearman's Rho	.5967	< .001
Kendall's Tau	.5446	< .0001

If the partial correlations are compared with the zero-order correlations above, one sees a small drop in the correlation coefficient. This indicates that a small part of the relationship between the social relations of production and social stratification displayed in Table 3.3 was due to an underlying interaction between social relations and forces of production. However, when the partial-correlation method is used to factor out the effects of the forces of production, a very strong correlation remains between social relations and stratification. On this basis, I can claim that Hypothesis 2 is upheld.

Hypotheses 1 and 2 express the basic materialist paradigm of stratification in a measurable form: The mode of production (forces and social relations of production) is the most important factor underlying the form of social stratification in a society. The data show that both the forces and social relations are independently correlated with the level of stratification. Examining the relative strength of the two relationships, one finds that the social relations of production are a much stronger predictor of the degree of stratification than are the forces of production, but both are independent and statistically significant predictors of social stratification.

Another method for determining the relative contribution of these two variables toward predicting social stratification is to utilize a linear-regression equation. Such an equation will also indicate the extent to which these two variables taken together adequately account for the variance in level of social stratification. The equation tested is:

$$\text{Stratification} = b_1 \times \text{Forces of production} + b_2 \times \text{Relations of production} + \text{Constant}$$

where b_1 and b_2 are the regression coefficients that express the relative contribution of each variable in predicting stratification.

The adjusted R^2 statistic for the regression equation above is 0.44929. This means that forces of production and social relations of production together account for 44.93% of the variance in level of social stratification. By the standards typically employed by quantitative social scientists, this is a strong result.

The relative contributions of the forces and social relations of production in predicting stratification can be determined from the regression by comparing the "beta weights" for the two variables. This comparison indicates that the social-relations measure is 2.78 times as strong a predictor of stratification as the forces variable. (The full statistics for the regression analysis are listed and discussed in Appendix 6.)

This completes the analysis of the Standard Cross-Cultural Sample data. I now consider the subsample of sixty societies and the materials on legal institutions.

Social stratification and legal institutions

In the section above, I established that the two elements of the mode of production will successfully predict the degree of social stratification across a sample of societies. The next step in the analysis is to move from stratification to legal institutions. First, I must assess the extent to which the level of stratification predicts the type of legal institution found in any given society in the subsample. Thus, where social stratification was the dependent variable in the previous section, it now becomes the independent (or predictor) variable. The "new" dependent (predicted) variable is that of legal complexity.

The reader will recall that data were collected on the legal institutions of sixty societies, for a representative subsample. I have already outlined the eight-level legal variable that will be used for testing the next hypotheses. The codes assigned to each of the sixty societies are listed in Appendix 7. With these codes in mind, let us consider the next proposition:

> Hypothesis 3. The more stratified a society, the more complex its legal institutions.

In the interests of clarity, I will analyze Hypothesis 3 according to the same procedures employed in the prior sections. First, Table 3.4 presents cross-tabulations that show the distribution of the eight types of legal institutions across the three categories of social stratification. The patterns in this table are straightforward: Within societies that have no wealth distinctions or class stratification, the majority of them (68.2%) have only the simplest forms of legal institutions, namely self-redress and advisor systems. The remaining 31.8% of the nonstratified societies have elders' councils, where each household (or, in most "communal" cases, all adult males) is represented.

When one considers the intermediate stratification category, societies *with* wealth distinctions but *without* class stratification, one finds the following: (1) Only 11.8% practice self-redress and none

Table 3.4. *Cross-tabulation of social stratification by legal institutions for 60-society subsample*[a]

	Stratification			
	Absence	Wealth distinctions	Class stratification	Row total
Type of legal institution				
Self-redress	10	2	0	12
	83.3	16.7	0	20.0
	45.5	11.8	0	
Advisor	5	0	1	6
	83.3	0	16.7	10.0
	22.7	0	4.8	
Mediator	0	3	0	3
	0	100.0	0	5.0
	0	17.6	0	
Elders' council	7	7	0	14
	50.0	50.0	0	23.3
	31.8	41.2	0	
Restricted council	0	0	3	3
	0	0	100.0	5.0
	0	0	14.3	
Chieftainship	0	5	5	10
	0	50.0	50.0	16.7
	0	29.4	23.8	
Paramount chief	0	0	6	6
	0	0	100.0	10.0
	0	0	28.6	
State-level	0	0	6	6
	0	0	100.0	10.0
	0	0	28.6	
Column total	22	17	21	60
	36.7	28.3	35.0	100.0

[a]The top figure in each cell is the cell count, the middle the row percent, and the bottom the column percent.

have advisory systems; (2) 41.2% have elders councils, a figure 10% higher than the comparable figure for nonstratified societies; (3) 17.6% have mediator systems, which do not appear at all in nonstratified societies; and (4) 29.14% of the societies with wealth distinctions have chieftainships, a system completely absent from nonstratified societies.

Finally, when I examine the class-stratified societies, the distribution of legal institutions stands in marked contrast to that outlined for the nonstratified societies or those with wealth distinctions. None of these societies practices self-redress (as a formal system of dispute settlement). Only 4.8% have advisor systems. Mediator systems and elders' councils are not represented among class-stratified societies at all. Fully 95.2% of the legal systems in these societies fall into the categories of restricted councils, chieftainships, paramount chieftainships, and state-level legal systems. Three of these four types of legal institutions are represented *only* in class-stratified societies.

These data indicate that the more stratified a particular society, the more likely it is to have a complex, institutionalized legal system. This observation is supported by the following nonparametric measures of correlation indicating the strength of the association between social stratification and legal institutions:

Correlations between degree of social stratification and complexity of legal institutions (zero-order correlations) for 60-society subsample

	Correlation coefficient	Level of significance
Statistic		
Gamma	.85009	
Spearman's Rho	.7914	< .001
Kendall's Tau C	.77500	< .0001
Somer's D (asymmetric)	.77955	

These are very high correlation coefficients and the significance tests indicate that the pattern that appears in Table 3.4 is highly unlikely to have occurred by chance. The magnitudes of the correlations indicates that the relationship between the degree of social stratification and forms of legal institutions is an extremely strong one.

On this basis, I conclude that Hypothesis 3 is well supported by the empirical data.

As an extension of this theory, I suggested that the relationship between stratification and legal institutions should hold even when one controls statistically for the effect of the forces of production. In other words, even among societies with the same subsistence technologies, and therefore similar rates of surplus production, the societies that are more stratified will have more complex legal institutions. This was expressed in Hypothesis 5 as follows:

> Hypothesis 5. Holding the forces of production constant (i.e., within each subsistence type), the more stratified a society, the more complex its legal institutions.

This hypothesis can be tested either by examining cross-tabulations of law by stratification within each subsistence type (see Appendix 8) or via the partial correlations below:

Partial correlations between degree of social stratification and legal institutions (first-order partial correlations, controlling for forces of production) for 60-society subsample

	Correlation coefficient	Level of significance
Statistic		
Gamma	.79487	
Spearman's Rho	.6782	< .001
Kendall's Tau	.5827	< .001

These statistics show that even after controlling for the influence of the forces of production, there remains an extremely strong and statistically significant relationship between social stratification and legal complexity. Hypothesis 5 is therefore corroborated.

However, from the materialist perspective, stratification should not be the *only* predictor of legal complexity. Stratification will increase conflict over the social surplus in any society and hence should lead to more complex mechanisms for dealing with heightened levels of conflict. But regardless of the level of stratification in a society, the development of the forces of production should be related to the total amount of surplus in a society. Because I take the position that legal institutions regulate property and forms of surplus, I expect to see a direct relationship between forces of production and legal complexity. For example, societies with relatively undeveloped forces of production (e.g., hunters and gatherers, fishers) have less surplus to conflict over than do societies at a higher level of surplus (e.g., agriculturalists). My theory suggests that legal institutions in hunting and gathering or fishing cultures would be less complex than those in agrarian societies, *even where such societies have equivalent scores on the stratification index.* This is a restatement of Hypothesis 4, which reads as follows:

> Hypothesis 4. Holding stratification constant (i.e., within each given level of stratification), the more developed the forces of production in a society, the more complex its legal institutions.

We can assess the validity of Hypothesis 4 by examining the following partial correlations:

Partial correlations between forces of production and legal institutions (first-order partial correlations, controlling for social stratification) for 60-society subsample

	Correlation coefficient	Level of significance
Statistic		
Gamma	.45507	
Spearman's Rho	.4067	< .001
Kendall's Tau	.3123	< .008

After the influence of stratification is factored out, these statistics indicate that there is a moderate and statistically significant relationship between the forces of production and legal complexity. Hypothesis 4 is therefore upheld.

In the above sections, Hypotheses 3, 4, and 5 have all been confirmed by the data analysis, indicating that stratification and forces of production both predict legal complexity independently. However, I need to assess the *relative* predictive power of the two variables and the extent to which, when combined, they adequately account for the variance in legal complexity. One way to do this is to compute a simple linear regression in which stratification and the forces of production are both predictor variables and legal complexity is the dependent variable, as follows:

Legal complexity = b_1 × Stratification + b_2 × Forces + Constant

where b_1 and b_2 are the regression coefficients that express the relative contribution of each variable in predicting legal complexity.

The adjusted R^2 statistic for this equation is 0.6789. Stratification and forces of production taken together therefore predict 67.89% of the variance in legal complexity, which suggests a very strong predictive model.

The relative contributions of stratification and the forces of production in predicting legal complexity is obtained from the regression by comparing the "beta weights" for the two variables. Thus the beta weight for stratification is 0.611, whereas for the forces of production it is 0.314. This indicates that stratification is approximately twice as strong a predictor as forces of production. The full statistics for the regression and a discussion of the attendant technicalities appear in Appendix 6.

The full model

In the preceding sections, I determined that the first five hypotheses were confirmed by the data. First, using the large Standard Cross-Cultural Sample, I found that the mode of production, understood as a composite of forces and social relations of production, was predictive of social stratification. Then, analyzing the sixty-society subsample, I determined that stratification itself was predictive of legal complexity.

To test a comprehensive model (Hypothesis 6), and to determine the relative power of all three independent variables (forces, social relations, and stratification) in predicting legal complexity, I shall now examine a subsample of fifty-six societies for which we have all the necessary data. Utilizing a regression equation containing *all* the predictor variables, we can test the full model as follows:

Legal complexity = b_1 × Forces of production + b_2 × Social relations of production + b_3 × Stratification + Constant

This regression equation yields these results: The adjusted R^2 was equal to .6646, which means that the equation explains 66.5% of the variance in legal complexity. The relative contribution of each predictor variable is as follows: Social stratification appears as the strongest predictor (beta = .417); social relations of production is second in power (beta = .292); and finally, forces of production was the least predictive (beta = .267); each predictor is significant at the .008 level of significance or better. The beta weights suggest that each of the three factors is important in determining legal complexity.

Overall, this regression equation indicates that the materialist paradigm for explaining legal complexity is fully supported by this empirical analysis. This finding confirms the hypothesis testing undertaken in the previous sections.

Nonstatistical summary
At the outset of this chapter, I advanced the thesis that the complexity of legal institutions could best be explained by the mode of production understood as both the development of the forces and the social relations of production. I argued that if a primary purpose of a legal system was the regulation of social relations of production, that is, the regulation of labor and the surplus it produces, then there should be a strong relationship between the rate of surplus production, the extent to which that surplus's distribution is controlled by a restricted group, and the complexity of the legal institutions that guarantee that distribution. In addition, I suggest that conflict will increase as the capacity of the forces of production for producing surplus grows (as the forces develop, to use Marx's phrase) and as the mechanisms for a restricted number of individuals or groups to appropriate that surplus multiply.

This theoretical paradigm was formulated in terms of six hypotheses that express predictive relations between the mode of production, stratification, and legal complexity. The first two of these broke the concept of mode of production down into its constitutive elements, forces and social relations, each of which was shown to be predictive of social stratification for the Standard Cross-Cultural Sample (184 societies). Regression analysis showed that social relations were roughly twice as powerful as the forces in accounting for stratification.

I next examined the predictive value of stratification in determining legal complexity. This hypothesis was examined using a subsample of sixty societies for which I collected data on legal systems. Subsequent analysis showed that social stratification was a powerful predictor of legal complexity. I also discovered that, for societies with the same levels of stratification, the greater the development of their forces of production, the higher their score on legal complexity – thus confirming the basic materialist model as well.

The final step in my analysis involved testing a comprehensive model on a subsample of fifty-six societies. All three predictors (forces, social relations, and stratification), were used simultaneously to predict the complexity of legal institutions. By performing a regression equation, I determined that the model is highly predictive of legal complexity, accounting for 67 percent of the variance. This is a strong result, which suggests that the materialist model as I have operationalized it here is a powerful theoretical tool for explaining the empirical problem of cross-cultural variation in legal institutions.

4

Modes of production and the functions of legal institutions

In this chapter, I focus on the substance of disputes and prescriptive rules rather than on the institutional apparatus of dispute management. In particular, I wish to explore the utility of the materialist paradigm for understanding the subject matter of disputes in preindustrial societies.

Anthropology has veered away from efforts to build a theory of substantive law in preindustrial societies. To the extent that the cross-cultural content of legal "codes" has been examined, the analysis has been concerned either with demonstrating that particular cultures do, in fact, have legal rules (e.g., Gluckman 1955, Hoebel 1968, and Pospisil 1958) or with demonstrating the ways in which substantive law reflects underlying cultural values (e.g., Nader 1969). These more traditional approaches have not attempted to build a theory linking sources of conflict with nonlegal, structural features of preindustrial society.

Although disputes come in many guises (adultery, debt disputes, ritual or status slights), in any given society some kinds of conflicts recur frequently while others are virtually absent. The ethnographic record suggests that disputes are rarely idiosyncratic. Certain types of societies are wracked with particular kinds of "trouble cases." Where stereotypical kinds of disputes prevail, I argue that there are underlying strains in the social relations of production, patterned inequalities in access to crucial resources, which are surfacing as disputes and which are addressed by prescriptive legal rules. It is in this sense that law should be viewed as regulating the social relations of production. I do not mean by this that legal institutions are always successful at this task, nor do they always return ruptured relations to the equilibrated state that the structural-functional school perceived. I am suggesting, however, that legal behavior is oriented toward and straining to accomplish the containment of structurally generated conflict. Thus, if the tensions generated within particular modes of production can be isolated, recurrent disputes and substantive rules should be interpretable as manifestations of these tensions.

It should be clear from this brief description that the theoretical approach I am recommending bears little resemblance to a "crude" materialist perspective that sees law as a passive reflection of economy. On the contrary, the notion of law as a regulatory institution that *actively* intervenes in processes of surplus allocation, labor organization, and the like, contradicts any imagery of "reflection." Nevertheless, the nature of law's activity should be understood in the context of modes of production. This should not be taken to suggest that law has *only* economic functions; it clearly plays other roles as well. Nevertheless, I am arguing that the regulation of social relations of production is a crucial function of law.

To explore this thesis, I first consider each of the six subsistence types (or forces of production) used in Chapter 3, one at a time. Within a given subsistence type, I classify societies according to their social relations of production. Societies that share modes of production are therefore grouped together. I shall then examine the content of disputes that constantly reappear in these modes of production.

I draw upon two types of data as sources of information on the substance of law. The first consists of the case materials and data on prescriptive rules included in some of the well-known ethnographies of law, such as *The Law of Primitive Man* (Hoebel 1968), *Ifugao Law* (Barton 1969), and *Ashanti Law and Constitution* (Rattray 1929). Supplementing these, I will return to the data collected for Chapters 2 and 3, the ethnographic materials on law in sixty preindustrial societies.

Food collectors: hunters, gatherers, and fishers
Although I distinguished between hunters and gatherers and fishers on the basis of subsistence technology in Chapter 3, many ecological-economic anthropologists (e.g., Cohen, Sahlins), group these societies into one category: the food collectors. The major portion of a food-collecting economy is devoted to gathering, capturing, or

otherwise amassing the resources provided by the natural environment. Food *production*, in the sense of active cultivation, is held to a minimum or is nonexistent. At this level in the development of the productive forces, human beings have the least amount of control over their habitats. Technology consists of hunting implements, foraging strategies, and a well-developed technical knowledge of environmental fluctuations.

To the extent that food collectors are categorized at all, categories are usually based on the extent to which their natural habitats require constant nomadism or permit semipermanent sedentism. In both instances, food collection remains the primary subsistence strategy. Yet the paucity of resources in certain environments and the abundance in others has an important impact on the ability of food-collecting populations to remain within a given area. Richness of the physical surroundings also has a critical affect on the labor process, social organization, political complexity, and (as will be shown) legal life in a given culture. In accordance with the accepted practice of distinguishing food collectors on the basis of the nomadic–sedentary dimensions (Blumberg 1978), I consider these two forms of production separately.

Nomadic food collectors

For tens of thousands of years, humans lived off the land, migrating from place to place seeking edible plants, fish, and small game animals.[1] This form of existence was the only one available for most of what we know of human history; in comparison, the history of

---

[1] Although, technically speaking, the Indian societies of the North American Great Plains may be considered hunters and gatherers, I have chosen not to consider them here. The ethnographic record on these societies documents a way of life that was so thoroughly altered through contact with the westward expansion of the United States that it can hardly be considered an accurate reflection of life prior to this unfortunate transition. Sahlins, in fact, considers the Plains Indians to represent a separate category of "equestrian hunters": "Today's stereotype of 'an Indian,' that intrepid mounted warrior of painted mein and feathered bonnet, was characteristic of the Plains and of no other area of America. Before the coming of the white man, this kind of Indian did not exist anywhere . . . Nor are there many ecological parallels elsewhere." The problem of contact could be raised with respect to other societies as well. However, the Plains cultures constitute a particularly thorny classification problem due to the drastic conditions they were forced to contend with; for this reason, I have chosen not to consider them in any detail.

agriculture occupies a rather small proportion of the time line. The character of life in foraging societies has been a subject of controversy. Many an eminent ethnologist has maintained that the existence of nomadic food collectors was "nasty, brutish, and short" at best.[2]

It took some solid ethnographic evidence (Lee 1968, 1979) and a strong dose of comparative analysis (Sahlins 1972) to dispel this dismal vision. Far from the specter of scarcity, fear of starvation, abandonment of the feeble, and constant labor for a meager living, Lee and Sahlins (among others) argued that hunting-and-gathering groups constitute the "original affluent society":

> A good case can be made that hunters and gatherers work less than we do; and rather than a continuous travail, the food quest is intermittent, leisure abundant, and there is a greater amount of sleep in the daytime per capita per year than in any other condition of society. (Sahlins 1972:14)

Even in some of the harshest territory inhabited by humans, the desert regions of Australia, food foragers were able to support themselves on short work hours.

Lee's (1979) study of the Kalahari desert Bushmen, the !Kung San of Botswana, was one of the first to track the subsistence practices of a nomadic population over a long period at close range. Lee notes that the !Kung diet is primarily composed of vegetable matter, with a comparatively minor amount of meat. Here one finds the first evidence of a sexual division of labor. Gathering is a female occupation practiced on a daily basis, whereas hunting is a male activity carried out in small cooperative groups intermittently (Cohen 1968:80).

---

[2] Simon Roberts (1979:98) has pointed out that this image is not necessarily misleading. Some hunting-and-gathering groups live where the "climate and terrain are so harsh that the margins between survival and death are narrow," whereas others exist amid abundance. He points out that dispute-resolution practices may be tied to these ecological realities: Where existence is marginal, cooperation is critical, group solidarity is emphasized, and ostracism (or the threat of it) has serious ramifications for individual survival. Conversely, in areas of plenty, a troublesome individual can withdraw from reciprocal obligations and suffer relatively little.

   Regardless of these variations, however, all known hunting-and-gathering groups depend on some form of cooperative foraging. High levels of internal conflict pose disruptive influences for the organization of production.

Although foraging can support a healthy, viable population, it clearly limits the demographic profile of hunting-and-gathering groups. The number of individuals who can be accommodated within a given area remains small; fifty persons in a living group appears to be the norm (Cohen 1968:79). The composition of these groups is in constant flux. Population is maintained at a low level by long intervals between births – a functional practice given the mobility demands on female gatherers (Blumberg 1978).

I now consider briefly the implications of the nomadic food-collecting economy for surplus production. Nomadic foragers epitomize the term "subsistence economy"; all indications are that they produce no surplus whatever. Sahlins points out that they fail to accumulate even though their technological sophistication would make this possible. Producers move out of camp every day or so to hunt and gather and return in the evening to share the day's catch, which renders surplus production virtually nil:

> Because of the strong emphasis on sharing, and the frequency of movement, surplus accumulation of storable plant foods and dried meat is kept to a minimum. There is rarely more than two or three days' supply of food on hand in a camp at any time. The results of this lack of surplus is that a constant subsistence effort must be maintained throughout the year. (Lee 1968:33)

Lee's account of foraging forces of production makes two important points. First, the need for constant mobility makes accumulation a practical impossibility. Second, the emphasis upon sharing means that whatever is produced is parceled out to the "residential" group. Under these circumstances, it is unlikely that stratification or exploitation in the Marxist sense will emerge. As Cohen (1968:71) put it, because "every member of a camp has equal rights to hunt and gather within its territory . . . no person can gain exclusive control over others because there are no resources over which he can exercise exclusive rights."

This does not mean that everyone works. The labor force is composed predominantly of married men and women, that is, members of the camp who are beyond adolescence and younger than "old." The ratio of producers to consumers is low. Lee (1978) estimates that 40 percent of a !Kung Bushmen camp contributes little to the food supplies, living off the production of those socially defined as adult workers. Young people are not expected to contribute in any substantial fashion, underlining once again the "underproduction" characteristics of foraging economies (Sahlins 1972).

Though producers are small in number compared to their dependents, this does not translate into social inequality, as it does in other settings. Whatever is produced is shared. Moreover, everyone is a producer at some point in his or her life cycle. Access to the means of production is wide open.

How is this egalitarianism reflected in conceptions of property and ownership? This, too, has been a subject of debate. For every ethnographer who proclaims food foragers as "primitive communists," there is one who points out that they *do* have concepts of personal possession. The issue is complicated by the fact that foragers produce few "things" apart from daily food and the tools needed to obtain it. Tools are often "owned," but they are not hoarded, for they are made from materials available in abundance. Lorna Marshall's discussion of Nyae Nyae !Kung property practices provides an apt description of this condition of material plenty:

> In their own life and with their own artifacts they were comparatively free from material pressures. Except for food and water . . . of which the Nyae Nyae !Kung have a sufficiency . . . they all had what they needed. . . . They lived in a kind of material plenty because they adapted the tools of their living to materials which lay in abundance around them and which were free for anyone to take. (Marshall, quoted in Sahlins 1972:10)

It is perhaps most appropriate to conceive of property among the nomadic food foragers as a form of territoriality, rather than as individual ownership of particular objects or individual control of the means of production. Territoriality should be understood as a system of prescriptive (hence legal) rules that govern access to critical means of production, namely the animal and vegetable resources within a defined locality, on a group level. These rules are often quite elaborate because they regulate access for members of different kinds of groups: "owners," neighbors, strangers, and so on. Generally, the complexity of territorial rules is an expression of the social relations of production that both distinguishes one band from another and links neighboring bands together in relations of reciprocity.

Godelier (1975) has pointed out that Australian hunting-and-gathering groups with elaborate "section systems" of kinship permit neighboring bands usufruct rights over each other's territory by virtue of overlapping section membership. These rights are exercised in "different times, such as prolonged droughts, famines, or epidemics," when the strain on local resources may be too great to accommodate the needs of the population. Kinship relations provide flexible and dependable social relations of production, widening the resource base of normally independent groups when they are most vulnerable. In fact, Yengoyan (1968) has shown that the more arid and inhospitable the desert area, the wider the territory occupied by each food-sharing group and the more complex the section system it develops.

Lee (1979) has provided the most comprehensive description of a hunting-and-gathering territorial property system in his work on the !Kung. He notes that !Kung land is divided into *n!ores*, large blocks of land surrounding each water hole. "Each *n!ore* is associated with a core group of owners (*k"ausi*), and these ownership rights are passed down from generation to generation" (Lee 1979:334). The *n!ores* are encircled by belts of land that are "shared by adjacent groups."

Within a *n!ore*, members of the camp constitute a sharing unit:

> The food is in or on the ground or in the trees, and any member of the camp may gather where she or he pleases. Visitors join residents in the exploitation of resources, and the day's take is unobtrusively distributed within the camp at the day's end. . . . No matter where they are from, as long as people are living together in a single camp the n!ore's food is theirs to share. (Lee 1979:336)

Neighboring groups do make use of *n!ore* land that does not "belong" to them. However, it is a mark of the territorial property system that they must seek permission to do so and that the food-sharing arrangements between owners and visiting groups must be cleared in advance.

Access to *n!ore* land is more tightly controlled when a distant group seeks to camp inside the boundaries of another's locality:

> Such a group must be especially careful to ask permission because it does not have a joint claim to the resources. . . . Usually if the visiting group is small and its stay is short, permission is freely given; but if the group is large and stays for months, the owner group may take steps to reassert its claim to the food resource. (Lee 1979:337)

As this description of !Kung San property relations suggests, territoriality is a general principle of inclusion and exclusion that regulates resource access. Within the limits of defined group membership, individuals have free and open access to the means of production. Prescriptive rules govern these usufruct rights.

Under these conditions, there are no mechanisms by which one person or group can monopolize the production process, a typical feature among nomadic food collectors. As a result, stratification is absent in these kinds of societies. Indeed, nomadic food foragers represent the egalitarian starting point of *The Evolution of Political Society* (Fried 1967).

The implications of this egalitarianism for the nature of legal authority are clear. There is nothing of a centralized hierarchy in nomadic bands. Self-redress, in the form of reprisals, shaming rituals, and the like constitute the only effective means of settling grievances. Failing this, the parties may simply leave the scene of the dispute, joining another camp on a temporary and sometimes permanent basis (Roberts 1979:85–6, Cohen 1968:74).

The Standard Cross-Cultural Sample, which I utilized in Chapter 3, provides variables measuring degrees of nomadism and sedentism. When I examine the sample of food foragers (in my subsample of sixty societies), with one exception (the Semang) the nomadic cultures all have self-redress systems of dispute settlement.

What are the most frequent causes of disputes in nomadic hunting-and-gathering communities? The major source of conflict at this level of social development revolves around women. Adultery and the failure to transact "marriage contracts" appropriately are the main sore points. Hart and Pilling (1960), whose fieldwork among the Tiwi of Australia focused on law in this nomadic foraging society, estimate that over 90 percent of all Tiwi disputes had to do with women. Most of these problems arose between younger and older men. In this polygamous society, where the older men had young wives (and the young men had none), disputes focused on adulterous relations between young men and the wives of their elders. Disputes between older men had to do with "nondelivery of bestowed daughters, or other types of broken promises" (1960:84).

A variation on this theme is present in Jules Henry's (1964) work on the Kaingang. Henry notes that adultery posed no particular problems within the band unit. However, should an enemy "take a woman away," this was grounds for an all-out feud. (As I pointed out in Chapter 2 under "Self- or kin-based redress," "enemies" are not foreigners; they are other Kaingang.) Indeed, during Henry's fieldwork he reports that Kaingang life was embroiled in a series of feuds and disputes that his informants claimed had resulted from attempts to abscond with women.

Almost without exception, the ethnographic materials on nomadic foragers indicate that women-related tensions are the primary occasion for disputes. This is, of course, not the only cause of conflict. Lee (1979:372) notes that "improper meat distribution, improper gift exchange . . . , laziness, and stinginess" are common topics of conflict. Theft and murder are mentioned, though (because property is minimal) theft is rarely the cause of a major upset. Individuals are simply expected to return what they have taken; this occurs without much fanfare. Murder is a more serious matter.[3] By definition, murder consists of killing someone who is in some way part "of one's own people." Murders within one's group (however that is defined) are avenged by the kinsmen of the deceased. However, as I noted for the Kaingang, murder is often related to the abduction of women, which results in a cycle of reprisal killings.

Why this emphasis on women? Anthropologists with demographic interests have puzzled over the paradox of female infanticide, shortages of marriageable women, and raiding for women. I cannot delve into these debates except to note that this situation heightens the frequency and seriousness of conflicts over women. What is worth comment, however, is the relationship between the contributions of women to subsistence production in nomadic food-foraging societies and the fact that most disputes center around them. This form of technology places a high premium on female labor power – the diet is largely composed of vegetable matter collected by women. Disruption of marital bonds through adultery,

---

[3] Lee (1979:383) records twenty-two cases of homicide among the !Kung between 1920 and 1969, a number of which occurred as a result of adultery. Many are impossible to interpret with respect to motivation, mainly because they occurred long before Lee's fieldwork and were reconstructed by informants from memory.

failure to "deliver" promised brides[4], and absconding with married women have important economic consequences in societies where the most valued producers are women. Such crimes threaten to remove a woman from a hunting-and-gathering band, which reduces the production capacities of the sharing unit. This is exacerbated in societies where demographic pressures and social practices limit the supply of women in the first place.

The economic consequences may extend beyond the removal of women's labor. Disputes between men over women also interfere with the cooperative arrangements necessary for group hunting expeditions, which are almost always male preserves. Where hunting is a communal male activity (e.g., for Nunamiut Eskimo Caribou hunters, Mundurucu wild peccary expeditions, Mbuti Pygmy net-hunts, etc. [Rosman and Rubel 1981:107]), intraband relations among men take on added significance. The social relations of production can be disturbed if conflicts over wives, daughters, or sisters become overt.

I hasten to add that social "capital" is clearly at stake in disputes over women. In emphasizing economic functions, the moral idiom within which disputes are conducted must not be overlooked. A man's status in societies such as these is intimately related to "success in competition for women" (Hoebel 1968:69). Conflicts over wives are therefore also conflicts over status and the source of tremendous stigma.

In summary, the legal life of nomadic food collectors is related to the form of the social relations of production typically found at this level of the development of the productive forces. There are few disputes over things, for things are in abundance and material wants are few. Women, however, often are in short supply. And even when they are not in short supply, their presence is a critical aspect of the daily production process. It is not surprising, therefore, that conflicts over them should be a common sore point in these cultures. The legal process intervenes in this trouble area to address

---

[4] Whereas the idiom of conflict focuses on women, a more abstract reading is possible: Disputes may concern failures to fulfill more general exchange obligations (which include the exchange of women). Rosman and Rubel (1971) and Rubel and Rosman (1978) provide an analysis of exchange systems that incorporates women, foodstuffs, domestic animals, and ceremonial objects into ideal-typical models for the societies of the Northwest Coast and New Guinea.

the strain and protect the continuity of sharing and production groups, though by no means always successfully.

Nonnomadic food collectors

Although the food collectors have been divided into two groups, this does not imply qualitative differences in subsistence technology. Nonnomadic foraging populations do, however, exhibit quantitative differences in food supply and a relative freedom from concerns of scarcity and environmental fluctuation. This creates a different demographic profile, which in turn influences labor requirements, surplus production, concepts of property, socio-political organization, and disputing practices.

A decline in nomadism occurs among hunting-and-gathering peoples when they live in lush habitats, where food resources are measurably greater and more dependable than those of the nomadic foragers.[5] Under these conditions, bands remain in one area longer and concentrate on a narrower range of food resources than the typical nomadic group. Fishing societies are often semisedentary, complementing their diet with the hunting of small game and the collection of local wild plants. The sheer abundance of these desirable goods in select locations allows the inhabitants to practice what Sahlins (1968:39) has called "natural agriculture," the harvesting of naturally occurring foodstuffs.

In her analysis of the origins of social stratification, Blumberg (1978) examined the mode of production characteristic of semisedentary and fully sedentary food foragers. She found that these groups share certain characteristics: They are found in lush environments; they have complex family structures; they live in larger and more densely populated settlements; and, unlike their nomadic counterparts, they tend to exhibit wealth distinctions and inherit-

---

[5] The literature on social evolution (e.g., Blumberg 1978) has long assumed that sedentary food collectors developed, in some sense, after nomadic foraging. It has been suggested that the abundance of certain habitats encouraged wandering groups to settle and thus permitted the quantum leap in food production, settlement density, and social stratification we see in the semisedentary hunters and gatherers. Don Melnick (personal communication) has suggested that the reverse chronology may have actually obtained, based upon his observations of primates in the wild. Melnick argues that sedentism may have been prior to nomadism, the latter developing as an adaptive strategy in the face of *declining* resources or competition.

ance systems that "typically favor sons over other potential heirs" (1978:14). She theorizes that these features are due to a decline in the practice of daily sharing. Sharing is an adaptive strategy in harsh environments, where pooled resources enhance the survival chances of a group as a whole. Bountiful resources in close proximity lessen the need for such a distribution process. Also, in Blumberg's view, as sharing declines, the relative productive power of different families begins to show itself in the accumulation of surplus. Those kin groups blessed with a favorable ratio of producers to consumers are likely to outstrip their "neighbors" who are less blessed. The sharing practices of nomadic food foragers have the fortuitous side effects of leveling differences in production capacity. Once sharing ends, differential accumulation is not far behind. Blumberg argues that this gives rise to social stratification, particularly in those cultures where inheritance practices and endogamous marriage rules allow for the institutionalization of inequalities.

However, at this level of the development of the productive forces, one person's wealth does *not* imply another's poverty. A number of potent mechanisms for leveling wealth distinctions remain in force and prevent the emergence of class stratification. First, the means of production are not controlled by any particular group, despite the fact that concepts of private property and individual ownership begin to emerge here. Second, the economies of sedentary hunters and gatherers are organized around redistribution ceremonies (e.g., the spectacular potlatch ceremonies of the Northwest Coast Indians; see Rosman and Rubel [1971]). Wealthy families are obliged to host frequent feasts, providing the necessary food and gifts for these ceremonial occasions. Generosity is a mark of high status. The result of redistribution ceremonies is the reduction of wealth inequalities. Yet such customs are not as effective as required daily sharing in eradicating emergent distinctions; they merely require the well-to-do to share the benefits of their surpluses.

Finally, there is little evidence of extrafamilial exploitation of labor. Unlike more "advanced" technological regimes, semisedentary food foragers show few signs of taxation, rent payments, labor power attachment, or any other mechanisms of surplus extraction. Without these devices, societies at this level attain at most a system of inequality based on wealth distinctions rather than the more solidified forms of class stratification.

Sedentism also brings with it important transformations in the concept of property. Nomadic hunters and gatherers have limited concepts of possession, which center on band-based territory rather than individual ownership. Territoriality and the importance of land boundaries are heightened by increasing sedentism (Forde 1963). The landholding unit consists of a group of families "which for some period of the year jointly occupies a settlement within well-defined territory" (Forde 1963:375). While land is held by multi-family groups, sedentary food foragers often practice *individual* ownership of other resources:

> Men own and transfer fishing territories and women patches of plants on the Northwest Coast, although these rights are more character-istically associated with larger units, extended families (lineages) or clans. (Forde 1963:375).

Gayton (1948) recorded a case in point – the property concepts of the Yokut, a semisedentary hunting-and-gathering people of south-central California:

> There was no mark of ownership on land or trees or seed areas, but a woman would verbally designate certain trees or grass spots as hers and would "growl" if some other woman took the products therefrom ahead of her ... There was a tacit, traditional ownership among families and in the larger sense among tribes, of desirable land and its concomitant hunting, fishing and seed gathering assets. The family "ownership" operated to the extent that a young married woman continued to gather vegetable products with her own mother, rather than with her mother-in-law. This was regardless of matrilocal or patrilocal residence, and surely led to inheritance of such plots, even though inheritance was not defined in set terms by any Yokuts people. (Gayton 1948:160)

Gayton's account makes clear that Yokut property practices followed the general trend of tribewide usufruct of common lands, and family-based, heritable usufruct rights of "private" resources. Radcliffe-Brown's description of ownership customs on the Andaman Islands is roughly parallel:

> The economic life of the local group, though in effect it approaches to a sort of communism, is yet based on the notion of private property. Land is the only thing that is owned in common. The hunting grounds of a local group belong to the whole group, and all the members have an equal right to hunt over any part of it. There exists,

however, a certain private ownership of trees. (Radcliffe-Brown
1948:41)

Lest it be concluded that private property has made its full-blown
appearance at this stage in the development of the productive forces,
I must add one further qualifying comment. Some of these privately
held resources fall under sharing norms requiring that the product
be distributed to those who ask for a portion. This is not the same
as the communal consumption of daily production described for
nomadic foragers. The sharing norms of sedentary hunters and
gatherers require that one accede to the *sporadic* demands of others
(and in so doing show generosity). The prevalence of these "on-
demand" sharing rules across cultures suggests that property concepts are not fully developed into total control over objects. Nevertheless, when compared to nomadic foragers, it is clear that the
sedentarists create readily identifiable concepts of property, be it
group- or family-owned land, trees, or particular objects.

How are these social relations of production and concepts of
ownership reflected in political and legal organization among sedentary foragers? Marshall Sahlins (1968) has dealt with the limitations of this mode of production and the development of tribal
structures. He notes that sedentary peoples tend to be organized
into independent villages, which are linked through kinship bonds
to other villages of the same tribe. Whereas I have emphasized the
increased dependability of food supply that makes sedentism possible, Sahlins stresses the opposite point: Uncertainty remains a
concern of all foragers. Although a larger population can be supported in lush environments, it must still be dispersed. Consequently, the political unification of hunting-and-gathering
communities fluctuates with the security of resources. Villages remain scattered beyond the optimal level required for the development of integrated political structures (Sahlins 1968:40).

Cohen notes that these conditions often give rise to quasi-hereditary "chieftainships," which are often "honorific, rudimentary, and
almost devoid of authority" (Cohen 1968:71). The reader will recognize this figure as the "advisor," whose authority is based mainly
on personal prowess and, in some cases, unusual wealth. There is,
however, variation in legal complexity among foragers, depending

on the degree of stratification. Among those sedentary foragers who are as egalitarian as their nomadic brethren, self-redress remains the major means of dispute settlement. As one continues to the scale of social inequality, one finds more complex legal institutions. The most frequently observed system of dispute settlement is that of the advisor; however, at the high end of the stratification scale there are a few mediator systems and chieftainships. The Eastern Pomo, Yokut, and Yurok are represented in these categories among the semisedentary and fully sedentary food gatherers.

Let me recap briefly before discussing disputes and prescriptive rules in these sedentary foraging societies. These cultures characteristically exhibit the following traits: (1) differential kin-based ownership of some valuable resources (e.g., trees, fishing weirs) and continued communal access to others; (2) no real exploitation of nonfamilial labor power; (3) differential potential for surplus production and accumulation in families with favorable producer/consumer ratios; (4) the lack of continuous interfamily sharing, but the presence of more sporadic redistribution of wealth and "on-demand" sharing; (5) the emergence of wealth distinctions, complemented (in some cases) by the development of inheritance rules; (6) variation in the extent of political integration, ranging from band-level to tribal systems; and (7) complex legal institutions, ranging from self-redress to advisor systems to mediators to (rarely) chieftainships.

When one examines the substance of disputes among nonnomadic food foragers, it comes as little surprise that women continue to be a sore subject. Thus Eduard Conzemius reports that among the Miskito Indians "most of the disputes and crimes that occasionally take place are the results of quarrels about women . . . " (Conzemius 1932:102). Radcliffe-Brown notes that among the Andaman Islanders adultery was regarded as a form of theft that emphasized the value of "possessing" women (Radcliffe-Brown 1948:50). Similar statements can be found in the ethnographic literature on each of the sedentary foraging societies included in this study.

However, women are not the sole point of discord. Frequent mention is made of "exploitative trespass," the uninvited use of familial resources by those who do not possess the requisite usufruct rights. Cooper notes that among the Ona Indians of Patagonia the territory belonged to the family as such. Each man of the family had the right to hunt on it wherever he chose. None of this family land could be alienated. Exploitative trespass on it by nonmembers of the family was deeply resented and was looked upon as ground for bloodshed. (Cooper 1946:118)

Similar remarks can be found for the Mataco, the Bellacoola, the Yurok, and most of the other semi- and fully sedentary foragers. Indeed, trespass is mentioned almost as often as problems with women as a source of disputes.

Another important category of disputes involves theft. Whereas theft plays a comparatively minor role in the dispute repertoire of nomadic foragers, for sedentary foragers it is mentioned more frequently and the consequences appear to be more serious.

Among the Yurok, an "elaborate scale of prices for each degree of injury" existed, such that any particular type of theft had to be compensated at a predefined rate (Waterman 1920:201). Failure to pay promptly resulted in retaliation by the aggrieved parties. Among the Mataco it was understood that the victim of theft could abscond with an equivalent item belonging to the thief and in so doing risk no retaliation. In some semisedentary societies, for example, the Copper Eskimo, Callinago, and Bellacoola, the penalties for theft were more severe. Breton (1957:23) reports that when the Callinago "catch [a thief] they make a slash with a point of the knife on his shoulders." These examples suggest a more pointed response to theft than is usually the case among the nomadic foragers.

Why do disputes over material possessions and conflicts over women crop up at this level in the development of the productive forces? I argued earlier that conflicts over women are best understood in terms of their value as producers. The same point can be made here. Women continue to play an important role in the daily production scheme and continue to be a focal point of conflict. I would argue that "exploitative trespass" and theft should be understood in terms of the emergence of property rights by kin-based groups. Possession of delineated territory by groups smaller than the entire tribal population suggests that the private ownership of resources has become a feature of sedentary food-foraging economies. In this light, it is not surprising that the violation of usufruct rights becomes a serious issue. The right to exact penalties for transgressions is further evidence for the significance of resource control. This applies both to group-held lands and to more individually controlled trees, fishing rocks, and seed grounds. Trespass and theft are sources of dispute because a system of property rights exists that excludes some and includes others. Legal norms, in the institutional form of self-redress or third-party intervention of some sort, stand as protectors of those rights, just as they regulated the most important production relations in foraging cultures, those obtaining between husbands and wives.

Pastoral societies

Ecological and economic anthropologists are of divided opinion regarding the evolutionary status of pastoral societies. This confusion results in part from the fact that even prior to colonial rule (and the attempts to forcibly sedentarize nomadic peoples) most pastoralists were found in quasi-permanent association with settled agriculturalists.[6]

In view of this complication it is difficult, and perhaps even questionable, to analyze pastoralism as a distinct type of production. Nevertheless, as an adaptation to semiarid open country, where dependable cultivation is difficult, pastoralism represents an important techno-economic system.

I will begin discussing pastoralism by considering those aspects of the forces and social relations of production that pastoral societies have in common. I will then take up the range of variation within pastoral production systems (especially differences in stratification).

Throughout this section, I will rely on the research of Frederik Barth (1964a, 1964b) on the pastoral Basseri tribe of Fars in South Persia. Barth has provided an excellent description of Basseri political life and jural relations while analyzing the complexities of Basseri economic relations. Wherever possible, I will comment on the extent to which Basseri legal traditions can be generalized to other herding cultures.

---

[6] Cohen has made this point: "There is growing conviction . . . that pastoralism represents a branch of the main line of social evolution rather than a stage along this line. This point of view is strengthened by the observation of Robert M. Adams and Hans Nissen that pastoralism has often been part of a mixed economy in which herding and settled cultivation are in reciprocal balance . . . Adams and Nissen are speaking here primarily of pastoralists in a state society, but their statement also applies to stateless pastoralists who are almost always associated with settled cultivators for at least part of the year."

Pastoralism is a system of production devoted to the care of animal herds. It is a mode of adaptation based upon "transhumance," the cyclical movement of animals and their caretakers from highlands to lowlands following seasonal fluctuations in the availability of water and pastureland. Transhumance differs from the nomadic existence of the simplest hunters and gatherers. The former activity involves movement from one relatively permanent spot to another: The herds are moved between two endpoints in a yearly cycle. In contrast, nomadic foragers move far more frequently and tend not to return to permanent camps.[7]

Pastoralism is the most extensive of the tribal economies. The Basseri migration covers roughly 600 miles in one seasonal cycle. For most of the year, herders travel in groups of 100 to 200 people and boast low population densities. Sahlins (1968:34) estimates that "population densities range mainly between one and five people per square mile." This compares favorably to hunting-and-gathering societies, where densities (in California, for example) ranged up to 11.12 per square mile (Baumhoff, cited in Sahlins 1968:40).

Along the pastoral migration route, one finds settlements of cultivators who are important participants in this production system. Herders can only provide some of their subsistence needs and must turn to agriculturalists for the remainder. Relations of mutual dependence develop whereby herders market livestock, hides, and dairy products in exchange for foodstuffs such as wheat, craft goods, clothing, and other items that sedentary peoples produce. The Fulani of West Africa are a case in point: They migrate along a route lined with sedentary grain growers, trading the milk produced by their cattle for grain in the market. The Kazak nomads of central Asia practiced a similar kind of pastoralism before the Russian Revolution, selling "the products of the herds and riding horses . . . to sedentary people in the market towns" (Rosman and Rubel 1981:106–7).

Although this may appear to be a symbiotic arrangement, in fact the relationship between transhumant herders and their agricultural neighbors is fraught with tension. The reputation of many pastoral

---

[7] Nomadic peoples do frequently return to the same areas on a seasonal basis. However, unlike pastoralists, foragers tend not to establish permanent camps to which they return.

groups for fierce militarism is not unjustified, for it is sometimes more convenient to raid than trade for what they cannot themselves produce. Understanding the pastoral production system therefore requires examination of the exchange relations prevailing between herders and farmers; I will consider these shortly.

The division of labor among pastoralists contrasts sharply with that of the food foragers. Herding tends to be "men's work." Men generally take exclusive control of the herds, the most valuable possession of a pastoral family. They watch over the livestock during the grazing periods, coordinate the movements of the herds over the yearly cycle, and determine the family's marketing and investment strategy. Women are relegated to "household chores," their only involvement with the family capital being milking animals, churning butter, and (in some cases) spinning and weaving wool. Women are involved primarily in the domestic economy, whereas men are involved in both the domestic and the external market economies. Across unrelated cultures, pastoralists place much higher value on the labor of menfolk. Women are spoken of as "providing so little and being economically so dependent," a testimony to the lack of value attached to domestic production (Forde 1963:409).

Unlike food foragers, who tend to practice multihousehold production and distribution, pastoralists are notable for independent household units. We do not find prescriptive rules requiring an individual or family to distribute the fruits of its labors on demand. Although a generous man is considered a virtuous man, by their own admission few nomadic pastoralists adhere to this proverb (Barth 1964a). On the contrary, a premium is placed on surplus accumulation within the household, and in this sense pastoral societies are intensely capitalistic.

Accumulation is achieved by building up as large a herd as the household can maintain. The wealth that the animals represent can be converted into less risky investments, including land in the farming villages along the migration route, or it can remain in its original animal form. The accumulation process entails the existence of certain social relations of production that have not been encountered before, including wage labor, anticipatory inheritance, credit, and market relations.

A household requires a minimum number of livestock to subsist independently. Among the Basseri, it was "estimated that a herd of sixty adult sheep/goats was about the minimum required by an elementary family" (Barth 1964b:73). The labor of at least three people is required to handle a flock this size: "A male of the household, who loads the pack animals and directs the migration, erects the tent, fetches water and wood, and keeps most equipment in repair; a woman, who does the cooking and housework, assists in packing and camping, and milks the flock; and a man who herds the animals, driving them to camp to be milked . . . " (1964b:73).

This is a "minimalist" picture. I should consider what happens to the fortunate households that are able to increase their herds. When the herd grows beyond the level that the labor supply within the household can handle, families hire additional help from less fortunate households. (According to Barth, the practice of contracting with nonfamily members occurs when the man:animal ratio exceeds 1:200.) Two types of contracts are frequently employed:

> (i) *dandune* contract: the shepherd pays 10–5 *Tomans* per animal per year and takes all produce. At the expiration of the contract period, he returns a flock of the same number and age composition as he originally received.

> (ii) *nimei* contract: the shepherd pays 30 *Tomans* per animal per year for a period of 3–5 years. He takes all the produce and at the expiration of the contract returns half the herd as it stands, and keeps the other half. (Barth 1964b:71)

The terms of these contracts reflect both the profit the owner derives and the losses he expects to endure from the borrower's pilfering and careless herding.

The use of contract labor is not a feature of every pastoral society. Yet, a household head can only increase his wealth if he can find the labor to cope with the growing burden, no matter what society he is part of. Among the Masai, the practice of polygyny is widespread and the average household is composed of the head, his wives, their married sons, and their wives and children. Labor needs can be satisfied through the organization of the extended family (which is not the case for the Basseri). Rwala Bedouin herders live in camps composed of male kinsmen, wives, chiefs, elders, and slaves.[8] The slaves are charged with the tasks of "watering camels,

---

[8] I use the term "slave" here because it is employed by Forde (1963:322). However, its connotations differ from those commonly associated with the notion of slavery (as it was practiced, for example, in the American South of the nineteenth century). In most "tribal" societies, slaves were war captives or other kinds of "strangers" (see Shack and Skinner [1979]) who were subsequently adopted into local lineages, freely married, and had property rights similar to nonslaves.

assistance in striking and setting up tents, and loading and guiding pack animals on the march" (Forde 1963:322).

The need for labor can clearly be accommodated in different ways. What is important here, however, is that the accumulation of surplus is achieved through the labor of individuals who often do not share equally in the benefits of this massing of wealth.

What does a successful Basseri herder do with his surplus? I have already pointed out that he has several choices. He can retain his wealth in the herds (although even in the best of times his flocks are vulnerable to disease, drought, and theft), *or* he can invest his funds by buying farming fields in the sedentary villages. The latter strategy has certain advantages: (1) The rent a nomadic landowner receives in the form of goods and food produced by tenants cuts his costs, for they replace items that would otherwise have to be purchased in the market; (2) investment in land is less risky than in animals; and (3) land returns a higher profit on investment than animals.[9]

Rent introduces an important dimension of the social relations of production because it is a means of extracting surplus labor:

> Vis a vis [*sic*] the tenants, the landlord's title gives him the right freely to dispose of his land – the peasants have no traditional usufruct rights, and in fact no legal security of tenure. In most places, fields are arbitrarily allotted on annual tenancy contracts as the landlord sees fit; where there is a very definite pattern of rotation of crops, the contract period is usually extended to the termination of one full cycle, or a period of 2–3 years. In most areas there is overpopulation and competition between tenants for contracts; few men are provided with as much land as they are able, and wish, to cultivate. The terms of the contracts are thus throughout very advantageous to the landowner. (Barth 1964a:104–5)

Barth reports that tenants must provide all labor, animals, and farm equipment in order to fulfill the obligations of their agreements. Moreover, they are required "to submit to the landlord's detailed control and supervision in most fields of life, not only in those directly connected with their work" (1964a:104–5).

---

[9] There is one further advantage to investment in land. Landholdings are not governed by the same inheritance rules as other aspects of property; on the contrary, the inheritance of land is governed by the rules of the sedentary villages. Thus land is not subject to anticipatory inheritance, as are flocks. A wealthy man can "shelter" his capital from premature divestment to his married sons by converting animals to landholdings. Land is passed on only upon the death of the owner.

Not all pastoral households have a disposable surplus to invest. Those families whose herds drop below the minimum level necessary to sustain an independent economic unit fall on hard times. When natural disasters strike, or mismanagement takes its toll, a family's capital can suffer a serious loss overnight. It takes a few years for this loss to destroy a household's overall economic status, but once initiated the downward spiral is regarded by the Basseri as inevitable.[10] In the end, the downfall of a marginal pastoral household results in its members taking up permanent residence in the agricultural community, usually as peasants or laborers. Barth claims that one out of every three Basseri men in his census were in this unfortunate position.

This portrait suggests that pastoral societies contain a potential for considerable social inequality. It is true that some herding societies develop highly stratified forms of social structure. However, there are also mechanisms that retard the growth of economic inequality.

The practice of inheritance is one feature of pastoral society that levels wealth differences. There are 15 pastoral societies in the Standard Cross-Cultural Sample (186 societies in all). Fourteen of them have movable property inheritance rules (the remaining 1 lacks the relevant data). Ten of them practice patrilineal inheritance, while the other 4 pass movable property either through the female line or through both sons and daughters. Most significantly, 11 of the pastoral societies distribute property *in equal proportion* to all heirs, while only 2 practice primogeniture and one practices ultimogeniture. Prescriptive legal rules therefore often dictate that a parental estate will be broken up into as many parts as there are eligible heirs. This subdivision of wealth prevents the accumulation of one "fortune" in the hands of a nuclear family indefinitely.

---

[10] To understand how this process unfolds, I return to an earlier point: Herders must purchase goods they cannot produce from settled agriculturalists along the migration route. The items are paid for in one of two ways: either with livestock or with credit against next year's flock. If a household suffers a significant loss, it must go into debt to farmers just to stay alive. If the herding family cannot recoup lost animals through breeding, the following year they will be forced to dip into their basic capital resources to repay creditors. Barth reports that poor nomads often become wage laborers in the town to make a dent in their debts, but doing so has short-term benefits and long-term liabilities. Unable to keep up with the pattern of transhumance, their remaining herds are depleted even further.

Among the Basseri, the custom of anticipatory inheritance adds to these leveling effects. Basseri men, who are the only eligible heirs, receive their full inheritance upon marriage, rather than at the death of the father. Each son receives an equal share of his father's flock on his wedding day, sets up his own household, and thereafter relinquishes claims on the estate of his natal family. Thus, well within a Basseri father's productive lifetime, he will see the divestment of his capital into the hands of his married sons. Although this does not prevent accumulation (after all, the herds multiply in between the marriages), it clearly puts a brake on the concentration of wealth in any particular household. Similar patterns of anticipatory inheritance are found among the Lapp reindeer herders (Paine 1971). Although numerous sons are a blessing for the labor power they provide, they are a liability for capital accumulation. Whether inheritance is transferred at marriage or upon the death of a father, the ultimate effect of equal inheritance provisions is to put constraints on the accumulation of capital within one nuclear family line.

Another related practice sets limits on the growth of wealth distinctions. Like his counterparts among the Masai, Rwala Bedouin, Chukchee, and Kazak pastoralists, the well-to-do Basseri man takes on multiple wives. Polygyny both boosts and drains the household economy. Additional wives provide not only prestige, but extra hands for the production of market and nonmarket valuables (e.g., butter and woven rugs). The more wives in a household, the more sons will be available to tend the herds. However, additional wives burden the household with demands for foodstuffs and luxury items, not to mention the extra beasts of burden that are needed to carry the increased weight of household goods.

I have now dealt with the more important aspects of the social relations of production in pastoral societies. The emergence of wage labor, slave labor or extended family labor, rent, and credit/debt, marks the pastoralists off from the food foragers discussed earlier in this chapter. As Chapter 3 showed, not all pastoral groups have the full complement of surplus-extraction mechanisms found among the Basseri. However, over half the pastoral groups in the Standard Cross-Cultural Sample have at least one source of income beyond the domestic sphere (e.g., either rent, wage labor, slavery, credit, or some other source). Those societies lacking these features are concentrated at the lower end of the stratification continuum, whereas pastoralists with several sources of surplus tend to have marked wealth distinctions or social classes. Variations in stratification have been linked to environmental conditions: Arid environments can support only small herds and therefore low levels of human populations, which tend toward small community size and minimal wealth inequalities. Lush environments tend toward the opposite: larger herds, denser populations, more hierarchical political organization, and social stratification. (See Krader's [1955] study of central Asian pastoral tribes for evidence of this thesis.)

Analyzing the herding societies in the sixty-society sample, there is a close relationship between the form of legal institutions and the level of stratification. In those groups where family-based production is central, where few external sources of labor power are used (or none at all), there are egalitarian forms of social organization and no basis for strong legal authority. There is little in the way of differential resource access to protect or regulate. As such, legal affairs are in the hands of elders' councils, where the disputing process gains authority from the consensus of a broad body. The Masai herders are representative of this sociolegal type.

Herders with wealth distinctions (but no class stratification) exhibit considerable variation in their legal institutions. The Goajiro use mediators in managing disputes. The Somali, Nama, Lapps, Chukchee, and Todas use elders' councils. The Rwala Bedouins have hereditary judges with the authority to decide disputes. This variation indicates the transitional state that ranked herding societies represent; some are clearly more like their egalitarian brethren, with weakly developed wealth differences. Others more closely resemble class-stratified societies.

Pastoral societies that are clearly stratified, such as the Tuareg and the Basseri, tend to have fully developed chieftainships functioning as legal institutions.[11] A closer look at Basseri legal-political organization reveals a two-tiered structure: At the local level (that is, among those herders who camp and travel together), headmen play a minor role in dispute settlement. Their main function is to link "the people" with the Basseri chief, who is the only real legal

---

[11] See Murphy (1964:1261) for a more detailed discussion of Tuareg political organization.

authority in the tribe. The chief has virtually unlimited authority over his tribesmen, and where disputes are not settled informally he has the first and last official word.

Given the close economic ties between the nomadic herders and the settled agriculturalists, it is not surprising that disputes tend to occur both within the pastoral group and between them and their farming neighbors. Intra-Basseri disputes focus on the violation of usufruct rights over pasturelands, theft of sheep, and inheritance disputes. The Basseri chief allocates pastureland to each *oulad*, a term which is translated as "family" but which refers to a group "on any level of subdivision below the section, in terms of strict descent or in more general terms of residence and polity unit." All pastureland is "owned" by *oulads*, and an individual has usufruct rights by virtue of membership in an *oulad*. Grazing land is a critical means of production in pastoral societies, as indicated by the value attached to usufruct rights. Those who trespass on grazing land belonging to another *oulad* are therefore violating a basic economic presupposition of Basseri society, and a serious dispute erupts.

No more valuable capital asset can be found in pastoral society than the herds. All Basseri have to cope with loss of animals due to natural disasters. However, pilfering is another matter. Barth reports that the thieving of sheep and goats is a constant thorn in the herder's side, particularly for the wealthy households. In many instances, the theft is perpetrated by a contract shepherd; the idiom of the dispute may then be in terms of contract violations rather than theft per se.

I have noted the significance of inheritance practices in the economic life of the Basseri household. Disputes over inheritance occur on the occasion of a son's marriage and are taken to the chief to adjudicate. The argument usually revolves around the appropriate amount due the son or the father's attempt to convert herd-wealth into land investments that are not subject to anticipatory inheritance. These disputes are particularly significant because a son's new herd represents the *only* resource he has for starting an independent household unit. Without the minimum number of sheep, his new household cannot survive. As such, conflicts over inheritance assume a heightened importance, as do brideprice disputes.

Two sources of conflict characterize relations between the nomads and the sedentary farmers, namely the practice of payment by credit for agricultural and craft products and the damage to crops that herds may cause. Credit relations are generally dependable if not amiable given the mutual dependencies of the parties. Defaults do occur, however, especially "through pauperization of . . . nomadic debtors, and their consequent sedentarization in other areas" (Barth 1964a:100). Crop damage is by far the most common form of aggravation pastoralists cause their agricultural partners.

Conflicts between villagers and nomads are difficult to resolve because the pastoral form of production requires frequent movement. Herders cannot remain in one place to use village courts; agriculturalists cannot leave their fields and travel with the nomads to use traditional tribal systems of dispute settlement. Sahlins (1968) points out that the political structures of the pastoralists are, in part, a response to this quandary: A chief can remain behind to represent his people in the legal forums of the agriculturalists. The Basseri chief does this when disputes arise between his herdsmen and local farmers.

I have detailed the topics of dispute that frequently arise among the Basseri because their case is well documented and because they evidence complex social relations of production when compared to other herding societies. However, it is important to determine the extent to which the Basseri are representative of pastoral nomads.

Without exception, the ethnographies on the eight herding societies in the sixty-society sample mention the problem of pilferage. In each instance, theft of animals is treated as a very serious offense. This contrasts sharply with nomadic foragers, for whom theft is a minor issue.

In sharp contrast to food-gathering economies, pastoralists seldom conflict over women.[12] This is understandable at least partly in terms of the very different roles that pastoral women play in the production process compared to women who gather for a living.

Although conflicts over adultery, wife absconding, and the like rarely appear in pastoral ethnographies, brideprice disputes certainly do (though on a smaller scale than elsewhere). Women's

[12] The Todas of India should be considered an exception to this generalization. Buffalo dairies form the main source of subsistence among the Todas, where women are important producers of clarified butter. Abduction of wives, marital arrangements, and the like are often the subject of dispute among them.

labor, though not as highly valued as men's, is nevertheless crucial to the domestic relations of production. The loss of a female member of a household through marriage does represent a loss of labor power, which is compensated by brideprice. Moreover, the woman's role in reproducing the male labor force for the household gives added emphasis to her material value. Given the economic significance of marriage, disputes that erupt in the process of completing "contractual" arrangements for it may be understood both as conflicts of status and as disruptions of the social relations of production.

Land, water, and grazing rights are also subject to dispute among pastoralists. These limited resources are closely guarded among herders, whereas they are more loosely held by foragers. Violations of usufruct rights call forth potentially lethal responses in pastoral societies.

Finally, pastoral peoples treat homicide as a serious crime. However, unlike the foragers, herders tend to respond to murder with demands for restitution rather than retaliation. This does not mean feuds are unheard-of. It does suggest that more elaborate methods of containing conflict through compensation of the bereaved (in the forms of livestock *weregild*) are common. Legal institutions in pastoral cultures tend to be able to intervene in murder disputes and require the payment of blood money, which suggests a degree of legal complexity beyond what has been seen for the food foragers.

The cultivators: extensive agriculture

The invention of plant cultivation represents a watershed in technological history. Up to its appearance, most societies derived their sustenance from food collecting[13], a system of production entailing low population densities, small dispersed bands, nomadic or seminomadic movement, and rather low levels of legal-political integration. With the growth of food-production technology, the possibilities for more sedentary forms of existence increased considerably. More productive methods of subsistence can support

---

[13] Pastoralism, which I place in an intermediate category (between foraging and cultivation), is a specialized adaptation to semiarid areas where cultivation is not feasible. It is, therefore, a "branch" of an evolutionary mainline in the view of most unilinear, ecological anthropologists (see Cohen 1968).

higher levels of population density, larger communities, and extra-local-level political systems.

G. P. Murdock's classification of the forces of production lists extensive agriculture, or horticulture, as the first form of food-cultivation technology. This technique involves tending vegetable gardens and fruit trees and/or growing cereals. One of the most widely used forms of extensive agriculture is shifting or swidden cultivation, which is common in tropical regions where heavily forested areas must be cleared through burning ("slash-and-burn"). Crops are planted after the vegetation covering the ground has been removed and are harvested at the end of the season. After several years of constant use, the land is exhausted and must be left fallow. Secondary forest growth returns after a period. Shifting agriculturalists reuse the plots years later.

Extensive agriculture depends on the use of nonpermanent fields and relies on tools such as hoes or digging sticks. There are no plows. The staple crops produced via swidden techniques include

> ... manioc (originally in South American tropical forests; now widely distributed in the tropical world), maize (in the Americas; now also widely distributed), millet and sorghum (Africa), rice (Southeast Asia and Indonesia), sweet potato and yam (Oceania; now Africa and elsewhere), taro and banana (Oceania and Southeast Asia; now wide-spread). (Sahlins 1968:30)

Extensive cultivation is a labor-intensive form of production. Sahlins estimates that the average adult contributes 500 to 1,000 hours per year toward the cultivation effort, exclusive of food-preparation time. Yet swidden systems provide high yields in proportion to expended labor. Given the length of the fallow periods (eight to ten years and longer), communities must control considerably more land than they actually have under cultivation at any one time. Population density tends therefore to be lower than that found among intensive agriculturalists (who use the plow or irrigation techniques).

Population growth, or its equivalent, land shortages, can have serious consequences for swidden production systems.[14] Food de-

---

[14] The population density of forest cultivators is frequently less than 10 people per square mile. Settlement size is likewise restricted: Villages larger on the average than 200 to 250 people are unusual in swidden areas (Sahlins 1968:31).

mands often cause cultivators to shorten fallow periods, which in turn causes soil nutrient deficiencies that can be irreversible. Thus people-to-land ratios in extensive agricultural areas are in a fairly delicate balance. Sahlins notes that this situation has potential for causing intercommunity conflict:

> Cultivation may pass directly into intercommunity competition over valuable land. The economic status-quo requires a balanced man-land ratio in each community, clearly a fragile equilibrium, easily upset by local variations in birth and death rates. Encroachment by larger groups on the garden-lands of smaller groups is not the only way to restore the balance, but it is at least a conceivable tactic, and the militant ethos of many forest tribes testifies to some readiness to adopt it. (Sahlins 1968:32)

Agricultural production is rarely the only source of sustenance in these economies. Domesticated animals are often important as well, particularly as capital resources. Extensive agriculturalists may also fish and hunt as a supplement, yet the staple diet depends on the gardens and the trees.

I have outlined some of the basic characteristics of extensive agriculture. However, there is a degree of variation in the size, complexity, and social organization of societies at this level of the development of the productive forces. Gerhard Lenski's (1966, 1970) cross-cultural studies of social stratification identified two distinct types of extensive agriculturalists. *Simple* horticulturalists are those for whom metallurgy is unknown, whereas *advanced* horticulturalists have a knowledge of metalworking. Simple horticultural societies therefore use the digging stick as their major tool; complex horticulturalists employ the hoe in weeding and planting. Lenski argues that this technological distinction predicts some important divergences in stratification, political complexity, warfare, and the economics of marriage transactions. Eighty-three percent of the simple horticulturalists in his study lack social classes, whereas only 46% of the advanced group lack classes, the majority having some form of inequality in resource access. Seventy-nine percent of the simple group are organized according to politically autonomous villages, whereas 71% of the advanced group are part of some form of political hierarchy. Finally, "marriage becomes almost invariably an *economic* transaction among advanced horticulturalists, which is not surprising in light of women's continuing importance as cultivators coupled with the increased emphasis on surplus production at this level" (Blumberg 1978:40). Ninety-seven percent of the advanced horticulturalists require brideprice or bride service.

Blumberg (1978) has argued that Lenski's scheme runs afoul in Africa, where the diffusion of iron technology from the Middle East and North Africa to the rest of the continent was extensive. She argues that at the broadest level African horticulturalists are of two types: One-third of them "have preclass, politically autonomous village societies. The remainder have more elaborate and inegalitarian stratification and political systems" (Blumberg 1978:38). Both groups have metalworking.

Blumberg offers a more detailed categorization of horticulturalists according to the extent to which surplus accumulation is developed among them. She suggests that four "paths" are possible in this regard: (1) "The first path involves a minimal journey along the road to surplus accumulation or population growth. Groups taking this route . . . have kept their lives simple, their production low, and their numbers well below the carrying capacity of their technology." (2) "The second path . . . is to produce a moderate amount of surplus, but to retain and distribute it *communally*. Often redistribution comes about in periodic festivals and feasts." (3) "The third and fourth paths involve the accumulation and retention of surplus at a level less inclusive than the total community – that of the family or even the individual. In the third path, *women* who are the chief cultivators, emerge as equal or better partners in the control of group resources and surplus." (4) "The fourth path emerges when men use women's labor in cultivation in order to deliberately produce surplus and prestige for their own benefit. Typically, the chief beneficiary is the man for whom the woman labors, in most cases, her husband" (Blumberg 1978:35–6).

Blumberg's argument is therefore different from Lenski's. Lenski suggests that variation in stratification and complexity flows from different subsistence technologies (hoe versus digging stick). He argues for categorization on the basis of *forces of production*. Blumberg, by referencing African societies, shows that technology is not the decisive factor. Horticultural societies sharing the same basic forces of production exhibit very different *social relations of production*. Some produce no surplus and have no method of exploiting the labor of others, while others have considerable surplus production and unequal forms of surplus appropriation. Blumberg's model is therefore conceptually closer to the materialist paradigm as it was discussed at the beginning of Chapter 3. As such, I will use a modified version of it to examine the links between the social relations of production, the form of legal institutions, and the content of disputes among extensive agriculturalists.

Blumberg was primarily concerned with the socioeconomic status of women in different types of horticultural societies. Because this is not my major interest, I will collapse her third and fourth paths into one. The resulting tripartite model – which consists of minimal surplus, low–redistributed surplus, and high–concentrated surplus societies – should provide a vantage point from which to view the variation among extensive agriculturalists. I will concentrate on one particular culture within each category to gain some understanding of the link between law and economy for each of the three types of horticulturalists.

The Jivaro

Famous for their headhunting practices, the Jivaro of eastern Ecuador are the subject of Michael Harner's sympathetic ethnography, subtitled *People of the Sacred Waterfall*. At the time of Harner's initial fieldwork (the mid-1950s), the interior Jivaro were among the few South American peoples whose way of life had not been destroyed by contact with the outside world. They were the only tribe of American Indians who ever successfully revolted against Spanish rule and, "despite the fact that they were known to occupy one of the richest placer gold deposit regions in all of South America," they managed to keep their traditional culture intact, at least until the mid-1960s.

The Jivaro are representative of those horticulturalists who produce little in the way of a surplus. Living off manioc and sweet-potato cultivation, a small amount of fish protein, monkey, bird meat, and domesticated chicken, the Jivaro do not lack for a varied diet. Each household has either a single large garden or several small ones, from which 65 percent of the daily diet is supplied. The gardens are abandoned after three manioc plantings (3–5 years), and new ones are created through slash-and-burn methods. The planting stick was the only tool of cultivation known to the Jivaro prior to the introduction of the machete. The planting and harvesting seasons of Jivaro staple foods overlap, thereby assuring constant and reliable sources of nutrition.

The sexual division of labor among the Jivaro finds the women doing most of the labor-intensive gardening work. They are exclusively responsible for manioc cultivation, the most important of Jivaro foods. Women undertake the onerous and never-ending task of weeding the gardens. Together, men and women plant peanuts, but it is the females alone who do the harvesting. Clearly, women are the major producers; men lead a rather leisured existence by comparison, their responsibilities limited to the clearing of forest land (once every few years) and regular hunting expeditions. This remains so today among the Aguaruna Jivaro of lowland Peru (Brent Berlin, personal communication).

Jivaro life centers on the individual household, normally inhabited by a polygynous nuclear family. Harner (1972) notes that households generally contain roughly nine members: a man, his two wives, and their children. Jivaro postmarital residence rules specify an uxurilocal pattern (the new couple live with the bride's family). When their first child is born, the couple forms its own nuclear household. Thus, one does not find extended-family households, as is the case among more complex horticulturalists. Population density is extremely low (approximately 1.19 persons/square mile). Jivaro households are not organized into villages but are widely dispersed throughout the forest. Each household may be located near one or two others composed of close relatives. There is an abundance of land, "accompanied by an absence of claims or definitions of territoriality" (Harner 1972:77).

Household productivity is closely correlated with the number of wives; thus polygyny is desirable. A modicum of surplus production is required to entertain friends and thereby gain status, a process that can only occur with additional wives:

> The Jivaro place a high value on drinking beer and eating (perhaps in that order), so that one's status in a neighborhood is greatly affected by one's generosity with beer and food. No one can expect to have many friends unless he is a good host; and he cannot easily meet the requirements of good hospitality without plural wives as a labor force. (Harner 1972:8)

Although a certain amount of surplus is generated by multiple wives, it is clear that this increased productivity does not translate into wealth accumulation, for the only reason for stepping up production is to increase one's capacity to be generous. In short, redistribution of the surplus product, such as it exists, is swift and direct.

One further mechanism for suppressing wealth distinctions is the practice of demanding gifts, something that nonshaman Jivaro do frequently. Harner notes that a request for a gift cannot be denied and that serious consequences befall the miser. Nonshamans "continually badger each other for gifts, thereby preventing the accumulation of wealth by a few individuals" (Harner 1972:117). This practice is reminiscent of sporadic gift demands common among sedentary foragers.

Gift giving and lavish manioc-beer and food parties drain enough income from a family to minimize wealth distinctions in traditional Jivaro society. The social relations of production do not provide any means for a household to exploit the labor of nonfamily members or otherwise seek to concentrate wealth in their own hands, and as such social stratification is virtually absent among the Jivaro.

The same might be said of politico-legal authority. The Jivaro are a paradigm case of self- or kin-based redress system of dispute settlement. Aggrieved parties, together with those kinsmen who are so inclined, take the law into their own hands, and take vengeance on an offender and his kin, a practice that has earned the Jivaro a fierce reputation. Normative ideals of proper and improper behavior govern retaliation.

What do the Jivaro dispute about? Unlike those of the pastoralists (and like those of the food collectors), Jivaro conflicts center on women. Polygyny creates an "artificial" shortage of women for young men to marry, and adultery is therefore rife. Young men visit married young women while their husbands are away on hunting expeditions. The sanctions against adultery are serious indeed, as extramarital affairs often result in the wife leaving to live with her lover permanently. Common punitive actions involve killing the lover and slashing the wife's scalp with a machete.

Similarly, "inheritance" disputes revolve not around material goods, but around who will marry the widow. The Jivaro practice levirate marriage, but this does not stop unrelated men from trying to abscond with willing widows. Similarly, the Jivaro prefer cross-cousin marriage; intense competition surrounds the decision as to which brother will marry a female cousin. Harner reports that this is a constant source of irritation.

A second major conflict among the Jivaro concerns sorcery. Jivaroans do not believe in death from "natural" causes. Death resulting from illness is caused by the shaman's curse. When a relative dies in this mysterious fashion, a Jivaro family engages another shaman to discover who was responsible. Retaliatory expeditions are then mounted.

Disputes over material goods are noticeably absent in Jivaro society. Harner reports that theft is "virtually unheard of." Similarly, land is not an object of conflict, for it is plentiful in supply and population density is low.

In sum, Jivaro society is composed of self-supporting families producing small surpluses, which are immediately redistributed through feasts and gift giving. Families do not live off the labor of others. The only resource in short supply is the labor power of female producers, which is critical to a Jivaroan man. Consequently, all areas of life that impinge on securing and keeping wives are fraught with conflict. This can be explained by the social relations of production and the emphasis on female productive capacity.

Malevolent sorcery is another matter; the materialist model cannot adequately account for it, though social-structural analyses may well be compatible with a materialist approach. Evans-Pritchard's (1937) research on Azande witchcraft practices has shown that witchcraft accusations are not randomly distributed, but exhibit observable patterns. Gluckman (1965:222) notes that further research in Africa has shown the same phenomenon of patterning, though the exact configuration of accusations differs from society to society. These findings have been analyzed as conflicts in social organization, but it is entirely possible that they are amenable to analyses that emphasize the relations of production as well.

Kapauku Papuans

The Jivaro typify the simplest form of horticultural society, one without wealth distinctions or significant surplus production and accumulation. The intermediate variety in Blumberg's categorization is typified by the Kapauku Papuans, who live in the central highlands of western New Guinea. Pospisil has written extensively on the economy, social structure, and legal institutions of the Kamu Valley Kapauku, who had "not yet met Western civilization or been brought under its legal control" at the time of his fieldwork in the 1950s (Pospisil 1963a:3). Pospisil observed Kapauku law in its pristine state, which is described in his well-known ethnography, *Kapauku Papuans and Their Law* (1958).

Kapauku horticultural technology differed only slightly from that practiced by the Jivaro. Kapauku territory encompassed two kinds of land: mountain land, which surrounded the Kamu Valley, and valley-floor land. Mountain plots were cleared by fire and planted with sweet potatoes, though they could bear only a single crop before being left to fallow. Valley-floor land was cultivated intensively, using drainage ditches, composting, and crop rotation, making possible three or more harvests from the same plot.

The importance of horticulture exceeded its contribution to the Kapauku diet. Sweet potatoes were fed to pigs, which represented the only means of capital accumulation in the society. Cultivation was therefore significant not only for the food it produced but for the direct support it lent to the maintenance of pig herds.

Unlike the Jivaro, where unclaimed land is plentiful, Kamu Valley land was owned *in toto*. Moreover, all land was owned by individuals rather than kin groups:

> All land of the Botukebo people is owned individually. There is no "lineage or sublineage land" free for the members of these groups to occupy and cultivate. In order to be able to make a new garden a cultivator has to have a specific title to the proposed site. He may either own it, or lease it for pay from another individual, or "borrow" it from a man without pay, with a tacit agreement to reciprocate in kind in the future. (Pospisil 1963b:88)

"Primitive capitalism" is the phrase Pospisil uses to describe the economic system of the Kamu Valley people: 59.8% of the garden land under cultivation during his first visit was owner cultivated, 33.58% was on "borrowed" land, and 6.84% was on land leased for shell money. Unlike other horticultural societies with less elaborate social relations of production, the Kapauku exhibited a definite tendency toward privatized control of material resources. The major means of production, the land, was owned by individuals whose control extended beyond cultivated land to virgin forest "where particular segments are owned by specific individuals who retain the most valuable rights to the economic exploitation of their wooded property" (Pospisil 1963b:131).

The Kapauku emphasis on private property is not necessarily characteristic of horticultural societies in the intermediate category of surplus production. Many groups, including well-documented New Guinea gardening societies, practice a mixture of individual title (usually assigned to the male household head) and corporate ownership. Rosman and Rubel describe the Kuma land-tenure system as such a mix:

> Clearing and cultivating unused land gives title to the land to the man who performs the labor and his descendants . . . Bush land . . . is owned by the sub-clan or sub-subclan. (1978:138–9)

Among the Kapauku, every plot of individually owned land was marked off from neighboring plots by fences or stakes (which also kept the pigs out). Lands left fallow were bounded by *ti* plants, which were removed from the interior of the plot and planted around its borders. Natural boundaries such as creeks, mountain ridges, and the like delineated the borders of virgin forest tracts.

The members of a nuclear or polygynous family "decidedly do not share common rights," either to the land or the produce cultivated on it. It was tacitly assumed that a father granted his sons permission to "fell trees of secondary growth and to trap and shoot rats in the fallow land as well as in the gardens." However, in the case of close relations usufruct rights were not automatically transmitted. On the other hand, a man had to ask permission of his adult sons to sell his land, lest the transaction be invalidated by them upon his death (which suggests some residual features of corporate tenure).

Women did not own land at all. Upon marriage, they obtained permission to cultivate and harvest a small portion of their husband's gardens, the produce of which technically belonged to the wife alone. However, these rights ceased upon divorce, which indicates the dependent status of womenfolk in the Kamu Valley. Though they were without their own means of production, women were critical to the Kapauku economy. In common with Jivaro women, the Kapauku female was exclusively responsible for the cultivation of the basic dietary staple (the sweet potato).

Women and pigs were closely linked in Kapauku society; the

more female producers, the larger the sweet-potato crop and the larger the pig herd that could be fed. Not surprisingly, polygynous marriages were highly desirable, for the female labor force at a man's disposal could be augmented through the acquisition of multiple wives.

Men did participate in the production process by digging the drainage ditches for the valley gardens, burning the forest lands on the hillsides, felling trees, building fences, and planting manioc squash and sugar cane. Theirs was not an especially leisured life; yet a man could not by himself produce the sweet potatoes he needed to accumulate pig capital.

Every Kapauku capitalist wanted to become a rich man. Unlike cultures where abundant possessions are an embarrassment, the Kapauku were devoted to the accumulation of wealth. A young man began his career by attempting to secure a contract as a pig breeder from a wealthy older man. Such an arrangement benefited both parties, in that the wealthy man increased the labor power at his disposal while the young man acquired some capital for breeding pigs and sought a reputation as a good breeder. If the young man was a success, he would be rewarded with "the respect and confidence of the wealthy man who may then be inclined to sell him the desired female piglet," thus enabling the novice to launch his own capital-accumulation efforts (Pospisil 1963b:215).

These initial breeding contracts were not easy to come by. The sons of rich men had an easier time than those of the poor:

> The first-born son of a rich man is assured of a good start in life. If the father dies while the son is still young, he receives a good inheritance. But even if his father is alive, the son has no need "to prove himself" as a good pig breeder before he can acquire pigs of his own, as a poor man's son must do. His father will usually give him a start on the way toward becoming a *tonowi* ("wealthy headman"), but if he proves to be negligent and careless, his loans and fortunes are easily dissipated. (Pospisil 1963b:387)

Clearly, some individuals were more successful than others in herd building. In the village of Botukebo, where Pospisil gathered most of his data, nineteen of the thirty-eight adult males owned all the pigs, which indicates the uneven distribution of capital among the Kapauku. Indeed, Pospisil (1963a:30) describes families with undernourished children sitting next door to the children of prosperous, well-fed households.

The cycle of capital accumulation followed a definite path. First, a man had to amass sufficient shell money to purchase a female piglet. Second, he had to furnish the piglet with an adequate supply of sweet potatoes. The first litter could be sold at a profit, although some pigs would be held off the market for breeding. However, feeding the pig(s) required land to plant and a wife to grow the sweet potatoes. A Kapauku entrepreneur had to go into debt to pay the brideprice and, unless he had already inherited land from his father, he also had to borrow to purchase or lease land. If his efforts paid off, he would accumulate a number of wives, raise many pigs, pay off his debts, and become a wealthy man. At this point, he would extend credit to the next generation of young men who would help raise his pigs, borrow shell money from him to "buy" their own wives, and so forth.

The benefits of becoming a rich man went beyond prestige. A wealthy man had economic power: He could affect the price of pork and thus derive high profits from his investments:

> The most conspicuous role of wealth lies in the marketing of pork. By extensive selling or buying a rich man may influence the prices of the local pig market. Furthermore, because he periodically accumulates pigs for slaughter, he is in a position to determine the frequency and dates of pig feasts, pig markets, . . . etc. From these events he not only gathers an enormous income and influences profoundly the distribution of goods, but he also receives a great amount of prestige. (Pospisil 1963b:392)

Wealthy men parlayed their riches into political power and elevated social standing. Typical of "big-man" societies, a Kapauku rich man extended credit to numerous less fortunate souls, thereby creating alliances and obligations of a social, economic, and political nature. These debtors became political followers.

The only form of political organization in Kapauku society rested on the shoulders of these capitalists, the *tonowi* or "big men" whom I described in Chapter 2. *Tonowi* had all the authority one typically associates with a chief. They initiated major "public works," acted as legal authorities in disputes, and "induce [their] followers to accept [their] opinions and decisions with regard to political alliances, diplomatic negotiations with outsiders and ultimately with regard to matters of war and peace" (Pospisil 1963b:381).

The position of a *tonowi* had its precarious aspects. He could go broke if he lent money unwisely. Bad business decisions could affect his pig herds and send him tumbling down. Loss of wealth meant loss of followers. However, if he remained successful, he had many obligations to fulfill. He had to sponsor pig feasts. He had to extend credit generously, for one who failed to spread the wealth around risked being murdered by outraged fellow citizens. Such a killing was viewed as justified and retaliatory steps were not taken.

I have already noted that *tonowi* served as legal authorities for their relatives and followers. I pointed out in Chapter 2 that they vied with one another to act as judges in disputes involving non-followers, rendering decisions according to a well-formed body of customary law. Pospisil's description makes it clear that the judgments of the *tonowi* were accepted as binding, for they were indeed powerful.[15]

The complexity of Kapauku economic relations was mirrored in their substantive law. Pospisil details five different categories of law that were derived from summaries of *tonowi* decisions distilled in the form of jural postulates recognized by the Kapauku. These include: (1) *offenses against property rights*, which included a complex of laws relating to land tenure, boundary rules, ownership of moveables, inheritance, usufruct, theft, etc.; (2) *contracts*, which encompassed sales agreements, land leasing, the extension of credit, and labor and pig-breeding contracts; (3) *offenses against persons*, which covered murder (which tended to occur as a result of property-right violations), relations between the sexes, accidental death, battery, suicide, and lying (it is interesting to note that the Kapauku regarded a woman's suicide as an offense against her husband or father, who was referred to as her "owner"); (4) *offenses against and by an authority* — here Pospisil refers to a *tonowi's* abuse of

---

[15] This is why the Kapauku fall into my category of chieftainships. Some might balk at this classification, preferring to discuss *tonowi* in terms of their roles as "big men." Such terminology is ordinarily employed to refer to the political functions of such individuals rather than their adjudicatory roles. At the risk of confusion, I place the Kapauku (and other similarly structured societies) in the chieftainship category to emphasize the ability of leaders to render authoritative judgments.

power and offenses committed against a *tonowi*; and finally (5) *delicts against society*, which included cases where a wealthy man refused to behave generously (this was taken as an insult directed against the body politic, rather than an affront to an individual).

In sum, in Kapauku society we see very complex social relations of production embedded within horticultural forces of production. There were various mechanisms by which the labor of men and women was appropriated by others (through marriage obligations, rent, labor contracts, and credit). These relations allowed for a much higher degree of surplus extraction compared, for example, with Jivaroan practices. There were also considerable wealth differences among Kapauku families (which was not true of the Jivaro), though full-fledged class distinctions were absent given the redistribution practices wealthy Kapauku had to follow.

Alongside the social relations of production, concepts of property rights abounded. Kapauku substantive law was far more complex than its Jivaro counterpart, for every aspect of social relations was represented therein. Labor was regulated through contract law; rights to land and inheritance were given legal expression; and credit and debt were similarly controlled. The legal process sustained production and redistribution relations.

Although the Kapauku and Jivaro share much the same forces of production, their social relations, legal institutions, and conflicts substances diverge considerably. However, in both cases law and economy mesh, the former addressing strains in the relations of production that repeatedly arise.

The Ashanti Kingdom

There can be no greater testimony to the variation in political organization within one category of the forces of production than the gap that separates the Jivaro horticulturalists from the Ashanti horticulturalists of West Africa. The simple local relations of the Jivaro give way among the Ashanti to "a massive military state with cities and towns that had all the elements of a nascent civilization save writing" (Hoebel 1968:211). The Gold Coast was the site of one of the most complex cultures on the continent, powerful enough to challenge the military might of the British Empire in the late nineteenth and early twentieth centuries.

The Ashanti Kingdom is an example of the way in which extensive

agricultural forces of production can be harnessed to produce sufficient surplus to support an administrative-legal bureaucracy, a
hereditary aristocracy, and a military machine. Through elaborate
social relations of production, the Ashanti built a pyramidal tribal
state "embracing more than 200,000 persons under
a . . . confederated monarchy" (Hoebel 1968:212).

The Ashanti subsistence base involved the cultivation of yams,
coco-yams, and plantains using rotational fallows. Women were
responsible for farming in the forest areas, whereas yams were
grown by men on a larger scale in open territory. Fishing and
hunting in the coastal and forest areas provided additional food
sources. The coastal zones permitted cattle and sheep husbandry;
the tsetse flies inhabiting the forest zone limited its livestock inven-
tory to poultry and pigs (Manoukian 1950). The similarities between Kapauku and Ashanti forces of production allow me to
proceed without further comment.

Describing the social relations of production of the kingdom will
be made easier by first describing the political organization of the
society, which functioned in part as a siphoning structure, extracting
surplus from the lower to the upper levels of the political pyramid.
Ashanti villages formed the lowest level of the pyramid. Matrilineal
lineages within each village held the usufruct rights to land (which
was attached to the village) and formed the basis of inheritance
rights and residence rules. The head of the senior lineage (whose
female ancestor was the first to settle in the area) was chosen by
the male members of his lineage to act as the village headman.
Together with a village council of senior elders from each lineage,
the headman administered the affairs of the village and served as
a conduit to the next level of political authority, the regional "stool."

The tribal division or region had its center in a capital city, where
the component lineages resided in special quarters. The head of the
most senior lineage (e.g., the founding lineage) and his advisory
council formed the political leadership of the division. The council
elders were responsible for representing the interests of the outlying
villages and as such were themselves drawn from each of the matrilineages in the division. The *Omahene*, the chief of a territorial
state, was a powerful figure commanding the administrative apparatus of his region.

All the territories of the Ashanti nation were subordinate in turn to a central authority, the king and his court. The *Ashantihene*, the paramount chief of the Kumasi region, was acknowledged as the king of the Ashanti. Together with the royal family, the members of the Kumasi matrilineage, he ruled the empire, leading conquests against neighboring tribes, subduing many, and adding them to the expanding kingdom.

The basic political structure of this society therefore resembles a series of hierarchical levels, with the village at the bottom, the territorial state in the middle, and the central government in the national capital at the top. The structure shares some features with European feudal states, where each level of authority owed allegiance to the level above but was fairly independent where the management of daily affairs was concerned. At each of the three levels, authority was vested in an executive figure, who was assisted by a group of bureaucratic administrators and advised by a council.

The legal structure of the Ashanti was identical to their political organization. Conflict within lineages within a village were dealt with by the village headman. However, if one party to a dispute chose to do so, he could "swear the oath" of the territorial chief, which automatically removed the case to his jurisdiction. Very serious cases, especially those involving capital offenses, were usually referred directly to the head of the regional state (the *Omahene*). Cases could be sent by the regional chief to the king and his advisory council, the highest appeal in the land.

An administrative-legal bureaucracy such as this required considerable revenues to support its activities. For, unlike the Kapauku *tonowi*, Ashanti kings and chiefs did not labor on the land for a living. Neither, for that matter, did their functionaries or the members of the royal family. Rattray (1929) notes that they lived in a state of relative splendor, though the rules of accession required that personal fortunes be converted to state property (thus political elites did not personally grow wealthy off their positions).[16]

In common with the Kapauku *tonowi*, Ashanti elites were expected to be generous in throwing feasts for their subordinates, and they too could be deposed if their followers were sufficiently dis-

---

[16] The personal property of Ashanti "stools" was converted to state property when they took office. However, officials frequently turned their personal property over to female relatives prior to taking office as insurance against the day they might be "destooled."

pleased. The resources that supported this generosity, as well as those that supported the daily needs of the bureaucracy, were garnered via elaborate relations of production; the legal system played a part in siphoning resources from below. Every time an oath was sworn or a case heard at any level of the judicial hierarchy, an *aseda* (court fee) was paid by the successful litigant. These fees were substantial, and court officials were paid out of the revenues (Rattray 1929:115).

Substantial fines could be levied by the courts, providing another lucrative source of revenue. Criminal cases were often settled in this fashion. Where capital offenses were concerned, special dispensation from the death penalty could be secured with a very large fee. Because a wide variety of offenses was considered capital, the coffers of the king and the subordinate chiefs were constantly supplemented by those trying to "buy back their heads."

The legal machinery of the Ashanti was not the only institutional instrument for the extraction of surplus. Upon a man's death, the chief could claim a portion of his personal moveable property by virtue of a "death tax" (Rattray 1929:108). (Inheritance taxes of this sort were strictly forbidden among the Kapauku.)

Chiefs had the right to tax their subjects to support certain obligatory activities:

> The chief had the capacity to make certain levies, with the concurrence of his council of elders and the approval of the people. These included such matters as paying for the expenses of a war, a chief's funeral, or a sacrifice of livestock on behalf of the tribe. (Carlston 1968:129)

Chiefs also had the right to demand a certain amount of corvée labor every year to work their own farms.

Trading monopolies constituted yet another important source of revenue:

> Kola went north to be exchanged for slaves and cloth. . .Gold and slaves were sent to the coast in exchange for European goods, trade goods. In Ashanti, trade played an important part in maintaining the King's power; he had a monopoly of certain trades, e.g., kola, for a certain period of every year. (Manoukian 1950:18)

Slavery provided a means of surplus extraction that was available to elites and nonelites alike. Rattray notes that "a condition of voluntary servitude was, in a very literal sense, the heritage of every Ashanti; it formed indeed the essential basis of his society (1929:33).

By this he means that every Ashanti was legally "subject" to a "master." In this matrilineal society, a man's nephew and niece were their uncle's "subjects"; a man's wife was her uncle's "subject," and so on.

However, it is clear from Rattray's account that some people were more "subject" than others. The Northern Territory of the Gold Coast provided the powerful Southern Kingdom with men and women who could be purchased for involuntary servitude (Schildkrout 1979:188). Rattray's descriptions of Ashanti slave markets at Salaga are as gruesome as accounts of the slave trade in the American colonies of the seventeenth and eighteenth centuries.[17] Men captured in war, or those sent "as a form of tribute from a subjugated foreign power," were transformed into slaves. Rattray claims that every free-born Ashanti could be "pawned" into slavery on a permanent or temporary basis if he or she were a troublemaker (or if their families were in need of capital).

Credit/debt relations were very complex. Individuals could lend and borrow against their personal property. The "stools" (chiefs) could borrow against the lands in their domains and pledge their subjects as slaves in surety. The interest paid on these loans was often quite high and therefore constituted another form of surplus extraction.

This description shows that the economic system of the Ashanti was built upon every form of surplus extraction in the index of the social relations of production constructed in Chapter 3. The right to appropriate these resources was guaranteed by the unwritten customary law of the Ashanti nation.

Rattray (1929) describes an elaborate "code" applied by legal authorities at each level of the hierarchy. Two categories of legal wrongs composed this code: "Sins" or "Things Hated by the Tribe"; and "Household" cases. This distinction involved both the formal relationship between the litigants and the type of offense.

---

[17] Rattray's descriptions of Ashanti slave markets were culled from an informant who had been a buyer in the days when the markets were active. A thorough understanding of the origins and role of the slave trade requires a discussion of the Atlantic Triangle and the interests of western European manufacturers as well as New World sugar-plantation owners. This is beyond my scope. However, there is evidence to suggest that slavery in some form had indigenous roots in African conquest states, including the Ashanti (see Schildkrout 1979).

Sins were subdivided into two types: (1) offenses that were automatically the concern of central authorities (the king, regional chiefs, or headmen) because they were regarded as threatening to the sociopolitical order. These included murder, suicide, the invocation of a curse upon a chief, treason and cowardice, witchcraft, violation of tribal taboos, and "refusal to obey any law or command issued and qualified by a 'conditional curse' " (Rattray 1929:293–4). (2) Offenses that concerned public officials only because they were perpetrated against authorities. For example, under Ashanti customary law, slander, assault, theft, and sexual offenses were not sins when committed by one commoner against another. However, any of the same offenses perpetrated against a chief, a public official, or one of their relatives automatically constituted a sin.

Up until the years of British domination, perpetrators of sins were liable to summary arrest and trial by a chief or the king himself. All sins were capital crimes, though, as I explained earlier, the death penalty could be commuted in exchange for a large fee.

Offenses categorized as sins involved (with a few exceptions) attacks against the aristocracy or its bureaucratic representatives through physical actions or symbolic insults (slanders or curses). It is testimony to the strength of the Ashanti administration that these challenges could be crushed with capital sanctions, which Rattray reports were considered legitimate exercises of legal power.

The other major branch of Ashanti law, household law, involved offenses such as theft, sexual misconduct, debt relations, land tenure, inheritance, labor obligations, and marital rules (including brideprice), where the aggrieved party was a commoner. These offenses were dealt with differently depending on the relations between litigants. Household offenses committed by one kinsman against another would be adjudicated by a family elder according to the customary law governing household matters. Disputes of this sort were considered private rather than public matters, though they were supposed to be resolved according to a body of law pertaining to household matters. Persuasion, conciliation, and a knowledge of local custom were the major tools at the disposal of the elders. Ridicule was used when necessary, and Rattray reports that it was a powerful sanction. The ultimate punishment within the lineage group was the threat of expulsion. Indeed, lineage members who repeatedly proved troublesome were candidates to be "pawned" (sold into temporary bondage).

If the resolution of an intralineage dispute was not to the satisfaction of a litigant, he or she could move it into the sphere of public sins by deliberately invoking the name of a deceased relative of the lineage head. At this point, it was mandatory to take the case to the lineage head, headman of the village, or regional chief. The subsequent investigation (of the swearing of the oath) would focus on the underlying dispute.

Interlineage disputes were handled differently. Ashanti matrilineages were corporate groups with corporate responsibilities for the behavior of members. If a member of a lineage failed to pay a debt, his kinsmen would either try to settle the issue informally or pay the debt themselves. This did not permit free license to commit offenses, knowing that one's kinsmen stood in the wings. On the contrary, an individual who put his lineage members in a compromising position risked severe treatment at their hands.

Chiefs tended to intervene in interlineage cases because they were able to raise revenue by imposing fines and levying court fees. Some regional chiefs went so far as to fine those who sought to settle interlineage disputes informally (thus avoiding the regional authorities). Loan holders often made use of this device by swearing the oath of the regional chief, who would then enforce a verdict against the debtor. This done, the creditor would pay a fee to the chief for his collection services. The aristocracy could, in this way, insert themselves into the regulation of private commerce, particularly when a profit could be derived from so doing.

Several points should be made in closing this section on Ashanti law. First, the social relations of production provided mechanisms whereby the hereditary aristocracy could "pump" surplus from its subjects; these arrangements were the subject of "public law," the "sins against the tribe." There were additional means whereby surplus could be accumulated by nonaristocrats through the use of slaves, the extension of credit, and the "pawning" of relations; these features were covered by "household law." On both levels, the law addressed aspects of resource control, be it labor or land.

The second point is that Ashanti law institutionalized the privileges of ruling elites. Among the Jivaro (and to a lesser extent the Kapauku), customary law applied equally to all. In the Ashanti case, there was a marked difference. The law of the land provided protection to and legitimation of a ruling elite.

Finally, the comparative centralization of the Ashanti kingdom affected the extent to which authorities could interfere in the "private" business of corporate kin groups. Although private adjudication continued in the Ashanti household-law system, legal authorities were able to intervene in this sphere. Rattray points out that such a tendency increased markedly as the kingdom became more and more centralized. Nevertheless, the Ashanti displayed a tension common to paramount chieftainships: a tug-of-war between the locally based kin groups and the central administration over legal control.

This discussion of the Ashanti Kingdom, in the context of legal systems in horticultural societies, points up the importance of using a fully developed version of the mode of production in analyzing the regulatory role of legal systems. If my analytic framework had only been the forces of production, there would have been tremendous and potentially inexplicable variations in the substantive law of societies like the Jivaro, Kapauku, and Ashanti. By adding the concept of social relations of production, I have been able to *differentiate between* these three extensive-agriculture societies and advance understanding of the variations among them with respect to substantive law.

They hold some aspects of substantive law in common. Women, who are the most important producers in horticultural societies, are the subject of conflict in each. However, the variation between the three cases is substantial when it comes to issues of land tenure, private property, corvée labor, and so on. By interjecting the social relations of production, one sees three different *modes of production* understood as the *combination* or forces and social relations, and the role of legal institutions in the economic life of these horticultural societies becomes clearer.

The cultivators: intensive agriculture

If horticulture represents the first great technological revolution after the invention of tools, the development of intensive agriculture probably constitutes the second (Lenski 1966). The productive capacities of intensive agriculture exceed those of any of the subsistence systems discussed thus far. This is not because returns to labor in agriculture are necessarily higher than the returns under swidden regimes (Sahlins 1968:43). But agricultural technology obtains higher yields *per acre* of arable land than swidden systems, because agriculture allows for continuous cropping, rather than lengthy fallow periods necessary for shifting cultivation.

There are two basic forms of intensive agriculture, one using the plow and the other employing hydraulic technology. The plow, coupled with the energy resources of draft animals and fertilizer, permits the cultivation of a larger area than can be farmed with a hoe or digging stick. Irrigated agriculture allows for the use of permanent fields by using water to replenish nutrients lost through the food-production process.

The increased yields that these techniques make possible mean that both the population density and the settlement size in agrarian societies is much larger than the typical horticultural tribe. Moreover, unlike extensive agriculturalists (horticulturalists), who must keep large tracts of land in reserve (in a fallow state), intensive agriculturalists can afford to populate the land, relying on permanent fields for the sustenance of relatively dense populations (Sahlins 1968:43).

Increasing productive capacity affects nondemographic aspects of social structure as well. Class stratification, a complex division of labor, the growth of urbanism, and the development of the state are all features associated with the great agrarian empires of the Old and New Worlds. Yet the category of agricultural societies contains a wide variety of legal-political structures. The empires of the Incas, the Aztecs, and the feudal states of Europe are representative of the most developed agrarian societies. Yet the Zuni, the Ifugao, and a host of other less centralized societies also practiced intensive agriculture.

As a prelude to my discussion of legal variation in intensive-agrarian societies, it will be necessary to note some of the general characteristics of these cultures that bear on their economic organization. Following Lenski's (1966) lead, I note that the higher productivity of agrarian societies makes possible a sharp increase in occupational specialization and the emergence of governing classes, retainers (officials, soldiers, servants), merchants, artisans, and the like. The vast majority of the populace remain peasant farmers, yoked to the land. However, unlike the other subsistence technologies I have discussed, the yields from intensive agriculture permit large numbers of people to be engaged in occupations unrelated to food production.

Urban centers develop in these societies because sufficient food supplies allow for densely populated areas. Occupational specialization is evident in these preindustrial cities, which often serve as centers of trade, commerce, and politics. Improvements in transportation and communications, particularly with the development of writing systems, make it possible to connect outlying agricultural areas with city centers, increasing the feasibility of central administration.

Land tends to become a scarce resource in agrarian societies, in that private ownership of the means of production begins to take precedence over kin-based systems of inalienable usufruct rights. Class stratification is far more common in agrarian societies than in any other subsistence system, and the most important economic base of the ruling classes is ownership and control of the land. The peasantry work the land, producing a surplus that is usually appropriated by a landlord class in the most stratified of the traditional agrarian societies.

Elites extract surplus in other ways as well. The collection of taxes, tribute, rents, and services contributes to the widening wealth disparities between the small governing classes and the large laboring classes:

> On the basis of available data, it appears that the governing classes of agrarian societies probably received at least a quarter of the national income of most agrarian states, and that the governing class and ruler together usually received not less than half. (Lenski 1966:228)

These inequalities bring about the development of the state as a means of protecting the privileges of the upper classes and facilitating control of the lower echelons of society. Government is in the hands of professional administrators (often relatives of the rulers), who share in the wealth flowing to the top as payment for loyal services.

Relations between rulers and their more decentralized nobility are a constant source of friction in many agrarian states. The nobility depends upon the monarchy for title to land, the major source of wealth. However, dependence runs both ways in these societies, for the nobility often has greater administrative control over the far corners of agrarian empires than do the rulers. Lenski argues that political life in agrarian states is best understood as a battle between these two groups – a battle whose outcome had little effect on the peasantry, whose function was the production of agricultural wealth for both classes.

The foregoing generalizations apply to the more complex end of the agrarian spectrum. Many agrarian societies fail to reach the dimensions of a state society. The productive capacities of irrigated agriculture based on diverted streams (rather than massive water works) is much lower. Technology of this sort does not usually lead to the kinds of population densities, political centralization, and stratification just described.

The Pueblo Indians of the American Southwest practiced floodwater farming, controlling the runoff from natural streams. Although the social organization of these peoples was more complex than that of the hunters and gatherers, or the small-scale horticulturalists, it was by no means equivalent to the feudal agrarian states.

Variation in the political complexity of hydraulic agricultural societies prompted Wittfogel to argue that large-scale irrigation could only be built and maintained by a mass labor force, which in turn could only be mobilized by a centralized political system. In *Oriental Despotism* (Wittfogel 1957), he suggested that a bureaucratic sector, interposed between the peasantry and a despotic ruler, would arise to oversee administrative tasks connected to large-scale irrigation.

The same kind of variation in societal complexity is evident in the "dry" (plow-using) agricultural economies. In my sixty-society sample, there were nine dry intensive-agricultural societies. Two of the nine showed no evidence of social stratification, whereas three had wealth distinctions only and four of them were classified as class stratified.

How are these variations reflected in the forms of legal institutions found in intensive-agricultural societies? Table 4.1 presents a cross-tabulation of legal institutions and social stratification within plow-using agrarian societies in the sample. The least stratified of the dry agriculturalists have elders' councils. The middle group, those with wealth distinctions but lacking class stratification, have either eld-

Table 4.1. *Cross-tabulation of legal institutions by social stratification in dry intensive-agricultural societies for 60-society subsample*[a]

	Social Stratification			
	Absence	Wealth distinctions	Class stratification	Row total
Type of legal institution				
Elders' council	2	2	0	4
	50.0	50.0	0	44.4
	100.0	66.7	0	
Headman-chief	0	1	2	3
	0	33.3	66.7	33.3
	0	33.3	50.0	
Paramount chief	0	0	1	1
	0	0	100.0	11.1
	0	0	25.0	
State-level	0	0	1	1
	0	0	100.0	11.1
	0	0	25.0	
Column total	2	3	4	9
	22.2	33.3	44.4	100.0

[a]The top figure in each cell is the cell count, the middle the row percent, and the bottom the column percent.

ers' councils or chieftainships. Finally, looking at the most stratified of the plow-using agriculturalists, one sees several chieftainships, one paramount chieftainship, and one fully centralized state-level legal system. There is clearly a spread of institutional forms, ranging from the more egalitarian and less powerful legal systems all the way to the most hierarchical and most powerful.

Table 4.2 presents the same data for the irrigated-intensive agricultural societies in the sample. Here one sees a different picture. There is still variation in legal complexity, but the concentration is at the high end; half the irrigated societies have state-level legal systems. The five cultures at that end are also all class stratified. The other two class-stratified cultures in the irrigated sample have restricted councils, also suggesting a more pyramidal distribution of legal authority. Finally, there are three cases of irrigated agri-

Table 4.2. *Cross-tabulation of legal institutions by social stratification in irrigated intensive-agricultural societies for 60-society subsample*[a]

	Social stratification			
	Absence	Wealth distinctions	Class stratification	Row total
Type of legal institution				
Mediator	0	1	0	1
	0	100.0	0	10.0
	0	100.0	0	
Elders' council	2	0	0	2
	100.0	0	0	20.0
	100.0	0	0	
Restricted council	0	0	2	2
	0	0	100.0	20.0
	0	0	28.6	
State-level	0	0	5	5
	0	0	100.0	50.0
	0	0	71.4	
Column total	2	1	7	10
	20.0	10.0	70.0	100.0

[a]The top figure in each cell is the cell count, the middle the row percent, and the bottom the column percent.

culturalists with legal institutions at the lower end of the complexity scale.

In Chapter 3, I argued that the social relations of production, coupled with stratification, could predict the variation in legal systems within a given level of the development of productive forces (e.g., within the category of irrigated intensive agriculture). I now consider the ways this materialist perspective can assist in understanding the variation in substantive law in intensive-agricultural societies.

I cannot examine substantive law for all nineteen of the intensive-agrarian societies in the sample. Instead, I will focus on two societies that represent different ends of the complexity spectrum: the Ifugao, rice cultivators of the Philippines; and the Inca Empire of sixteenth-century Peru.

The Ifugao

The mountainous interior of Luzon Island in the Philippines is the homeland of the Ifugao. These people are described in the ethnographic work of R. F. Barton, who spent nearly eight years among them during the 1910s, teaching in an American-sponsored educational system (a forerunner of the Peace Corps). Barton's admiration for the complexities of their jurisprudence is recorded in *Ifugao Law* (Barton 1969).

The Ifugao were rice growers who lived in rugged terrain, which had to be terraced with hard-river stones to irrigate the land along the steep mountainsides:

> It may safely be said that the Ifugao have constructed the most extensive and the most admirable terraces for rice culture to be found anywhere in the world. The Japanese terraces, which excite the admiration of tens of thousands of tourists every year, are not to be compared with them. (Barton 1969:2)

Reaching up to fifty feet high, the terrace walls held the rainwater back and guided the springs and streams into man-made irrigation ditches, which "sometimes creep for two miles along the mountain sides before reaching the fields they supply. From the upper terraces the water falls to the lower" (Barton 1922:410).

Although sweet potatoes were an important part of the Ifugao diet, rice was the most significant crop in the eyes of the people. For rice played a role in the Ifugao social system as well as in their nutritional regime. Wealth and status were measured almost entirely by rice production, which is, in turn, a function of the extent of one's landholdings.

Barton describes the social organization of the Ifugao as consisting of three basic "classes": *Kadangyang* were wealthy men, whose land produced a surplus of rice every year, enabling them to make loans to those less fortunate at interest rates up to 200 percent. The *natuwok*, or "middle classes" of Ifugao society, owned enough rice land to satisfy their yearly food requirements, though they often ran short before harvests and resorted to borrowing from *kadangyang*. Finally, Barton mentions the *nawatwat*, who had no rice fields (or only small ones); these were the "poverty-stricken" Ifugao, who subsisted mainly on sweet potatoes, a last-resort source of sustenance.

The social status of the *nawatwat* was equal to that of the "slaves" and indentured servants that well-to-do Ifugao households contained. Individuals from needy households were often "sold" or "mortgaged" to more fortunate families, thus enabling the poor ones to squeak by in a bad year. This practice was quite widespread among the Ifugao, as was the custom of mortgaging rice fields:

> Rice fields and children alike are mortgaged by the Ifugao . . . If a man finds himself under the necessity of raising some money and cannot raise it any other way, he mortgages either his rice fields or a child. In such case, his property reverts to him when he repays the money. Until then the one who lends the money uses the child as a servant; or if it be a field that was mortgaged, plants the rice field and reaps the harvest. (Barton 1922:420)

An Ifugao man needed money for practically every religious ceremony – of which there were many in a given year – for which he had to host a feast. Reserve capital was required for these occasions; non-*kadangyang* tended not to have it. Consequently, indebtedness was widespread, particularly among the *natuwok*. This situation gave rise to the creation of professional *monbaga*, debt collectors who worked in exchange for commissions.

Property relations were important in Ifugao society, particularly those covering landownership. Wealth inequalities were apparent to Barton. Within the three villages of the Kiangan district, roughly 18% of the families held 2 or more acres, 36% owned 1 to 2 acres, 36% owned less than 1 acre, and the remaining 10% owned no land at all (Barton 1922:412). These figures indicate that both property ownership and wealth were unevenly distributed among the Ifugao.

There was both upward and downward social mobility in Ifugao society. A rich man's son had an advantage in his efforts to attain *kadangyang* status, but his fortunes were not completely guaranteed by birthright. Ifugao inheritance practices followed a pattern of primogeniture, which left the eldest son in a privileged position. His siblings inherited little and were therefore not much better off than their *natuwok* counterparts in the capital-accumulation effort. Conversely, a successful middle-class rice cultivator could parlay his holdings into the wealth and status that befit a *kadangyang*, particularly through the judicious extension of credit. The similarities between Kapauku horticulturalists and Ifugao rice farmers are strong: Well-managed capital could be augmented in both cases by lending and collecting on the interest.

The commonalities extend to the issue of surplus redistribution as well. For, as with the Kapauku, the obligations of the Ifugao *kadangyang* included throwing lavish feasts on a regular basis, a practice that the poor depended upon for sustenance. A rich man could not retain his social standing if he failed to provide in this fashion, and the more opulent the redistribution the better.

With this general overview of Ifugao social structure in mind, I turn to *Ifugao Law*. The reader may recall that the Ifugao go-betweens (*monkalun*) served as prototypes for mediator systems of dispute settlement (of the "shuttle diplomacy" variety). *Monkalun* were invariably drawn from the *kadangyang* class and the weight of their social status was always thrown behind settlement efforts.

Barton's account of substantive law in Ifugao society delineated three legal "branches" that covered all the social relations of production just discussed: (1) *Family law*: rules of marriage and re-marriage of widows, divorce, obligations toward dependents, the status of illegitimate children, and "reciprocal obligations of parents and their children"; (2) *property law*: land tenure, property transfer, contracts for property sale, family property, irrigation law, and debt law; and (3) *penal law*: sorcery, adultery, murder, theft, arson, kidnapping, incest, rape, and a host of "minor offenses" (Barton 1969:10–82).

Family law was important in Ifugao culture, where bilateral kin groups were the backbone of social organization. An individual's family consisted of relatives of both his parents to the third degree, ascending and descending. The family "corporation" jointly held the rice and forest lands as heirlooms:

> The Ifugao attitude is that land and articles of value that have been handed down from generation to generation cannot be the property of any individual. Present holders possess only a transient and fleeting possession, or better, occupation, insignificant in duration in comparison with the decades and perhaps centuries that have usually elapsed since the field or heirloom came into the possession of the family. (Barton 1969:32)

Monogamous marriage was considered a contractual arrangement among the Ifugao. There were two forms of marriage: *trial marriages*, which involved little ceremonial activity or property transfer (and were basically formed by cohabitation for a period of time) and *contract* marriages, prearranged unions. The latter form of marriage was commonly utilized in cases where a substantial inheritance was at stake:

> The contract marriage is usually arranged for, and its first ceremonies at least performed while the children are quite small. Its purpose is to guard against the commission of such a folly on the part of the child who will be wealthy as marriage to a less wealthy spouse. The danger is that such a child, sleeping in the common dormitory, will give way to the ardor of youth and temporarily mate with one below him in station, and that the union will prove permanent. (Barton 1969:12)

Protection of the family's property and its social standing was clearly a concern in the betrothal of its progeny. The division of family property was designated at the time of initial ceremonies in contract marriages, each child receiving an amount roughly equal to that which his or her intended partner would receive. Parents were enjoined from the sale of this property except under clearly specified conditions: the illness or death of the child or his or her intended. Family property was transferred to the children when they actually married and formed a separate household. The remaining property was passed on to the oldest son upon the death of the parents, following the rule of primogeniture.

Family law therefore governed one of the most important aspects of economic life, the division of the means of production. Moreover, it specified the obligations parents had to their children (legitimate and illegitimate) for support and education (knowledge of tribal customs). Finally, it governed the treatment and acquisition of indentured servants.

Property law was highly specific. It divided property into two kinds, personal and family, and specified ownership rights, transfer procedures, and terms of sale for each. Transactions were carefully "recorded" in that they were accompanied by public ceremonies and the presence of required observers. The sale of family property, the capital mainstay of the corporate kin group, was undertaken only under circumstances of dire need and only with the permission of male and female members of the corporation.

Property law also governed the conditions of land mortgaging, a practice described earlier. Each transaction had to be witnessed

by the agent of the borrower, who obtained the loans and received
a commission that Barton estimates at 5 to 12 percent of the loan
obtained (1969:38).

Irrigation rights were clearly and elaborately specified in the Ifugao property code:

> If all the land below a spring or small stream located on ownerless
> land be common land – that is, land without an owner – he who
> makes the first rice field below the source of the water supply is
> entitled to all the water needed for his rice field. Another man, making
> a rice field between the field of the first comer and the source of the
> water supply, may not use the spring or stream to the detriment of
> the first comer.
>
> But should a man make a field, be it on common or on owned
> land, below a spring or stream, and should another man make a field
> between the first field and the source of the water supply on *owned
> land*, the second comer would have the right to whatever water might
> be useful to him. (Barton 1969:52)

This excerpt represents only a small part of the section of the property law that dealt with one principal means of production: water.
The diversion of water, the ownership and upkeep of irrigation
ditches, and a host of other water-related issues were covered in
minute detail by the law.

Criminal law among the Ifugao is of interest for two reasons.
First, it demonstrated the significance of corporate liability for individual conduct and for enforcing collective rights in disputes involving criminal conduct. Penalties in criminal cases were generally
in the form of fines for which the offender's corporate group was
fully responsible, underlining the corporate nature of resource management in Ifugao culture.

Second, the criminal code included differential penalties for offenses according to the economic status of the parties involved. A
kadangyang could demand higher compensation for an injury than
a middle-class man suffering the identical fate. Likewise, the wealthier man had to pay more for a wrong he committed than his less
well-to-do counterpart who inflicted the same injury. In the end, a
compromise was reached through the services of a *monkalun*, though
the penalties varied according to the status of the parties (Barton
1969:55).

The social relations of production in this irrigated agricultural
society were clearly delineated in Ifugao substantive law. Major

sources of surplus extraction, including rent, interest on loans, and
the labor of servants or slaves, were all reflected in and controlled
by legal norms. Property relations specified landownership and the
division of family resources, and underscored a major feature of
the social relations of production, namely the corporate group's
control of resources.

This elaborate substantive law existed in the absence of fully
differentiated legal institutions. At the other end of the institutional
spectrum were irrigated agriculturalists with state-level legal systems, including the sixteenth-century empire of the Andes to which
I now turn.

The Inca Empire

The land mass encompassed by the Inca Empire[18] at the time of
the Spanish conquest included a variety of ecological environments
suitable for the growth of a great diversity of domesticated plants.
Although draft animals were introduced by the Spaniards, the natives of the area had made their living from agricultural production
using foot plows and hand-held hoes for centuries. Inhabitants of
the high valleys planted potatoes and quinoa among many crops
suitable to the Andean altitudes. Lowland areas were better suited
to maize, sweet manioc, and a variety of other fruits and vegetables.

Irrigation technology was critical to the success of agriculture in
the Andean valleys, where bottomland was limited. Rainy-season
runoff was enough to flood the available flatland. Consequently,
the valley sides were terraced to capture the rains and provide
additional arable land. Before the consolidation of the empire, the
terraces were "small and irregular, and probably the work of in-

---

[18] Readers who wish to consult additional sources on the political organization of
the Inca state are referred to the following sources: John Murra's (1980) authoritative account, *The Economic Organization of the Inka State*; John Rowe's
(1948) classic piece, "Inca Culture at the Time of the Spanish Conquest"; and
Richard Schaedel's (1978) recent article, "Early State of the Incas." Sally Falk
Moore's (1958) book, *Power and Property in Inca Peru*, is the most comprehensive work available on law in the empire. The material on legal/political
organization presented here is drawn principally from these four sources.

Readers interested in recent studies of the process of political incorporation
of local areas by the central state are referred to Terence D'Altroy's (1981) recent
study, *Empire Growth and Consolidation: The Xauxa Region of Peru Under
the Incas*.

dividual family groups," but by the time the state had entrenched itself large labor forces were assembled to construct elaborate water-works (Rowe 1948:210). The scale of these waterworks far sur-passed that of the Ifugao. Ethnohistorical records indicate that the irrigation works were constructed by corvée labor, organized by the state and supervised by specialized engineers (Murra 1980:15).

Land tenure in the dominions of the Inca state was based upon an elaborate division, which Richard Schaedel has described as follows:

> In each province, at least ideally, there were three types of land: (1) Land belonging to the dominant ethnic group, which was to be exploited through the extant hierarchical arrangements for its own sustenance. (2) Land dedicated to the cultivation of crops necessary for the sustenance of the state religion . . . (3) Land to be exploited for the maintenance of the secular state apparatus at the provincial and national level. (1978:295)

In each case, the land was worked by the commoners, labor obli-gations having been set at the provincial level and levied on male household heads. The produce from the state lands was used to support the central bureaucracy, which lived entirely off this income.

The state bureaucracy was staffed exclusively by ethnic Incas or "Incas-by-privilege," members of ethnic groups from the circum-Cuzco area (Quechua speakers) who were considered loyal to the state. Provincial elites lived off the surplus of their constituents and the largesse of the dominant Inca caste. A parallel system of ex-ploitation supported the extensive priesthood and the maintenance of religious shrines.

The remaining portion of the land was cultivated by and belonged to the commoner classes. The landholding unit, the *ayullu*, was the endogamous kinship group of pre-empire days. The term *ayullu* later came to include villages, which many of the *ayullus* became under the colonization and reorganization efforts of the Inca rulers. Each *ayullu* owned a specific area of cultivated land, and "each married couple cultivated as much of it as they needed for their support" (Rowe 1948:225). These family lots were supposed to be distributed anew every year, taking into account changes in the composition of each household.

Many people in the empire were supported by the labor of the common classes. The surplus capacity of the economy was substantial, and it went toward the upkeep of the royalty, the nobility, and the priesthood. In exchange, the taxpayers could expect their needs to be met from birth to death. The aged and infirm, no longer able to contribute to the tax base, were supported from government stores. Taxes, in the form of corvée labor (not in rent), were assessed according to a complex system of age grades, each of which was obligated to contribute a different amount of *mit'a* (labor) service.

Mobilization of this massive labor force enabled the construction of elaborate public works: a road system that spanned the length of the empire, consisting of two highways (inland and coastal) that connected the provincial capitals with each other; a post service that permitted efficient communications between Cuzco and the provincial cities; a system of storage houses for the use of the military and administrative officials of the empire (D'Altroy 1981); and, finally, the formidable state-constructed irrigation works.

Officials of the central bureaucracy kept a close watch on the available labor supply through carefully maintained census counts, which were regularly sent to Cuzco. Census data provided the base for assessing taxes and military conscription. The *quipu*, knots tied in colored string, kept the Inca aware of the capacities of the various provinces to provide labor for the fields and plantations, the husbandry of animals, gold mining, and the like.

Some scholars regard the empire as the first experiment in state socialism. Economic planning reached a high point in the empire, and land and technical resources were owned by the state. Yet surplus extraction for the benefit of the nonlaboring classes also climbed to new heights, a feature not generally associated with socialism.

The coordination of such an economic system required a well-developed political hierarchy; indeed, that of the Inca was as pyramidal as any considered thus far. At the head of the state was the emperor, who ruled by divine right:

> The Inca Emperors were absolute rulers, with power checked only by the influence of ancient custom and the fear of revolt. They not only ruled by divine right, but claimed lineal descent from the Sun and were worshipped as divine during their lifetimes. While the emperor and his government were merciless toward their enemies and demanded an obedience which amounted to virtual slavery from their subjects, they were in theory obliged to care for their people

in every sort of need and keep them comfortable and happy. The unquestionable success of the system is due chiefly to a sincere effort by the Imperial Government to live up to its theoretical obligation. (Rowe 1948:257)

The emperor stood at the head of the ruling classes of Inca society. The descendants in the male line of each emperor formed the most privileged of these classes, and were considerable in number owing to the practice of taking secondary wives (thus multiple progeny). At the time of the Spanish conquest, the descendants of Manco Capac, the founder of the dynasty, numbered approximately 500. Members of the emperor's family lived in splendor. At the same time, they constituted "a useful court circle of educated men trained in the imperial ideology and interested in its perpetuation. The emperors chose their top administrators from this group when possible" (Rowe 1948:257).

The remainder of the nobility were known as "curacas," designated "Incas by privilege" by the Emperor Pachacuti, the great organizing genius of the Inca state. As the conquests of the Inca militia expanded the boundaries of the empire, Pachacuti found the Inca ethnic group itself too small to furnish the administrative labor power to run the outlying regions. He remedied this shortage and promoted the linguistic unification of the empire by proclaiming Quechua speakers as a secondary nobility, exempting them from taxation, and placing them in positions of political responsibility.

With the emperor and his royal *ayullus* at the top of the hierarchy, the next level of political jurisdiction below was the "quarter" (*suyu*). As the name implies, there were four such divisions, headed by *apocunas*. These positions were not hereditary, but were drawn from among the near relatives of the emperor. Representatives of the four *suyus*, together with one member of each moiety of Cuzco Incas, formed a royal "council of twelve" that sat in the capital city. This council was apparently responsible for maintaining a "liaison between the central government and the provinces in their respective *suyus*, affecting levies for campaigns" and "marshalling special troop levies" (Schaedel 1978:303).

Below the quarter were the provinces, each of which was administered by an imperial governor (*tocricoc*). The governors "represented the interests of the federal government at the provincial level and supervised or corrected the highest echelon of provincial officials" (Schaedel 1978:303). Each province was divided into a number of divisions, headed by *curacas*. From the level of the *curacas* and below, the political hierarchy was composed of elites of local origin, as opposed to those of Inca descent. Sally Falk Moore has pointed out that this arrangement is best understood as a colonial structure of indirect rule:

> In each new territory, they superimposed Inca government on the already existing one . . . The Inca altered the apportionment of some of the land, but they did not do away with the local government and replace it. They did not disturb local hereditary interests. They simply added themselves at the top and made full use of the already existing administrative machinery, incorporating the local hereditary aristocracy into the decimal system. (1958:100)

Curacas were ranked according to the number of taxpayers under their administration. These officials filled hereditary positions and were drawn from the ranks of preconquest elites of the (non-Inca) ethnic groups subsequently incorporated into the empire. Their appointments required state approval. Below them stood the nonnoble headmen, who were in charge of household units of ten.

Apart from this hierarchy, with its emphasis on indigenous ethnic elites, the Inca political system included a group of official emissaries of the central bureaucracy, who represented the emperor's interests in the conquered territories. They operated as a surveillance system, watching over the activities (and loyalties) of local functionaries:

> Field inspectors, special delegates – traveling and possibly resident – were used for census, tax, judicial and other matters. Some were assigned only in emergencies, while others were sent out in the ordinary course. (Moore 1958:101)

These representatives of the imperial elite were particularly involved with cases of "cheating or interference with conscription and taxation," which indicates the direct connection between legal-political structure and the highly stratified social relations of production in the empire. These special judges were also involved in prosecuting "political" offenses, including refusal to accept the state religion, witchcraft against the Inca, and "having relations with one of the chosen women or women of the Inca or Sun" (Moore 1958:119). The roving emissaries were therefore concerned with the steady flow of surplus appropriation from the lower rungs of the political ladder and with the ideological hegemony of the Inca state.

There were no courts as such in the empire. Cases were settled by individual officials of the state hierarchy and were assigned according to the locus of the disputes and the seriousness of the issues. Disputes involving two or more communities were handled by provincial governors. Boundary conflicts involving "large administrative subdivisions" were adjudicated by special royal delegates or the emperor himself (Moore 1958:120). The priestly hierarchy had jurisdiction over religious personnel.

The provincial governor was responsible for handling cases pertaining to the property or prerogatives of the Inca. Moore (1958:118) suggests that "crimes and private contentions in which the Inca government had no such direct interest were tried by the various levels of *curacas*. One would also guess in this case that local customary laws applied." The principal judicial concerns of the *curacas* had to do with the allocation of shares of communal land. Local *curacas* were responsible for adjudicating other property conflicts, including theft.

Moore's study of Inca judicial practices indicates that the transformation of local law into state law was complex. Some sources suggest that "the Inca imposed their law wherever they ruled," but she warns that this should not be taken literally. Local customs of no concern to the state were tolerated, though the cultural continuity of the Andean area meant that extreme differences were not a problem. What was universally instituted was strict adherence to the requirements of the taxation and conscription edicts; "the universal acceptance of [the state's] authority; the acceptance of the Sun cult; and of the Quechua language" (Moore 1958:102).

The state adamantly prohibited private vengeance and self-help (Moore 1958:118). Those cases that could not be settled by lower-level authorities or *curacas* were taken as high as the provincial governors. Lower "judges" were required to report the substance of all cases and their decisions to higher authorities by means of the *quipu*. There were no appeals as such (1958:118).

The punishment of crimes of interest to the central bureaucracy, especially those involving taxation and military service, was in the hands of emissaries from the central court:

> These judges were sent out when the inspectors disclosed that there had been violations of law. The judges punished crimes and fixed penalties as they saw fit. . .They apparently received presents from

the local *curaca* when they came on their much feared business. (Moore 1958:112–13)

The emperor himself or his council of state was responsible for handling "serious offenses such as treason as well as all crimes committed by Incas and Curacas" (Murdock 1934:432). In a sense, two different judicial systems existed in the empire: one for the nobility and the royal family and one for commoners. The bifurcation of the judicial system extended to punishment as well. Punishment for misconduct on the part of commoners and civil officials was severe "on the principle that the act of breaking any law was disobedience to the Emperor and hence to be classed with treason and sacrilege" (Rowe 1948:271). Murder, robbery, and causing death through witchcraft were capital crimes for commoners, though permission to impose the death penalty had to be granted by a governor, a representative of the central state. If committed by a member of the nobility, the very same offense warranted nothing more than a public reprimand:

> Justice was not equal and common to all; for although it was considered important that any offense and crime should be denounced, other kinds of punishment were given to the high-born and rich than those given to the humble and poor. The practice originated in the belief that to an Inca of royal blood a mere public reprimand was by far a greater punishment than death was to a plebian. . . .Chastisement was regarded as so shameful that it very seldom happened that a man of noble birth was punished. (Cobo, quoted in Hyams and Ordish 1963:89)

Death, imprisonment in a pit of vipers in Cuzco (Schaedel 1978:304), the breaking of his or her back with a large stone dropped from a height, and banishment to work in the mines and plantations (Murra 1980:108) – these were the nasty fates awaiting a commoner who broke the imperial law.

In both institutional form and punitive sanctions, the law of the empire was, in practice, class justice. It kept commoners in their places and protected and legitimated the positions of the privileged. Bureaucratic officials standing in between the nobility and the commoners were no less subject to imperial control. There was no pretence of equality before the law.

The social relations of production I have described as the economic backbone of the empire were part and parcel of the Inca state's civil law. The amount and kind of corvée labor required was detailed through yearly edicts, and the general authority to issue these demands was part of the imperial code. The responsibilities of public officials and the laws of debt, tribute, and land tenure were all specified by Inca law.

We see in this legal system the use of law not merely as a device for settling disputes between individuals, but also as a mechanism of social control and a means of maintaining class distinctions. The state reached into the organization of production, extending its control through an indirect-rule system that nevertheless held local officials accountable to a centralized power.

Intensive agriculture: law and economy
In summarizing my findings on legal systems in intensive-agricultural societies, I return to the distinctive features of such societies (adapted from Lenski 1966) in order to evaluate the legal systems of the Ifugao and the Inca against the general characteristics of agrarian society.

Lenski's first point is that occupational specialization takes a leap forward in agrarian societies because much of the populace is freed from the food-production process. Very little evidence of this division of labor is present in the Ifugao case. Labor is divided according to gender, with men engaged in heavy physical tasks (constructing irrigation ditches and retaining walls, turning soil) and women engaged in intensive cultivation (tending rice seedlings, transplanting, etc.). There are no individuals in Ifugao villages who do not labor for a living, though there are those who are more successful and wealthy than others.

In contrast, the Inca economy was composed of highly diverse occupational groups. Although the largest number of people were engaged in agricultural labor, the surplus production of these laborers sufficed to support specialized artisans, road builders, weavers, mine workers, religious personnel, an enormous political bureaucracy, a professional military, and a nonworking aristocracy.

The substantive law of the two cultures reflects their fundamental differences in economic specialization. Among the Ifugao, the major categories of law are concerned with property transactions (through marriage or sale, rent, mortgage, loan, etc.) occurring between members of corporate groups. Inca law, on the other hand, mandated the contributions of specialized labor groups and provided for the coordination and distribution of their products, be these food products or bureaucratic services. We do not see a laissez-faire market system among the Inca; we do see a planned economy in which the administration of law through royal edict played an important role.

Class distinctions are embodied in both Ifugao and Inca law, but, curiously, the outcomes are almost opposite. Among the Ifugao, the privileges of the *kadangyang* are protected through the law of rent, mortgage, and interest. However, the rich are subject to harsher fines than their middle-class counterparts for criminal offenses. Ifugao criminal law evens out the status differences between individuals.

The contrast with the Inca case could not be stronger. Inca law protected the ruling classes and placed them above serious prosecution. Beyond the criminal law, the elites were exempt as well from *mit'a* service, the labor tax, which further institutionalized class differences.

Lenski notes that agrarian states boast major urban centers as loci of trade, commerce, and political administration. This is clearly not the case for the Ifugao, whose political organization was diffuse and decentralized. The Inca were much closer to Lenski's vision. Their impressive communications system (of roads, postal "runners," etc.) linked the central state to the outlying areas and thus assured a much higher degree of accountability of the lower-level authorities than we find in paramount chieftainships, for example.

The variation in legal complexity and substantive law at this level of the development of the productive forces is considerable, as these two cases show. This variation is, however, understandable in view of the differences in forms and intensity of surplus extraction, that is, in terms of their social relations of production.

Summary

In this chapter, I have analyzed the relationship between modes of production, areas of dispute, and the substance of prescriptive legal rules. My principal concern has been to indicate the ways in which substantive law regulates aspects of the social relations of production in preindustrial societies. I have analyzed "trouble" spots in foraging, pastoral, extensive-agricultural, and intensive-agricultural societies with respect to the organization of labor, the potential for surplus accumulation and extraction, the nature of property ownership and inheritance, and control over the means of production.

I have argued that much of the content of preindustrial law amounts to efforts to contain the strains inherent in the inequalities of the social relations of production. Rather than expand on these points here, I will move to the final chapter, in which the findings and arguments from this chapter's case studies of substantive law can be integrated with the material from the previous three chapters.

5

Conclusion: Materialism and legal systems

The goal of this book has been to explore the relationships between legal organization, substantive law, and preindustrial modes of production. My findings suggest that the degrees of development of the forces of production, "exploitive" social relations of production, and social stratification are strong independent predictors of legal complexity, defined according to my fivefold variable. Moreover, I determined that the social relations of production are imprinted on the substantive, prescriptive rules of preindustrial legal orders. Strains that these relations produce surface as patterns of recurrent disputes.

An objection might be raised: that I simply have shown that as general social complexity increases, so does legal complexity – an observation that is self-evident. I do not hold to this position. If legal complexity were simply a function of general social complexity, one could choose any of a number of dimensions of social existence and argue that as it became more complex, so would legal institutions (a view that Donald Black finds persuasive in his book *The Behavior of Law*). I have argued at some length against this sort of approach.

Lenski's theory – that technological complexity predicts numerous other aspects of social complexity, including law – is an example of such a view, and it is inadequate for explaining legal development. Nomadic and sedentary hunters and gatherers have very similar subsistence technologies; yet, when we look at their systems of stratification and law, we see considerable differences that cannot be explained in terms of technology. Similarly, Lenski distinguishes between horticulturalists who practice metallurgy and those who do not. Yet, among both groups, one finds societies that are not stratified and have very similar legal institutions. In short, at any given level of *technological* sophistication, a range of legal institutions may be observed.

Similarly, if any aspect of social complexity could be taken as a predictor of legal development, it should be the case that the substantive complexity of customary law would be strongly correlated with the development of, for example, political institutions. Although it is true that politically complex societies typically have well-developed systems of substantive law, the reverse is not always the case. Within certain societies lacking differentiated political bodies, we nevertheless find very complex systems of substantive law. Neither the Ifugao nor the Kapauku is politically centralized, and neither has an organized polity; yet they both have elaborate bodies of legal principles that are used to settle disputes.

In sum, one cannot simply take any dimension of social life and argue that the more complex that dimension, the more complex the law. All aspects of social reality are *not* equally effective in predicting levels of legal development. Even within the model developed here, it is the *interaction* between three distinct dimensions – the forces and social relations of production, and social stratification – that seems to best explain the variance in legal complexity.

At the heart of my analysis is the concept of surplus production as used by Blumberg (1978). The forces of production constitute the key determinant of a society's capacity for generating surplus. The forces simultaneously point to those material resources that are potentially in short supply. Unequal access to these limited means of production is the primary mechanism by which social inequalities develop. The social relations of production enter the picture at this point. Where some kin groups can gain a disproportionate access to scarce resources, wealth inequalities arise. The next stage, which may or may not develop, occurs when families are able to utilize this differential access to make others work for them (i.e., to make others pay rent, deliver labor services, etc.). This sets the stage for class stratification in the classic sense of the term.

Let us trace this development in more detail with reference to legal complexity. In societies where the supply of land and natural resources equals or exceeds the demand and where property relations provide for open access to these resources (for example, in nomadic food-collecting societies) we see little in the way of conflict over these means of production. However, the availability of labor (especially women's labor) obtained through marriage may be a critical factor in such a production system. Labor is a crucial "means of production" in all societies; in cultures where female labor power is both important and "artificially" in short supply (e.g., through unequal distribution due to polygyny, or in cases of female infanticide), access to wives is an ongoing source of conflict. In the simplest societies, the disputing process focuses on betrothal, marriage, adultery, wife stealing, and any other behavior that threatens to remove women from a domestic unit. Even though other resources are abundant and universally available, and surplus production is held to a minimum, the distribution of female labor power is the recurrent locus of trouble and the subject of most legal control.

Once we move beyond nomadic hunters and gatherers to more complex subsistence types, access to means of production other than labor power may be restricted. Notions of property become greatly elaborated in societies where productive land, water supply, and domestic animals can be monopolized. In many of the societies we have considered, the proliferation of property rights is kin based rather than individual. With the first sign of kin-based territoriality, we begin to see a sharper definition of usufruct rights, and a concomitant rise in the number and kinds of disputes that have as their focus the violation of those rights.

Under conditions of corporate property, disputes tend to occur between family groups. Even where individuals are concerned, they tend to be viewed as representatives of larger kinship units, which stand behind them in the disputing process.

Wealth distinctions first emerge when some families have access to better land, animal, or labor resources than others. In many such "wealth-distinction" societies, however, we find social norms that force the redistribution of accumulated wealth (feasts, exchanges, sharing norms, and the like) such that wealth inequalities are held within certain boundaries.

As soon as control over the means of production can be used as a lever for obtaining the labor of non–family members, we see a distinct shift in patterns of stratification and law. One of the earliest forms of labor extraction involves the practice of wealthy (usually older) men loaning capital to poorer (younger) men for required brideprice payments. Poor people work for wealthier ones, and the latter cease to live solely off the fruits of their own productive capacities. This is not the only mechanism whereby the labor of non–family members can be attached. In some cultures (e.g., the Basseri, the Kapauku), labor contracts (for shepherding and pig breeding) are also important forms of surplus extraction.

Once the productive resources of a society (land, labor, animals, water, etc.) are unequally controlled, the likelihood of disputes over these tools of survival grows. The effect of private ownership of the means of production *combined with* the extraction of nonfamilial labor power is to stimulate the growth of such phenomena as rent, interest on debts, wage labor, and the like. This in turn affects social stratification. Where previously one might have societies with wealthier and poorer families, but where all have sufficient basic resources to produce a livelihood, one starts to find societies with propertiless individuals who have access to insufficient means of production to survive and who are dependent on others for work, credit, or charity. At this level of complexity in the mode of production, law expands to address the rights and obligations of parties on either side of these socio-economic relations: Contract law, debt law, inheritance law, and other aspects of property control are well-developed topics of legal "doctrine." This transition in the substantive complexity of law typically occurs *in the absence of a centralized polity.* Indeed, neither the Ifugao *monkalun* nor the Kapauku *tonowi* represents centralized government, yet both operate in the midst of complex bodies of legal rules. Thus, the elaboration of law's content precedes the development of complex legal institutions.

With the proliferation of exploitive social relations of production, distinct social classes begin to form. These classes are able to hand down their privileges and property from generation to generation, bolstered by class-endogamous marriage practices. At the same time, more powerful legal institutions appear, and democratic or popular control over the disputing process fades in favor of elite power and patrimonial bureaucracy. Classes attain formal recognition in law, and legal concepts develop that identify "crimes" against the social order (e.g., treason, threatening the property or person of state officials or members of the nobility).

Two features of law in class societies are worthy of mention. First, we see a marked increase in the complexity and authority of legal institutions. Areas of conflict that were previously the concern of kin groups or local-level communities fall under "external," or centralized, control. The administration of law becomes part of a general trend toward political consolidation. It is usually administered by an elite, though it is often handled on a daily basis by a professional bureaucratic sector of trusted (and often familially related) officials.

The second point to be made involves the nature of substantive law in preindustrial *class* societies. In addition to providing legal rules for the governance of labor, rent, and the like, these legal systems also institutionalize the differential rights and privileges of the classes. The Ashanti and Inca materials are cases in point. Unequal treatment before the law is the rule rather than the exception. One set of legal principles applies to the conduct of the commoner classes, whereas a different code regulates the conduct of elites. Under these conditions, law plays a role in maintaining the dominance of the upper classes, the subordination of the lower classes, and the loyalty of the middle sector of bureaucratic functionaries (who share some of the privileges of the elites and some of the liabilities of the peasantry).

To what extent can the diachronic-evolutionary orientation of this theory be substantiated? Up to this point, I have been concerned with a prior question: the identification of various stages of institutional and substantive development of law and the distribution of these stages synchronically across preindustrial modes of production. I have not marshalled evidence that speaks to the movement or metamorphosis of one stage into the next. Indeed, as the driving force in my model is the mode of production and law figures as a dependent variable, the critical evidence for an evolutionary or diachronic model of legal development depends upon the articulation of a diachronic paradigm for modes of production.

Nevertheless (in keeping with Maine's methodology), we can examine transitional cases for which there is historical evidence documenting the intensification of social relations of production in a particular society, with a concomitant transformation in legal structure. R. S. Rattray's (1929) account of the development of the Ashanti "nation" out of independent regional ethnic groups is a case in point. Prior to the rise of the dominant Ashanti lineage as a conquering power, the area was organized as a discontinuous series of decentralized peoples, each with its own chiefs or elders' councils handling dispute settlement within their own localities. As the paramount chieftainship – the proto-state of the Ashanti Kingdom – expanded its dominions over these independent polities, new mechanisms of surplus extraction developed; these grew principally through tribute and trade monopolies, which incorporated the subordinate territories into a single mode of production. Part and parcel of this drive to centralize power was the creation of a legal system that subordinated the authority of local, indigenous leaders to the paramount chief and his provincial representative.

The paramount created a whole category of offenses against the "crown" (sins), which could be adjudicated only by his court:

> With the expansion of the isolated kindred groups into the larger Territorial Divisions, and the absorption of many petty heads under one paramount ruler, the evolution in the punishment of [slander] tended to follow the same lines . . . as other offenses (e.g., adultery), until the sin came to be regarded as a Tribal taboo, only when practiced against the supreme tribal authority. (Rattray 1929:309)

Offenses that, under decentralized conditions, had been amenable to local settlement became the paramount "stool's" concern and were interpreted as high crimes when directed against the king or members of the royal aristocracy. Capital offenses (which included all tribal sins) were removed from the jurisdiction of local officials. In fact, attempting to hear capital cases outside the paramount's court became a punishable offense in and of itself, thus reinforcing the top-down control of the ascendant caste.

On the civil-law side, the *Ashantihene* developed elaborate bodies of law concerned with land tenure, inheritance (of which the king could always claim a portion through "death duties"), and taxation (to which the outlying areas of the kingdom became subject). Whereas land law and inheritance had always been, in some fashion, in existence in the independent polities, incorporation into the Ashanti nation meant that a more uniform code was instituted to regulate these aspects of property and revenue. Law became one administrative device for drawing formerly isolated villages into one economic and political system, thereby creating an infrastructure that could siphon surplus production from the commoner classes to those at the top of the economic hierarchy.

This historical example demonstrates a movement from one type of production system, with less exploitive relations of production, to one where surplus was extracted from the bottom and an elite or royal caste was thereby sustained. Both the institutional form of the legal system and the substantive law codes altered as integral parts of a transformation in the mode of production.

More evidence of this kind, particularly for the less developed forces of production, would be necessary to claim substantiation for an evolutionary-materialist theory of legal development. For the moment, however, I am content to argue for the synchronic veracity of the theory.

Although I have stressed the role of economic factors in shaping law, and the functions of law in regulating economic relations, not all aspects of law can be accounted for in this fashion. Indeed, the "idiom" of law, the language in which its concepts and conflicts are expressed, is surely a matter of cultural determination. Conflicts over women in hunting-and-gathering societies may be expressed as insults to the social status of men. Similarly, offenses against the Ashanti monarch are articulated using religious symbols and values. Obligations for labor service are often expressed in the idiom of familial responsibilities or more generalized respect for elders. In short, economic disputes may well be articulated in noneconomic language.[1] This in no way negates cultural influences over the disputing process. The approach suggested here points to the need to examine these cultural processes in the light of their role in sustaining modes of production. Moreover, there are realms of law for which, in my view, a strict materialist explanation is of limited value. Many ritual taboos, religious practices, and normative values embodied in legal codes appear to have little connection to economic relations.

However, traditional legal anthropology has long kept itself analytically isolated from the materialist approach. My findings suggest it is time for a rapprochement – one that subjects cross-cultural and particularistic legal ethnography to a theoretical analysis based on a mode-of-production framework of the sort I have employed

---

[1] Ritual and religious law is, of course, not completely impenetrable to formal analysis. One suspects that as more detailed comparative studies of preindustrial production systems from a Marxist perspective (e.g., Meillasoux 1964) or from a structuralist–exchange theory viewpoint (e.g., Rosman and Rubel 1971; Rubel and Rosman 1978) are conducted, we will be better able to account for these aspects of law using a historical-materialist approach.

here. For the analytic tools of the traditional approach, which emphasize the role of law as "peacemaker" responding to the demand for mending broken ties in "multiplex" societies (Gluckman 1955), do not allow us to differentiate Tiwi foragers very well from Barotse horticulturalists; both live in face-to-face communities, but their legal institutions, substantive law, and patterns of recurrent disputes are strikingly different.

In closing, I want to return briefly to the classical theories examined in Chapter 1 and in particular consider the views of Maine, Durkheim, Weber, and Marx in light of the findings presented in this book.

Maine (1970) divided legal development into four distinct stages: (1) primitive law, (2) ancient law (as epitomized by Roman law), (3) medieval law, and (4) modern law. Through these four stages, Maine saw a developmental trend, which was summarized in the movement "from status to contract."

According to Maine, in the earliest epochs of human history legal authority was in the hands of the omnipotent patriarch, who governed internal family relations. To the extent that extra-kin group conflict was legally regulated, it was handled through ritualized relations between corporate bodies. Maine argued that legal judgments were rendered uniquely and that no systematic body of legal principles could evolve under these circumstances.

At the opposite end of Maine's developmental scheme is law based on contract. Unlike primitive law, where legal relations are based on membership in kinship groups, in the contemporary period law is universal in orientation and applies to individuals without reference to birthright. Moreover, contract law is elaborate, codified, and based upon general principles that can be applied in particular circumstances to render consistent judgments. Legal authority becomes differentiated, permanent, and endowed with the power to enforce its commands.

The ethnographic record suggests that Maine's scheme is inaccurate in certain respects. The simplest forms of law are not those in which corporate groups constitute the major legal actors. In food-collecting societies, individuals are held accountable as such for their transgressions, though they may receive assistance in seeking vengeance from their kinsmen. The rise of corporate kinship groups as legal entities comes at a more advanced stage of socioeconomic development. Indeed, this principle tends to develop where land access is restricted to members of kin groups.

Maine was also mistaken in his assumption that relations between corporate entities are devoid of general principles. Many of the cultures we have considered that had corporate groups as the principal legal actors also possessed very elaborate bodies of legal principles and procedural rules.

The regulation of legal relations between individuals via contract is not necessarily a feature of modern legal systems alone. Among the Kapauku Papuans, Pospisil (1958) describes a comprehensive system of interindividual contracts. So, too, among the Ifugao we find evidence of agreements between individuals backed by universalistic legal sanctions. Anthropological analysis suggests that *Ancient Law* underrates the variation and complexity of legal systems which Maine would categorize as "primitive" or "patriarchal."

Turning to Emile Durkheim, we recall his thesis that the major movement in law is the transition from repressive to restitutive sanctions. In constructing his theory, Durkheim was clearly influenced by the reputation of simple societies for bloodthirsty retribution; in contrast, "civilized" society's ways of dealing with conflict seemed to aim at the calm restoration of the status quo. Many legal anthropologists have stated that ethnological research points to the opposite trend. Although at the simplest levels of societal complexity, self-redress is the major mechanism of legal control, it does not always consist of physical punishment. Shaming, ridicule, loss of prestige, and the like are important and potent tools of self-redress that fall outside Durkheim's conception of "repression."

In slightly more complex societies, self-redress fades in favor of complex procedures of mediation; these are often aimed at reaching compromise agreements, thereby enabling the parties to regain the status quo. *Weregild*, blood money, is an early invention whose function is to restore harmony between conflicting parties without violence. Similarly, an emphasis on returning stolen goods, paying fines for damages done, and the like, is common among the very simplest food-collecting, pastoral, and horticultural peoples.

If anything, punitive legal orientations reach their zenith among the advanced preindustrial societies, where state authorities use capital punishment to consolidate the domination of a ruling elite. I have already mentioned Rattray's observation that capital punishment became the sole prerogative of the royal lineage of the Ashanti. A similar statement could be made of Inca law, where central authorities assumed control of the forces or organized coercion. Localities were specifically prohibited from taking certain aspects of the law into their own hands – those of immediate concern to the state and those involving the ultimate sanction of the death penalty.

In sum, the punitiveness of legal systems seems to vary a great deal across societies. If there is a trend to be found, it would appear to be the reverse of Durkheim's. Restitutive orientations seem to give way to repressive ones as societal complexity increases.

Max Weber's historical theory of rationalization stands as his most definitive statement on the development of law. His thesis was that a shift from substantive to formal rationality can be discerned over the course of legal history. The practice of making legal decisions based upon the particular circumstances of a conflict gave way to the process of legal decision making based on general principles brought to bear without consideration for special or individual circumstances. Primitive people were said to consider all legal problems on a situational basis, without regard to general rules. Among them, the social context of legal conflict is taken into account and given emphasis to the detriment of abstract rules.

In contrast, Weber saw modern law as consisting of the impartial evaluation of an action solely in terms of abstract rules. The issue for legal authorities under these circumstances is not why an individual broke a rule, but simply what rule was broken and what regular sanction should therefore be invoked.

It is true that many preindustrial societies consider a wide range of circumstances in evaluating an action. Both Gluckman (1955, 1965) and Nader (1969) have argued that these cultures are interested in the underlying causes of an individual's actions as much as the actions themselves. Curiously, however, when we look at the societies at the low end of my complexity scale, we see little concern for these contextual elements. The Tiwi do not consider the context of adulterous encounters before initiating dispute-settlement procedures. The Jivaro do not stop to ask why women have been "stolen" before retaliating. This is not the same as saying that there are no rules or procedures. In both these cases, it must be determined that adultery has, in fact, occurred, or that a woman is actually the victim of a raid, before reaction is mounted. However, at this end of the complexity spectrum, the relevant question is whether an actionable transgression has occurred; if so, a prescribed response must be made.

Weber generally downplays the systematicity of legal principles in such societies. He wrote as if decisions were not rendered with normative prescriptions in mind, but were reactive or guided by unsystematic sources (e.g., oracles). My investigation of the substantive law of simple societies suggests that this is not the case. There is a strong normative element to legal decision making, which is often overtly articulated in the form of legal-moral principles.

The bulk of this book has been dedicated to elaborating an empirically substantiated theory of legal development based on the historical-materialist approach developed by the last of the classical theorists covered in Chapter 1, Karl Marx and his collaborator Friedrich Engels. Their writings on law are scattered throughout the immense corpus of their scholarship; as Greenberg and Anderson (1981:294) have pointed out, their remarks do not constitute a well-developed or consistent theory of law, even for capitalist society. Even less is available in their writings on the relationship between law and precapitalist economic formations. However, this volume has tried to fill that gap by showing the utility of a materialist approach for explaining the distribution of legal institutions and the role they play in regulating the social relations of production.

Appendix 1.

Sixty-society subsample by geographical region and subsistence type

Africa

Hunting and gathering
Kung (Bushmen)

Fishing
0

Herding
Nama (Hottentot)
Masai

Extensive agriculture
Bemba
Ashanti (Twi)
Mende
Tiv
Azande

Dry intensive agriculture
Kikuyu
Ganda
Bambara
Tallensi

Irrigated intensive agriculture
Tanala

Asia

Hunting and gathering
Semang

Fishing
Andamandese

Herding
Toda
Chukchee

Extensive agriculture
Muria Gond

Dry intensive agriculture
Lepcha

Irrigated intensive agriculture
Burmese
Korea
Santal

Circum-Mediterranean

Hunting and gathering
0

Fishing
0

Herding
Somali
Rwala
Lapps
Tuareg

Extensive agriculture
Wolof

Dry intensive agriculture
Amhara
Turks
Albania (Gheg)

Irrigated intensive agriculture
Fellahin
Hausa

North America

Hunting and gathering
Eastern Pomo
Yokut

Fishing
Copper Eskimo
Yurok
Bellacoola
Ojibwa (N. Salteaux)

Herding
0

Extensive agriculture
Pawnee

Dry intensive agriculture
0

Irrigated intensive agriculture
Zuni
Aztec

Pacific

Hunting and gathering
Tiwi
Aranda

Fishing
Manus
Truk

Herding
0

Extensive agriculture
Trobrianders
Marquesans
Kapauku
Samoa

Dry intensive agriculture
0

Irrigated intensive agriculture
Ifugao

South America

Hunting and gathering
Mosquito
Nambicuara
Ona
Botocudo (Kaingang)

Fishing
Callinago
Mataco

Herding
Goajiro

Extensive agriculture
Jivaro

Dry intensive agriculture
Paez

Irrigated intensive agriculture
Inca

Appendix 2.

Bibliographic sources for sixty-society subsample

Amhara
Hoben (1973), Levine (1965), Lipsky (1962), Pankhurst (1955)

Andaman Islanders
Man (1883), Radcliffe-Brown (1948), Temple (1903)

Aranda
Basedow (1925), Chewings (1936), Roheim (1933, 1945), Spencer and Gillen (1927)

Ashanti
Busia (1951), Danquah (1928), Manoukian (1950), Rattray (1929, 1932)

Azande
Evans-Pritchard (1971), Seligman and Seligman (1932)

Aztec
Bandelier (1975), Bray (1968), Sahagun (1953), Thompson (1933), Vailliant (1944)

Bambara
Monteil (1924), Paques (1954)

Bellacoola
Boas (1894), McIlwraith (1948), Rosman and Rubel (1971)

Bemba
Richards (1940, 1961, 1971b), Whitely (1950)

Botocudo
Henry (1964), Metraux (1946)

Burma
Aung (1962, 1967), Furnivall (1948), Hall (1950), Stevenson (1944), Yoe (1927)

Callinago
Breton (1957), Breton and Paix (1929), Neveu-Lemaire (1921), Taylor (1938, 1946, 1951)

Chukchee
Bogaraz-Tan (1904), Sverdrup (1938)

Copper Eskimo
Jenness (1917, 1922, 1959)

Fellahin
Ammar (1954), Blackman (1968)

Ganda
Fallers (1960), Haydon (1960), Mair (1934), Murdock (1934), Richards (1960), Roscoe (1911), Southwold (1965)

Gheg
Coon (1950), Durham (1909, 1928), Hasluck (1954)

Goajiro
Armstrong and Metraux (1948), Gutierrez de Pineda (1950), Petrullo (1937), Pineda Giraldo (1950), Santa Cruz (1960)

Ifugao
Barton (1922, 1969), Villaverde (1909)

Incas
D'Altroy (1981), de la Vega (1961), Hewett (1968), Markham (1969), Means (1973), Moore (1958), Murdock (1934), Murra (1980), Radin (1942), Rowe (1948), Schaedel (1978), Steward and Faran (1959)

Jivaro
Harner (1972), Radin (1942), Steward and Metraux (1948), Stirling (1938)

Kapauku Papuans
Pospisil (1958, 1963a, 1963b)

Kikuyu
Kenyetta (1965), Lambert (1956a), Leakey (1952), Middleton (1953), Prins (1953)

Korea
Grajdanzev (1944), Heydrich (1931), Moose (1911)

Kung
Hahn et el. (1928), Lee (1968, 1979), Marshall (1965), Schapera (1930)

Lapps
Anderson (1949), Collinder (1949), Nikul (1948), O'Leary (1975), Pehrson (1957), Vorren and Manker (1962), Whitaker (1955)

Lepcha
Gorer (1938)

Manus
Fortune (1935), Mead (1937)

Maria Gond
Elwin (1947), Fuchs (1960), Grigson (1949), Singh (1944)

Marquesans
Handy (1923), Linton (1939)

Masai
Bernardi (1955), Fosbrooke (1948), Gulliver (1963), Hailey (1950), Huntingford (1953), Leakey (1930, 1952)

Mataco
Fock (1974)

Mende
Little (1951), McCullough (1950a, 1950b)

Mosquito
Conzemius (1932), Kirchoff (1948)

Nama Hottentots
Schapera (1930), Schapera and Farrington (1933)

Nambicuara
Levi-Strauss (1948), Oberg (1953), Steward and Faran (1959)

Ojibwa
Hallowell (1942), Skinner (1911)

Ona
Cooper (1917, 1946), Radin (1942)

Paez
Bernal Villa (1954), Hernandez de Alba (1946), Nachtigall (1955), Pittier de Fabrega (1907)

Pawnee
Dorsey (1940), Dorsey and Murie (1940), Weltfish (1965)

Eastern Pomo
Gifford (1923, 1926), Kroeber (1925), Loeb (1926), Powers (1877), Stewart (1943)

Rwala
Chelhod (1971)

Samoa
Keesing (1934), Mead (1930), Stanner (1953)

Santal
Biswas (1956), Culshaw (1949), Datta-Majumder (1956), Kochar (1970), Mukherjea (1962), Orans (1965), Skrefsrud (1942)

Semang
Dentan (1979), Murdock (1934)

Somali
Lewis (1955)

Tallensi
Fortes (1940, 1945), Rattray (1932)

Tiv
Bohannan (1957), Bohannan and Bohannan (1953, 1958), Crocker (1936), Downes (1933)

Tiwi
Hart and Pilling (1960)

Todas
Marshall (1873), Rivers (1906)

Trobriands
Malinowski (1921, 1922, 1926), Powell (1967)

Truk
Bollig (1927), Goodenough (1951), Gladwin (1953), Kramer (1932)

Tuareg
Briggs (1958), Lhote (1955), Murphy (1964), Rodd (1926)

Turks
Magnarella (1974), Makal (1954), Mango (1968), Pierce (1964), Stirling (1965), Starr (1978), Szyliowicz (1966)

Wolof
Berenger-Feraud (1879), Gamble (1957)

Yokut
Gayton (1930, 1948), Kroeber (1925)

Yurok
Kroeber (1925, 1926), Waterman (1920)

Zazzagawa
Hassan and Shuaibu (1952), Nwabueze (1963), Smith (1960)

Zuni
Cushing (1920), Kroeber (1919), Leighton (1963), Parsons (1917), Smith and Roberts (1954), Stevenson (1904)

Appendix 3.

Nonparametric measures of association

I have used several nonparametric measures of association to assess the
relationships between variables in Chapter 4. *Functionally*, these measures
are equivalent. Each answers the questions: Is variable "A" related to
variable "B"? How strongly are they related? In which direction are they
related? However, each measure is sensitive to different aspects of statistical
association, as I will explain below.

Gamma is a measure of association for ordinal (i.e., ranked) variables.
Gamma can have values from +1 to −1. A gamma of +1 means that
two variables are perfectly related, such that as the value of one variable
increases the value of the other variable increases as well. A gamma of −1
indicates a perfect correlation, but in the opposite direction; as one variable
increases, the other variable decreases. A gamma of zero means that there
is no relationship between the variables. Gamma is frequently used as a
measure of association; however, it has two weaknesses. First, gamma
varies according to the dimensions of the table. Second, it is insensitive to
"ties", that is, situations where the ranking of a case on one variable equals
the ranking of the same case on the other variable.

Spearman's Rho and *Kendall's Tau* also take values from −1 to +1.
As before, the value of 0 indicates no relationship between the variables.
Both these measures make a correction for "ties." The two measures are
calculated somewhat differently, and in general Kendall coefficients tend
to be smaller than Spearman's Rho. Kendall's Tau C is used for rectangular
tables, that is, where the number of rows is not equal to the number of
columns.

Somer's D provides yet another method of measuring the relationship
between two ordinal variables. Unlike the other three above, it presumes
that one variable is independent (i.e., the cause) and the other is dependent,
(i.e., the effect). It then measures the extent to which knowing the value
of a case on one variable enables one to predict the value of that case on
the other variable.

For the sake of completeness, I have given the values for all these different
measures of association to show the reader that the relationships observed
in the data hold under all these conditions.

Appendix 4.

Social stratification by forces of production for each of the values of the social relations of production (Standard Cross-Cultural Sample)[a]

[a]For definitions of variables, see Chapter 3.)

"Social stratification" by "forces of production" for those societies that have a value of 0 on the index of "social relations of production"[b]

	Forces of production							
	Hunting-gathering	Fishing	Pastoralism	Incipient agriculture	Extensive agriculture	Dry intensive agriculture	Irrigated intensive agriculture	Row total
Stratification								
Absence	25	8	3	13	13	4	2	68
	36.8	11.8	4.4	19.1	19.1	5.9	2.9	66.7
	89.3	57.1	42.9	76.5	56.5	50.0	40.0	
Wealth distinctions	2	5	4	1	8	4	2	26
	7.7	19.2	15.4	3.8	30.8	15.4	7.7	25.5
	7.1	35.7	57.1	5.9	34.8	50.0	40.0	
Class stratification	1	1	0	3	2	0	1	8
	12.5	12.5	0	37.5	25.0	0	12.5	7.8
	3.6	7.1	0	17.6	8.7	0	20.0	
Column total	28	14	7	17	23	8	5	102
	27.5	13.7	6.9	16.7	22.5	7.8	4.9	100.0

[b]The top figure in each cell is the cell count, the middle the row percent, and the bottom the column percent.

"Social stratification" by "forces of production" for those societies that have a value of 1 on the index of "social relations of production"[a]

	Forces of production						
	Fishing	Pastoralism	Incipient agriculture	Extensive agriculture	Dry intensive agriculture	Irrigated intensive agriculture	Row total
Stratification							
Absence	0	0	2	3	0	3	8
	0	0	25.0	37.5	0	37.5	19.5
	0	0	40.0	27.3	0	42.9	
Wealth distinctions	2	2	1	1	5	0	11
	18.2	18.2	9.1	9.1	45.5	0	26.8
	50.0	40.0	20.0	9.1	55.6	0	
Class stratification	2	3	2	7	4	4	22
	9.1	13.6	9.1	31.8	18.2	18.2	53.7
	50.0	60.0	40.0	63.6	44.4	57.1	
Column total	4	5	5	11	9	7	41
	9.8	12.2	12.2	26.8	22.0	17.1	100.0

[a]The top figure in each cell is the cell count, the middle the row percent, and the bottom the column percent.

"Social stratification" by "forces of production" for those societies that have a value of 2 on the index of "social relations of production"[a]

	Forces of production				Row total
	Pastoralism	Extensive agriculture	Dry intensive agriculture	Irrigated intensive agriculture	
Stratification					
Wealth distinctions	1	4	0	0	5
	20.0	80.0	0	0	18.5
	50.0	44.4	0	0	
Class stratification	1	5	7	9	22
	4.5	22.7	31.8	40.9	81.5
	50.0	55.6	100.0	100.0	
Column total	2	9	7	9	27
	7.4	33.3	25.9	33.3	100.0

[a]The top figure in each cell is the cell count, the middle the row percent, and the bottom the column percent.

"Social stratification" by "forces of production" for those societies that have a value of 3 on the index of "social relations of production"[a]

	Forces of production				
	Pastoralism	Extensive agriculture	Dry intensive agriculture	Irrigated intensive agriculture	Row total
Stratification					
Wealth distinctions	1 100.0 100.0	0 0 0	0 0 0	0 0 0	1 9.1
Class stratification	0 0 0	3 30.0 100.0	4 40.0 100.0	3 30.0 100.0	10 90.9
Column total	1 9.1	3 27.3	4 36.4	3 27.3	11 100.0

[a] The top figure in each cell is the cell count, the middle the row percent, and the bottom the column percent.

"Social stratification" by "forces of production" for those socie-ties that have a value of 4 on the index of "social relations of production"[a]

	Forces of production	
	Irrigated intensive agriculture	Row total
Stratification		
Class stratification	1 100.0 100.0	1 100.0
Column total	1 100.0	100.0

[a]The top figure in each cell is the cell count, the middle the row percent, and the bottom the column percent.

"Social stratification" by "forces of production" for those societies that have a value of 5 on the index of "social relations of production"[a]

	Forces of production		
	Dry intensive agriculture	Irrigated intensive agriculture	Row total
Stratification			
Class stratification	1 50.0 100.0	1 50.0 100.0	2 100.0
Column total	1 50.0	1 50.0	2 100.0

[a]The top figure in each cell is the cell count, the middle the row percent, and the bottom the column percent.

Appendix 5.

Social stratification by social relations of production for each of the levels of the forces of production (Standard Cross-Cultural Sample)[a]

"Social stratification" by "social relations of production" in hunting-and-gathering societies[b]

	Social relations of production	
	0	Row total
Stratification		
Absence	25	25
	100.0	89.3
	89.3	
Wealth distinctions	2	2
	100.0	7.1
	7.1	
Class stratification	1	1
	100.0	3.6
	3.6	
Column total	28	28
	100.0	100.0

[a]For definitions of variables, see Chapter 3.
[b]The top figure in each cell is the cell count, the middle the row percent, and the bottom the column percent.

*Social stratification by social relations of production
in fishing societies*[a]

	Social relations of production		Row total
	0	1	
Stratification			
Absence	8	0	8
	100.0	0	44.4
	57.1	0	
Wealth distinctions	5	2	7
	71.4	28.6	38.9
	35.7	50.0	
Class stratification	1	2	3
	33.3	66.7	16.7
	7.1	50.0	
Column total	14	4	18
	77.8	22.2	100.0

[a]The top figure in each cell is the cell count, the middle the row percent, and the bottom the column percent.

*Social stratification by social relations of production
in pastoral societies*[a]

	Social relations of production				Row total
	0	1	2	3	
Stratification					
Absence	3	0	0	0	3
	100.0	0	0	0	20.0
	42.9	0	0	0	
Wealth distinctions	4	2	1	1	8
	50.0	25.0	12.5	12.5	53.3
	57.1	40.0	50.0	100.0	
Class stratification	0	3	1	0	4
	0	75.0	25.0	0	26.7
	0	60.0	50.0	0	
Column total	7	5	2	1	15
	46.7	33.3	13.3	6.7	100.0

[a]The top figure in each cell is the cell count, the middle the row percent, and the bottom the column percent.

Social stratification by social relations of production in incipient agricultural societies[a]

	Social relations of production		Row total
	0	1	
Stratification			
Absence	13	2	15
	86.7	13.3	68.2
	76.6	40.0	
Wealth distinctions	1	1	2
	50.9	50.0	9.1
	5.0	20.0	
Class stratification	3	2	5
	60.0	40.0	22.7
	17.6	40.0	
Column total	17	5	22
	77.3	22.7	100.0

[a]The top figure in each cell is the cell count, the middle the row percent, and the bottom the column percent.

Social stratification by social relations of production in extensive-agricultural societies[a]

	Social relations of production				Row total
	0	1	2	3	
Stratification					
Absence	13	3	0	0	16
	81.3	18.8	0	0	34.8
	56.5	27.3	0	0	
Wealth distinctions	8	1	4	0	13
	61.5	7.7	30.8	0	28.3
	34.8	9.1	44.4	0	
Class stratification	2	7	5	3	17
	11.8	41.2	29.4	17.6	37.0
	8.7	63.6	55.6	100.0	
Column total	23	11	9	3	46
	50.0	23.9	19.6	6.5	100.0

[a]The top figure in each cell is the cell count, the middle the row percent, and the bottom the column percent.

Social stratification by social relations of production in dry intensive agricultural societies[a]

	Social relations of production					Row total
	0	1	2	3	5	
Stratification						
Absence	4 100.0 50.0	0 0 0	0 0 0	0 0 0	0 0 0	4 13.8
Wealth distinctions	4 44.4 50.0	5 55.6 55.6	0 0 0	0 0 0	0 0 0	9 31.0
Class stratification	0 0 0	4 25.0 44.4	7 43.8 100.0	4 25.0 100.0	1 6.3 100.0	16 55.2
Column total	8 27.6	9 31.0	7 24.1	4 13.8	1 3.4	29 100.0

[a]The top figure in each cell is the cell count, the middle the row percent, and the bottom the column percent.

Social stratification by social relations of production in irrigated intensive-agricultural societies[a]

	Social relations of production						Row total
	0	1	2	3	4	5	
Stratification							
Absence	2	3	0	0	0	0	5
	40.0	60.0	0	0	0	0	19.2
	40.0	42.9	0	0	0	0	
Wealth distinctions	2	0	0	0	0	0	2
	100.0	0	0	0	0	0	7.7
	40.0	0	0	0	0	0	
Class stratification	1	4	9	3	1	1	19
	5.3	21.1	47.4	15.8	5.3	5.3	73.1
	20.0	57.1	100.0	100.0	100.0	100.0	
Column total	5	7	9	3	1	1	26
	19.2	26.9	34.6	11.5	3.8	3.8	100.0

[a]The top figure in each cell is the cell count, the middle the row percent, and the bottom the column percent.

Appendix 6.

Regression equations

The major statistical tool that I have used in my analyses is partial correlation. This is the most appropriate measure because most of the variables are ordinal (ranked), rather than interval or continuous. However, regression analysis is a convenient method for assessing the total explanatory power of a statistical model. The adjusted R^2 statistic signifies the percentage of variance in the dependent variable that is "explained" by the various predictor variables. There is no such simple summary statistic for partial correlation.

I have therefore decided to use regression analyses as a supplement to the partial correlation analyses. Because regression is a "robust" method, the use of ordinal variables in certain cases is considered acceptable even though, strictly speaking, regression should use normally distributed interval-level variables.

Three regression equations were tested. For the Standard Cross-Cultural Sample (184 societies), I was concerned to predict the degree of social stratification, from the forces of production and the social relations of production. In terms of the computer variable names, this equation was expressed as:

$$\text{CLASS} = b_1 \times \text{SUBS3} + b_2 \times \text{IND6} + \text{CONSTANT}$$

where CLASS = degree of social stratification
      SUBS3 = forces of production
      IND6 = index of social relations of
             production
The remainder of this appendix summarizes the results of this regression.

Full statistics for regression equation, N = 184

| | | | F | Beta |
| | | Standard | ――――― | ――――― |
	B	error B	Significance	Elasticity
Variable				
IND6	.45083063	.52351773	76.814291	.5537481
			0	.18250
SUBS3	.87549502	.27836727	9.8917015	.1987132
			.002	.19202
(CONSTANT)	1.2135586	.11493888	111.47760	
			0	

Variables in the equation

Multiple *R*	.67477
R square	.45531
Adjusted *R* square	.44929
Standard deviation	.64988

For the sample of sixty societies, I was concerned to predict the degree of legal complexity (variable name "NEWD2") from the forces of production (SUBS4) and the degree of social stratification (CLASS). Thus the regression equation is:

$$NEWD2 = b_1 \times SUBS4 + b_2 \times CLASS + CONSTANT$$

A summary table for this regression follows in this appendix.

Finally, for the sample of fifty-six societies, I wanted to predict the degree of legal complexity (variable name "NEWD2"), from the three predictor variables: forces of production (SUBS4), social relations of production (IND6), and social stratification (CLASS). The regression equation is:

$$NEWD2 = b_1 \times SUBS4 + b_2 \times IND6 + b_3 \times CLASS + CONSTANT$$

The remainder of this appendix lists all the statistics for this equation.

Full statistics for regression equation, N = 60

		Variables in the equation		
		Standard	F	Beta
	B	error B	Significance	Elasticity
Variable				
CLASS	1.6803825	.24602204	46.651784	.6113568
			0	1.03075
SUBS4	.43279311	.12337032	12.306635	.3140005
			.001	.47295
(CONSTANT)	−1.6286276	.46551153	12.240036	
			.001	

Multiple R	.83051
R square	.68974
Adjusted R square	.67885
Standard deviation	1.32930

Full statistics for regression equation, N = 56

		Variables in the equation		
		Standard	F	Beta
	B	error B	Significance	Elasticity
Variable				
SUBS4	.35977967	.12962372	7.7037867	.2669778
			.008	.38520
CLASS	1.1461110	.28841819	15.790942	.4171347
			.000	.71009
IND6	.57328371	.20689546	7.6778619	.2918596
			.008	.15267
(CONSTANT)	−.81471866	.55518876	2.1534461	
			.148	

Multiple R	.82744
R square	.68465
Adjusted R square	.66646
Standard deviation	1.35203

Appendix 7.

Legal institution codes for sixty-society subsample

Variable	Description
0	Self- or kin-based redress
1	Advisors system
2	Mediator system
3	Elders' council
4	Restricted council
5	Chieftainship
6	Paramount chief
7	State-level system

Legal institution code	Society name	Legal institution code	Society name
0	Kung	3	Maria Gond
5	Bambara	3	Toda
3	Somali	4	Tanala
6	Wolof	7	Burmese
3	Gheg	1	Semang
7	Korea	2	Ifugao
3	Santal	0	Tiwi
1	Andaman	1	Marquesans
0	Aranda	0	Copper Eskimo
5	Kapauku	2	Yukok
1	Truk	5	Yokut
5	Trobriand	3	Zuni
4	Samoa	7	Aztec
0	Ojibwa	0	Jivaro
0	Callinago	1	Nambicuara
7	Inca	6	Mende
0	Mataco	1	Ona
3	Nama	0	Botocudo
6	Bemba	6	Ganda
3	Kikuyu	5	Pawnee
6	Ashanti	3	Paez
5	Tallensi	0	Manus
3	Tiv	0	Miskito
6	Azande	2	Goajiro
3	Masai	0	Bellacoola
4	Fellahin	5	Eastern Pomo
3	Lapps	5	Turks
5	Rwala	7	Amhara
3	Chukchee	5	Tuareg
3	Lepcha	7	Zazzagawa

Appendix 8.

Legal institutions by social stratification within each level of the forces of production for 60-society subsample[a]

Legal institutions by social stratification in hunting-and-gathering societies[b]

	Stratification		Row total
	Absence	Wealth distinctions	
Type of legal institution			
Self-redress	5	0	5
	100.0	0	50.0
	62.5	0	
Advisor	3	0	3
	100.0	0	30.0
	37.5	0	
Chieftainship	0	2	2
	0	100.0	20.0
	0	100.0	
Column total	8	2	10
	80.0	20.0	100.0

[a]For definitions of variables, see Chapter 3.
[b]The top figure in each cell is the cell count, the middle the row percent, and the bottom the column percent.

Legal institutions by social stratification in fishing societies[a]

	Stratification		Row total
	Absence	Wealth distinctions	
Type of legal institution			
Self-redress	4	2	6
	66.7	33.3	66.7
	66.7	66.7	
Advisor	2	0	2
	100.0	0	22.2
	33.3	0	
Mediator	0	1	1
	0	100.0	11.1
	0	33.3	
Column total	6	3	9
	66.7	33.3	100.0

[a]The top figure in each cell is the cell count, the middle the row percent, and the bottom the column percent.

Legal institutions by social stratification in pastoral societies[a]

	Stratification			Row total
	Absence	Wealth distinctions	Class stratification	
Type of legal institution				
Mediator	0	1	0	1
	0	100.0	0	11.1
	0	16.7	0	
Elders' council	2	4	0	6
	33.3	66.7	0	66.7
	100.0	66.7	0	
Chieftainship	0	1	1	2
	0	50.0	50.0	22.2
	0	16.7	100.0	
Column total	2	6	1	9
	22.2	66.7	11.1	100.0

[a]The top figure in each cell is the cell count, the middle the row percent, and the bottom the column percent.

*Legal institutions by social stratification in
extensive-agricultural societies*[a]

	Stratification			
	Absence	Wealth distinctions	Class stratification	Row total
Type of legal institution				
Self-redress	1	0	0	1
	100.0	0	0	7.7
	50.0	0	0	
Advisor	0	0	1	1
	0	0	100.0	7.7
	0	0	11.1	
Elders' council	1	1	0	2
	50.0	50.0	0	15.4
	50.0	50.0	0	
Restricted council	0	0	1	1
	0	0	100.0	7.7
	0	0	11.1	
Chieftainship	0	1	2	3
	0	33.3	66.7	23.1
	0	50.0	22.2	
Paramount chief	0	0	5	5
	0	0	100.0	38.5
	0	0	55.6	
Column total	2	2	9	13
	15.4	15.4	69.2	100.0

[a] The top figure in each cell is the cell count, the middle the row percent, and the bottom the column percent.

Legal institutions by social stratification in irrigated
intensive-agricultural societies[a]

	Stratification			
	Absence	Wealth distinctions	Class stratification	Row total
Type of legal institution				
Mediator	0	1	0	1
	0	100.0	0	10.0
	0	100.0	0	
Elders' council	2	0	0	2
	100.0	0	0	20.0
	100.0	0	0	
Restricted council	0	0	2	2
	0	0	100.0	20.0
	0	0	28.6	
State-level	0	0	5	5
	0	0	100.0	50.0
	0	0	71.4	
Column total	2	1	7	10
	20.0	10.0	70.0	100.0

[a]The top figure in each cell is the cell count, the middle the row percent, and the bottom the column percent.

*Legal institutions by social stratification in dry intensive-
agricultural societies*[a]

| | Stratification | | | |
	Absence	Wealth distinctions	Class stratification	Row total
Type of legal institution				
Elders'	2	2	0	4
council	50.0	50.0	0	44.4
	100.0	66.7	0	
Chieftainship	0	1	2	3
	0	33.3	66.7	33.3
	0	33.3	50.0	
Paramount	0	0	1	1
chief	0	0	100.0	11.1
	0	0	25.0	
State-	0	0	1	1
level	0	0	100.0	11.1
	0	0	25.0	
Column total	2	3	4	9
	22.2	33.3	44.4	100.0

[a]The top figure in each cell is the cell count, the middle the row percent,
and the bottom the column percent.

Bibliography

Abel, Richard. 1973. A comparative theory of dispute institutions in society. *Law and Society Review* 8:217–437.

Althusser, Louis. 1969. *For Marx*. Harmondsworth, England: Allen Lane.

Ammar, Hamed. 1954. *Growing Up in an Egyptian Village*. London: Routledge & Kegan Paul.

Anderson, Robert. 1949. Some aspects of Lapp culture history. M.A. thesis, University of California, Berkeley.

Armstrong, John, and Alfred Metraux. 1948. The Goajiro. In *Handbook of South American Indians*, vol. 4, pp. 369–385. J. Steward, ed. Washington D.C.: Government Printing Office.

Asad, Talal, and H. Wolpe. 1976. Concepts of the mode of production. *Economy and Society* 5(4):470–506.

Aung, Maung Htin. 1962. *Burmese Law Tales: The Legal Element in Burmese Folklore*. London: Oxford University Press.

——— 1967. *A History of Burma*. New York: Columbia University Press.

Bailey, Fred. 1965. *Decisions by Consensus in Councils and Committees*. ASA Monographs 2:1–20. New York: Praeger.

Balandier, Georges. 1970. *Political Anthropology*. New York: Random House.

Bandelier, A. F. 1975. *On the Social Organization and Mode of Government of the Ancient Mexicans*. New York: Cooper Square Publisher, Inc. (Orig. pub. 1879.)

Barkun, Michael. 1968. *Law Without Sanctions*. New Haven, Conn.: Yale University Press.

Barth, Frederick. 1964a. *Nomads of South Persia: The Basseri Tribe of the Khamseh Confederacy*. New York: Humanities Press.

——— 1964b. Capital, investment and the social structure of a pastoral nomad group in South Persia. In *Capital, Saving, and Credit in Peasant Societies*, pp. 69–81. R. Firth and B. Yamey, eds. Chicago: Aldine.

Barton, Roy. 1922. *Ifugao Economics*. Berkeley: University of California Press.

——— 1969. *Ifugao Law*. University of California Publications in Archaeology and Ethnology, vol. 15. Berkeley (Orig. pub. 1919.)

Basedow, Herbert. 1925. *The Australian Aboriginal*. Adelaide, Australia: F. W. Preece.

Benedict, Ruth. 1934. *Patterns of Culture*. Boston: Houghton Mifflin.

Berenger-Feraud, L. J. B. 1879. *Les peuplades de la Senegambie*. Paris: Librarie de la Societie Asiatique.

Bernal Villa, S. 1954. Medicine and magic among the Paez. *Revista Colombiana de Antropologia* 2:219–64.

Bernardi, B. 1955. The age-system of the Masai. *Annali Laternensi* 18:257–318.

Biswas, P. C. 1956. *Santals of the Santal Parganas*. Delhi: Bharatiya Adimjati Sevak Sangh.

Black, Donald. 1976. *The Behavior of Law*. New York: Academic Press.

Blackman, Winifred. 1968. *The Fellahin of Upper Egypt*. London: Cass.

Blumberg, Rae Lesser. 1978. *Stratification: Socioeconomic and Sexual Inequality*. Dubuque, Iowa: William C. Brown.

Blumberg, Rae L., and Robert F. Winch. 1973. The rise and fall of the complex family: some implications for an evolutionary theory of societal development. Paper read at annual meeting of American Sociological Association, New York.

Boas, Franz. 1894. *The Social Organization and the Secret Societies of the Kwakiutl Indians*. Washington D.C.: U.S. National Museum Report.

Bogaraz-Tan, Vladimir. 1904. *The Chukchee*. New York: G. E. Stechert.

Bohannan, Laura, and Paul Bohannan. 1953. *The Tiv of Central Nigeria*. Ethnographic Survey of Africa, part VIII. London: International African Institute.

1958. *Three Source Notebooks in Tiv Ethnology*. New Haven, Conn.: Human Relations Area Files.

Bohannan, Paul. 1957. *Justice and Judgment Among the Tiv*. London: Oxford University Press.

Bohannan, Paul, ed. 1967. *Law and Warfare: Studies in the Anthropology of Conflict*. Garden City, N.Y.: Natural History Press.

Bollig, Laurentius. 1927. *Die Bewohner der Truk-Inseln* (The Inhabitants of Truk Island). Munster in Westphalia: Aschendorffsche Verlagsbuchhandlung.

Bray, Warwick. 1968. *Everyday Life of the Aztecs*. New York: Putnam.

Breton, Raymond. 1957. *Observations of the Island Carib: A Compilation of Ethnographic Notes*. M. McKusick and P. Verin, trans. New Haven, Conn.: Human Relations Area Files.

Breton, Raymond, and Armand de la Paix. 1929. Relations de L'Ile de la Guadeloupe (An account of the island of Guadeloupe). In *Les Caraibes, La Guadeloupe*, pp. 45–74. Joseph Rennard, ed. Paris: Libraire Generale et Internationale.

Briggs, L. Cabot. 1958. *The Living Races of the Sahara Desert*. Papers of the Peabody Museum of Archaeology and Ethnology, vol. 28, no. 2. Cambridge, Mass.: Peabody Museum.

Busia, Kofi. 1951. *The Position of the Chief in the Modern Political System of the Ashanti: A Study of the Influence of Contemporary Social Changes on Ashanti Political Institutions.* London: Oxford University Press.

Cain, Maureen, and Alan Hunt. 1979. *Marx and Engels on Law.* London: Academic Press.

Carlston, Kenneth. 1968. *Social Theory and African Tribal Organization.* Champaign: University of Illinois Press.

Chagnon, Napoleon. 1968. *Yanomamo: the Fierce People.* New York: Holt, Rinehart and Winston.

Chelhod, Joseph. 1971. *De droit dan la societe Bedouine.* Paris: Libraire Marcel Riviere et Cie.

Chewings, Charles. 1936. *Back in the Stone Age: The Natives of Central Australia.* Sydney: Angus and Robertson.

Cieza de Leon, Pedro de. 1883. *The Second Part of the Chronicles of Peru.* Clements Markham, trans. London: Hakluyt Society.

Cohen, Ronald, and John Middleton. 1967. *Comparative Political Systems: Studies in the Politics of Pre-Industrial Societies.* Austin: University of Texas Press.

Cohen, Yehudi. 1968. *Man in Adaptation: The Cultural Present.* Chicago: Aldine.

Collinder, Bjorn. 1949. *The Lapps.* Princeton, N.J.: Princeton University Press.

Collins, Henry B., Austin H. Clark, and Egbert H. Walker. 1945. *The Aleutian Islands: Their People and Natural History.* Washington, D.C.: Smithsonian Institution.

Colson, Elizabeth. 1953. Social control and vengeance in plateau Tonga society. *Africa* 23:199–211.

Colson, Elizabeth, and Max Gluckman. 1951. *Seven Tribes of British Central Africa.* Oxford: Oxford University Press.

Conzemius, Eduard. 1932. *Ethnographical Survey of the Miskito and Sumo Indians.* Bureau of American Ethnology, Bulletin 106. Washington, D.C.: Government Printing Office.

Coon, Carleton. 1950. *The Mountains of Giants.* Papers of the Peabody Museum of American Archaeology and Ethnology, vol. 23, no. 3. Cambridge, Mass: Peabody Museum.

Cooper, John M. 1917. *Analytical and Critical Bibliography of the Tribes of Tierra del Fuego and Adjacent Territory.* Bureau of American Ethnology, Bulletin 63. Washington, D.C.: Government Printing Office.

1946. The Ona. In *Handbook of South American Indians,* vol. 1, pp. 107–26. J. Steward, ed. Washington, D.C.: Government Printing Office.

Crocker, Walter R. 1936. *Nigeria: A Critique of British Colonial Administration.* London: Allen and Unwin.

Culshaw, W. J. 1949. *Tribal Heritage: A Study of the Santals.* London: Lutterworth Press.

Cushing, Frank H. 1920. *Zuni Breadstuff.* New York: Museum of the American Indian.

D'Altroy, Terence. 1981. Empire growth and consolidation: the Xauxa region of Peru Under the Incas. Ph.D. dissertation, University of California, Los Angeles.

Danquah, Joseph. 1928. *Gold Coast: Akan Laws and Customs and the Akim Abuakwa Constitution.* London: G. Routledge.

Datta-Majumder, Nabend. 1956. *The Santal: A Study in Cultural Change.* Calcutta: Government of India Press.

Davis, Shelton. 1977. *Victims of the Miracle: Development and the Indians of Brazil.* Cambridge: Cambridge University Press.

Davis, Shelton, and Robert Mathews. 1976. *The Geological Imperative: Anthropology and Development in the Amazon Basin.* Cambridge, Mass.: Anthropology Resource Center.

de la Vega, Garcilasco. 1961. *The Incas: The Royal Commentaries of the Inca.* Maria Jolas, trans. New York: Avon Books.

Dentan, Robert K. 1979. *The Semai: A Nonviolent People of Malaya.* New York: Holt, Rinehart and Winston.

Dorsey, George A. 1940. *Traditions of the Skidi Pawnee.* Memoirs of the American Folk-Lore Society, vol. 8. Boston: Houghton Mifflin.

Dorsey, George, and James Murie. 1940. *Notes on Skidi Pawnee Society.* Anthropological Series, vol. 27, no. 2. Chicago: Field Museum of Natural History.

Downes, Roger. 1933. *The Tiv Tribe.* Kaduna, Nigeria: Government Printer.

Durham, M. E. 1909. *High Albania.* London: Edward Arnold.

1928. *Some Tribal Origins, Laws and Customs of the Balkans.* London: Allen and Unwin.

Durkheim, Emile. 1933. *The Division of Labor in Society.* New York: Free Press. (Orig. pub. 1893.)

Edwards, Richard, Michael Reich, and Thomas Weiskopf. 1972. *The Capitalist System: A Radical Analysis of American Society.* Englewood Cliffs, N.J.: Prentice-Hall.

Elwin, Verrier. 1947. *The Muria and Their Ghotul.* Calcutta: Oxford University Press.

Engels, Friedrich. 1942. *The Origin of the Family, Private Property and the State.* New York: International Publishers.

Epstein, A. L. 1974. *Contention and Dispute.* Canberra: Australian National University Press.

Evans-Pritchard, Edward. 1937. *Witchcraft, Oracles and Magic Among the Azande of the Anglo-Egyptian Sudan.* Oxford: Oxford University Press (Clarendon Press).

1940. *The Nuer.* London: Oxford University Press.

1971. *The Azande: History and Political Institutions.* Oxford: Oxford University Press (Clarendon Press).

Fallers, Margaret C. 1960. *The Eastern Lacustrine Bantu (Ganda and Soga).* London: International African Institute.

Felsteiner, William. 1974. Influences of social organization on dispute processing. *Law and Society Review* 9 (1):63–94.

Firth, Raymond. 1970. *Preface to Ancient Law*. Boston: Beacon Press.
    1975. The sceptical anthropologist. In *Marxist Analyses and Social Anthropology*, pp. 29–60. Maurice Bloch, ed. New York: Wiley.
Fock, Niel. 1974. Mataco law. In *Native South Americans: Ethnology of the Least Known Continent*, pp. 221–5. P. Lyons, ed. Boston: Little, Brown.
Forde, Daryll. 1963. *Habitat, Economy and Society*. New York: Dutton.
Fortes, Meyer. 1940. The political system of the Tallensi of the Northern Territories of the Gold Coast. In *African Political Systems*, pp. 239–71. M. Fortes and E. E. Evans-Pritchard, eds. London: Oxford University Press.
    1945. *The Dynamics of Clanship Among the Tallensi*. London: Oxford University Press.
Fortune, R. F. 1935. *Manus Religion*. Philadelphia: American Philosophical Society.
Fosbrooke, H. A. 1948. An administrative survey of the Masai social system. *Tanganyika Notes and Records* 26:1–50.
Foster-Carter, Aiden. 1978. The modes of production controversy. *New Left Review* 107:47–77 (Jan./Feb.).
Freeman, L., and R. Winch. 1957. Societal complexity: an empirical test of a typology of societies. *American Journal of Sociology* 62:461–6.
Fried, Morton. 1967. *The Evolution of Political Society: An Essay in Political Anthropology*. New York: Random House.
Friedman, Jonathan. 1974. Marxism, structuralism and vulgar materialism. *Man* 9(3):444–69.
Friedman, Lawrence. 1969. On legal development. *Rutgers Law Review* 24(1):11–64.
Fuchs, Stephen. 1960. *The Gond and Bhumia of Eastern Mandla*. Bombay: New Literature Publishing House.
Furnivall, John S. 1948. *Colonial Policy and Practice: A Comparative Study of Burma and Netherlands India*. New York: New York University Press.
Gamble, David. 1957. *The Wolof of Senegambia*. Ethnographic Survey of Africa; Part XIV: Western Africa: International African Institute.
Garfinkel, Harold. 1956. Conditions of successful degradation ceremonies. *American Journal of Sociology* 61:420–4.
Gayton, A. H. 1930. *Yokuts-Mono Chiefs and Shamans*. Berkeley: University of California Press.
    1948. *Yokuts and Western Mono Ethnography II: Northern Foothill Yokuts and Western Mono*. Anthropological Research, vol. 10, no. 2. Berkeley: University of California Press.
Giddens, Anthony. 1978. *Emile Durkheim*. New York: Viking Press.
Gifford, Edward W. 1923. *Pomo Lands on Clear Lake*. Berkeley: University of California Press.
    1926. *Clear Lake Pomo Society*. University of California Publications in American Archaeology and Ethnology, vol. 18, no. 2. Berkeley.

Gladwin, Thomas, and Seymour B. Sarason. 1953. *Truk: Man in Paradise.* New York: Wenner-Gren Foundation for Anthropological Research.

Gluckman, Max. 1955. *The Judicial Process Among the Barotse of Northern Rhodesia.* Manchester: Manchester University Press.

1965. *Politics, Law and Ritual in Tribal Society.* New York: New American Library.

1967. The judicial process among the Barotse. In *Law and Warfare: Studies in the Anthropology of Conflict,* pp. 59–92. P. Bohannan, ed. Garden City, N.Y.: Natural History Press.

Goddard, David. 1969. The limits of British anthropology. *New Left Review* 58:79–89.

Godelier, Maurice. 1975. Modes of production, kinship, and demographic structures. In *Marxist Analyses and Social Anthropology,* pp. 3–27. Maurice Bloch, ed. New York: Wiley.

1977. *Perspectives in Marxist Anthropology.* Cambridge: Cambridge University Press.

Goodenough, Ward H. 1951. *Property, Kin and Community on Truk.* New Haven, Conn.: Yale University Press.

Gorer, Geoffrey. 1938. *Himalayan Village: An Account of the Lepchas of Sikkim.* London: Thomas Nelson and Sons.

Grajdanzev, Andrew J. 1944. *Modern Korea.* New York: International Secretariat, Institute of Pacific Relations.

Greenberg, David, and Nancy Anderson. 1981. Recent Marxisant books on law. : a review essay. *Contemporary Crises* 5:293–322.

Grigson, Wilfrid V. 1949. *The Maria Gonds of Bastar.* London: Oxford University Press.

Gulliver, Phillip. 1963. *Social Control in an African Society: A Study of the Arusha: Agricultural Masai of Northern Tanganyika.* London: Routledge & Kegan Paul.

1969. The conservative commitment in Northern Tanzania: the Arusha and Masai. In *Tradition and Transition in East Africa,* pp. 223–42. P. Gulliver, ed. Berkeley: University of California Press.

1979. *Disputes and Negotiation: A Cross Cultural Perspective.* New York: Academic Press.

Gusinde, Martin. 1975. *Folk Literature of the Selknam Indians.* Los Angeles: University of California Latin American Center Publications.

Gutierrez de Pineda, Virginia. 1950. *Organizacion Social en La Guajira* (Social Organization in La Guajira). Bogota: Universidad Nacional de Colombia.

Hahn, C.H., H. Vedder, and L. Fourie. 1928. *The Native Tribes of South West Africa.* New York: Barnes and Noble.

Hailey, Lord. 1950. *Native Administration in the British African Territories,* Part 1. East Africa: Uganda, Kenya, Tanganyika. London: His Majesty's Stationery Office.

Hall, Daniel G. 1950. *Burma.* New York: Hutchinson's University Library.

Hallowell, A. Irving. 1942. *The Role of Conjuring in Saulteaux Society.*

Publications of the Philadelphia Anthropological Society, vol. 2. Philadelphia: University of Pennsylvania Press.

Handy, Edward W. 1923. *The Native Culture of the Marquesans*. Honolulu: Bernice P. Bishop Museum.

Harner, Michael. 1972. *The Jivaro: People of the Sacred Waterfalls*. Garden City, N.Y.: Natural History Press.

Harris, Marvin. 1968. *The Rise of Anthropological Theory*. New York: Crowell.

Hart, C. W., and Arnold Pilling. 1960. *The Tiwi of Northern Australia*. New York: Holt, Rinehart and Winston.

Hart, H. L. A. 1961. *The Concept of Law*. London: Oxford University Press.

Hasluck, Margaret. 1954. *The Unwritten Law in Albania*. Cambridge: Cambridge University Press.

Hassan, Malam, and Malam Shuaibu. 1952. *A Chronicle of Abuja*. Nigeria: Ibadan University Press.

Haydon, E. S. 1960. *Law and Justice in Buganda*. London: Butterworths.

Henry, Jules. 1964. *Jungle People*. New York: Vintage Books.

Hernandez de Alba, G. 1946. The Highland Tribes of Southern Colombia. In *Handbook of South American Indians, vol. 2*, pp. 915–27. Julian Steward, ed. Washington, D.C.: Government Printing Office.

Hewett, Edgar. 1968. *Ancient Andean Life*. New York: Biblio and Tamen.

Heydrich, M. 1931. *Koreanische Landwirtschaft* (Korean Farming). Dresden: Museen fur Tierkunde und Volkerkunde, Abhandlungen and Berichte.

Hindess, Barry, and Paul Hirst. 1975. *Pre-Capitalist Modes of Production*. London: Routledge & Kegan Paul.

Hoben, Allan. 1973. *Land Tenure Among the Amhara of Ethiopia: The Dynamics of Cognatic Descent*. Chicago: University of Chicago Press.

Hoebel, E. Adamson. 1968. The Law of Primitive Man: A Study in Comparative Legal Dynamics. Cambridge, Mass.: Harvard University Press.

Huntingford, G. W. 1953. *The Southern Nilo-Hamites*. London: International African Institute.

Hyams, Edward, and George Ordish. 1963. *The Last of the Incas: The Rise and Fall of an American Empire*. New York: Simon and Schuster.

Jenness, Diamond. 1917. The Copper Eskimos. *Geographical Review* 4:81–91.

——— 1922. *The Life of the Copper Eskimos*. Report of the Canadian Artic Expedition 1913-1918. vol. 12. Ottawa: F. A. Acland.

——— 1959. *The People of the Twilight*. Chicago: University of Chicago Press.

Keesing, Felix M. 1934. *Modern Samoa: Its Government and Changing Life*. London: Allen and Unwin.

Kenyatta, Jomo. 1965. *Facing Mt. Kenya: The Tribal Life of the Gikuyu*. New York: Vintage Books.

Kirchoff, Paul. 1948. The Caribbean Lowland Tribes. In *Handbook of*

South American Indians, vol. 4, pp. 219–29. Julian Steward, ed. Washington, D.C.: Government Printing Office.

Kluckholn, Clyde. 1944. *Navajo Witchcraft*. Boston: Beacon Press.

Kochar, Vijay. 1970. *Social Organization among the Santals*. Calcutta: Editions Indian.

Krader, Lawrence. 1955. Ecology of Central Asian Pastoralism. *Southwestern Journal of Anthropology* 12:301–26.

Kramer, Augustin. 1932. *Truk*. Hamburg: Friederichsen de Gruyter.

Kroeber, Alfred. 1919. *Zuni Kin and Clan*. Anthropological Papers of the American Museum of Natural History, vol. 18, part 2. New York: American Museum.

——— 1925. *Handbook of the Indians of California*. Washington, D.C.: Bureau of American Ethnology.

——— 1926. *Law of the Yurok Indians*. International Congress of Americanists, Proceedings 22, vol. 2.

Kuper, Adam. 1971. Council Structure and Decision-Making. In *Councils in Action*, pp. 13-28. A. Richards and A. Kuper, eds. Cambridge: Cambridge University Press.

Lambert, H. E. 1956. *Kikuyu Social and Political Institutions*. London: Oxford University Press.

Leakey, L. S. B. 1930. Some notes on the Masai of Kenya Colony. *Journal of the Royal Anthropological Institute of Great Britain and Ireland* 15:185–210.

——— 1952. *Mau Mau and the Kikuyu*. London: Methuen.

Lee, Richard, 1968. What hunters do for a living, or, how to make out on scarce resources. In *Man the Hunter*, pp. 30–48. R. Lee and I. DeVore, eds. Chicago: Aldine.

——— 1979. *The !Kung San: Men, Women, and Work in a Foraging Society*. Cambridge: Cambridge University Press.

LeGros, Dominique. 1977. Chance, necessity and mode of production: a Marxist critique of culture evolutionism. *American Anthropologist* 79:26–41.

Leighton, D., and J. Adair. 1963. *Peoples of the Middle Place: A Study of the Zuni Indians*. New Haven: Human Relations Area Files Press.

Lenski, Gerhard. 1966. *Power and Privilege: A Theory of Social Stratification*. New York: McGraw-Hill.

——— 1970. *Human Societies* New York: McGraw-Hill.

Levine, Donald. 1965. *Wax and Gold: Tradition and Innovation in Ethiopian Culture*. Chicago: University of Chicago Press.

Levi-Strauss, Claude. 1948. The Nambicuara. In *Handbook of South American Indians*, vol. 3, pp. 361–70. Julian Steward, ed. Washington, D.C.: Government Printing Office.

——— 1967. The social and psychological aspects of chieftainship in a primitive tribe: the Nambikuara of northwestern Mato Grosso. In *Comparative Political Systems*, pp. 45–62. R. Cohen and J. Middleton, eds. Austin: University of Texas Press.

Bibliography 251

Lewis, I. M. 1955. Peoples of the Horn of Africa. Ethnographic Survey of Africa. Part I: North Eastern Africa. London: International African Institute.
Lhote, Henri. 1955. Les Touaregs du Hoggar. Paris: Payot.
Linton, Ralph. 1933. The Tanala: A Hill Tribe of Madagascar. Field Museum of Natural History Publications 317, Anthropological Series: Vol. XXII. Chicago: Field Museum.
1939. Marquesan culture. In The Individual and His Society, pp. 138–96. Abram Kardiner, ed. New York: Columbia University Press.
Lipsky, George. 1962. Ethiopia: Its People, Its Society, Its Culture. New Haven: Human Relations Area Files Press.
Little, Kenneth L. 1951. The Mende of Sierra Leone: A West African People in Transition. London: Routledge & Kegan Paul.
Llewellyn, K., and E. Adamson Hoebel. 1941. The Cheyenne Way. Norman: University of Oklahoma Press.
Loeb, Edwin M. 1926. Pomo Folkways. University of California Publications in Archaeology and Ethnology 19 (2). Berkeley.
Lukes, Steven. 1972. Emile Durkheim: His Life and Work. New York: Harper & Row.
McCullough, Merran. 1950a. Peoples of Sierra Leone Protectorate. London: International African Institute.
1950b. Peoples of Sierra Leone. Ethnographic Survey of Africa. Part II: Western Africa. London: International African Institute.
McIlwraith, Thomas F. 1948. The Bella Coola Indians. Toronto: University of Toronto Press.
Magnarella, Paul J. 1974. Tradition and Change in a Turkish Town. New York: Wiley.
Maine, Sir Henry. 1970. Ancient Law. Gloucester, Mass.: Peter Smith Press. (Orig. pub. 1861.)
Mair, Lucy P. 1934. An African People in the Twentieth Century. London: G. Routledge and Sons.
Makal, Mahmt. 1954. A Village in Anatolia. Sir W. Deedes, trans. London: Vallentine, Mitchell and Co.
Malinowski, Bronislaw. 1921. The primitive economics of the Trobriand Islanders. Economic Journal 31:116.
1922. Argonauts of the Western Pacific. London: George Routledge and Sons.
1926. Crime and Custom in Savage Society. London: Routledge & Kegan Paul.
1945. The Dynamics of Culture Change. New Haven, Conn.: Yale University Press.
Man, E. H. 1883. On the aboriginal inhabitants of the Andaman Islands. Journal of the Anthropological Institute of Great Britain and Ireland 12:69–116.
Mango, Andrew. 1968. Turkey. London: Thames and Hudson.
Manoukian, Madeline. 1950. Akan and GaAdangme Peoples of the Gold Coast. London: Oxford University Press.

Markham, Sir Clements. 1969. *The Incas of Peru.* New York: AMS Press. (Orig. pub. 1910.)

Marshall, Lorna. 1965. The !Kung bushmen of the Kalahari Desert. In *Peoples of Africa*, pp. 241–278. James Gibbs, ed. New York: Holt, Rinehart and Winston.

Marshall, William E. 1873. *A Phrenologist Amongst the Todas.* London: Longmans, Green.

Marx, Karl. 1965. *Pre-Capitalist Economic Formations.* New York: International Publishers.

———. 1970. *Capital*, vol. 1. London: Lawrence and Wishart.

Mead, Charles. 1924. *Old Civilizations of Inca Land.* New York: American Museum of Natural History Press.

Mead, Margaret. 1930. *Social Organization of Manua.* Honolulu: Bernice Bishop Museum.

———. 1937. The Manus of the Admiralty Islands. In *Cooperation and Competition Among Primitive Peoples*, pp. 210–239. M. Mead, ed. New York: McGraw-Hill.

———. 1956. *New Lives for Old: Cultural Transformation of the Manus 1928–1953.* New York: Morrow.

Means, Philip. 1973. *Biblioteca Andina.* Detroit: Blaine-Ethridge Books. (Orig. pub. 1928.)

Meillasoux, Claude. 1964. *L'anthropologie economique des Gouro de Cote d'Ivoire.* Paris: Mouton.

Metraux, Alfred. 1946. The Caingang. In *Handbook of South American Indians, vol. 1.* pp. 445–76. Julian Steward, ed. Washington, D.C.: Government Printing Office.

Middleton, John. 1953. *The Central Tribes of the North-Eastern Bantu.* London: International African Institute.

Monteil, Charles V. 1924. *Les Bambara du segou et du Kaarta.* Paris: LaRose.

Moore, John H. 1977. The evolution of exploitation. *Critique of Anthropology* 8 (2):33–58 (Spring).

Moore, Sally Falk. 1958. Power and Property in Inca Peru. New York: Columbia University Press.

Moose, J. R. 1911. *Village Life in Korea.* Nashville: Publishing House of the Methodist Episcopal Church.

Morgan, Lewis H. 1912. Ancient Society. Chicago: Charles H. Kerr and Co.

Mukherjea, Charulal. 1962. *The Santals.* Calcutta: A. Mukherjee.

Murdock, George P. 1934. *Our Primitive Contemporaries.* New York: Macmillan.

———. 1967. *Ethnographic Atlas*: a summary. *Ethnology* 6(2):109–236.

Murdock, George, and Douglas White. 1969. Standard cross-cultural sample. *Ethnology* 8(4).

Murphy, Robert. 1964. Social distance and the veil. *American Anthropologist* 66(6): 1257–74.

Murra, John V. 1980. *The Economic Organization of the Inka State.* Research in Economic Anthropology, supplement 1. Greenwich, Connecticut: JAI Press.

Nachtigall, H. 1955. *Tierrandentro, Archaelogy and Ethnography of a Colombian Region.* Zurich: Origo

Nader, Laura. 1969. Styles of court procedure: to make the balance. In *Law in Culture and Society*, pp. 69–91. L. Nader, ed. Chicago: Aldine.

Neveu-Lemaire, M. 1921. Les Caraibes des Antilles. *Geographie* 35:127–46.

Nie, Norman H., et al. 1975. *Statistical Package for the Social Sciences.* 2nd edition. New York: McGraw-Hill.

Nikul, Karl. 1948. *The Skolt Lapp Community Suenjelsijd During the Year 1938.* Stockholm: Hugo Gebers Forlag.

Nonet, Phillipe, and Philip Selznick. 1978. *Law and Society in Transition: Toward Responsive Law.* New York: Harper & Row.

Nwabueze, B. O. 1963. *The Machinery of Justice in Nigeria.* London: Butterworths.

Oberg, Kalervo. 1953. *Indian Tribes of Northern Matto Grosso, Brazil.* Smithsonian Institution Institute of Social Anthropology, publication no. 15. Washington, D.C.: Government Printing Office.

O'Leary, Timothy, and Joan Steffens. 1975. *Lapps Ethnographic Bibliography.* New Haven, Conn.: Human Relations Area Files Press.

Orans, Martin. 1965. *The Santal: A Tribe in Search of a Great Tradition.* Detroit: Wayne State University Press.

Paine, Robert. 1971. Animal as capital: comparisons among northern nomadic herders and hunters. *Anthropological Quarterly* 44(3):157–72.

Pankhurst, Sylvia. 1955. *Ethiopia: A Cultural History.* Essex, England: Lalibela House.

Paques, Viviana. 1954. *Les Bambara.* Paris: Presses Universitaires de France.

Parsons, Elsie C. 1917. *Notes on Zuni, Part II.* Memoirs of the American Anthropological Association, vol. IV. Lancaster, Pa.: New Era Printing Co.

Pashukanis, Evgenii. 1978. *Law and Marxism: A General Theory.* London: Ink Links.

Pehrson, Robert N. 1957. The bilateral network of social relations in Konkama Lapp District. *International Journal of American Linquistics* 23 (1).

Petrullo, Vincenzo. 1937. *The Composition of 'Torts' in Guajira Society.* Publications of the Philadelphia Anthropological Society, Vol. 1. Philadelphia: University Press.

Pierce, Joe E. 1964. *Life in a Turkish Village.* New York: Holt, Rinehart and Winston.

Pineda Giraldo, Roberto. 1950. *Aspectos de la Magia en La Guajiro.* Bogota: Universidad Nationale de Colombia.

Pittier de Fabrega, Henry. 1907. *Ethnographic and Linguistic Note on the*

Paez Indians of Tierra Adentro, Cauca, Colombia. Memoirs of the American Anthropological Association, vol. 1, part 5. Lancaster, Pa.: New Era Printing Co.

Pospisil, Leopold. 1958. *Kapauku Papuans and Their Law.* New Haven, Conn.: Yale University Press.

  1959. Multiplicity of legal systems in primitive societies. *Bulletin of the Philadelphia Anthropological Society* 12 (3):1–4.

  1963a. *Kapauku Papuan Economy.* New Haven, Conn.: Yale Department of Anthropology.

  1963b. *The Kapauku Papuans of West New Guinea.* New York: Holt, Rinehart and Winston.

  1967. The attributes of law. In *Law and Warfare: Studies in the Anthropology of Conflict,* pp. 25–42. P. Bohannan, ed. Garden City, N.Y.: Natural History Press.

  1974. *Anthropology of Law: A Comparative Theory.* New Haven, Conn.: Yale University Press.

Pound, Roscoe. 1930. *Interpretations of Legal History.* London: Macmillan.

Powell, H. A. 1967. Competitive leadership in Trobriand political organization. In *Comparative Political Systems,* pp. 155–92. R. Cohen and J. Middleton, eds. Austin: University of Texas Press.

Powers, Stephen. 1877. *Tribes of California.* Washington, D.C.: Government Printing Office.

Prins, Adriaan H. 1953. *East African Age-Class System.* Groningen, Netherlands: J.B. Wolters.

Radcliffe-Brown, A. R. 1948. *The Andaman Islanders.* Glencoe, Ill.: Free Press.

  1952. *Structure and Function in Primitive Society.* Glencoe, Ill.: Free Press.

Radin, Paul. 1942. *The Indians of South America.* Garden City, N.Y.: Doubleday, Doran.

Rattray, R. S. 1929. *Ashanti Law and Constitution.* London: Oxford University Press.

  1932. The Tribes of the Ashanti Hinterland. Oxford: Oxford University Press (Clarendon Press).

Reinhardt, H., R. L. Blumberg, and R. Winch. 1975. Theory guided coding: a pilot study coding fertility, the status of women and the economic function of the family. Paper presented to the Society for Cross-Cultural Research, Chicago.

Renner, Karl. 1949. *The Institutions of Private Law and Their Social Functions.* London: Routledge & Kegan Paul.

Rheinstein, Max. 1954. *Introduction to Max Weber on Law in Economy and Society.* New York: Simon and Schuster.

Richards, Audrey I. 1940. The political system of the Bemba Tribe. In *African Political Systems,* pp. 83–120. Meyer Fortes and Edward Evans-Pritchard, eds. London: International African Institute.

  1960. *East African Chiefs: A Study of Political Development in some Uganda and Tanganyika Tribes.* New York: Praeger.

1961. *Land, Labour and Diet in Northern Rhodesia: An Economic Study of the Bemba Tribe*. Oxford: Oxford University Press.

1971a. The nature of the problem. In *Councils in Action*, pp. 1–12. A. Richards and A. Kuper, eds. Cambridge: Cambridge University Press.

1971b. The conciliar system of the Bemba of Northern Rhodesia. In *Councils in Action*, pp. 100–29. A. Richards and A. Kuper, eds. Cambridge: Cambridge University Press.

Rivers, William H. 1906. *The Todas*. New York: Macmillan.

Roberts, Simon. 1979. *Order and Dispute: An Introduction to Legal Anthropology*. Harmondsworth, England: Penguin Books.

Rodd, Francis R. 1926. *People of the Veil*. London: Macmillan.

Roheim, Geza. 1933. Women and their life in central Australia. *Royal Anthropological Institute of Great Britain and Ireland Journal* 63:207–65.

1945. *The Eternal Ones of the Dream: A Psychoanalytic Interpretation of Australian Myth and Ritual*. New York: International Universities Press.

Roscoe, John. 1911. *The Baganda: An Account of Their Native Customs and Beliefs*. London: Macmillan.

Rosman, Abraham, and Paula Rubel. 1971. *Feasting with Mine Enemies: Rank and Exchange Among Northwest Coast Societies*. New York: Columbia University Press.

1981. *The Tapestry of Culture*. Glenview, Ill.: Scott, Foresman.

Rowe, John H. 1948. Inca culture at the time of the Spanish conquest. In *Handbook of South American Indians*, vol. 2, pp. 138–330. Julian Steward, ed. Washington, D.C.: Government Printing Office.

Rubel, Paula, and Abraham Rosman. 1978. *Your Own Pigs You May Not Eat*. Chicago: University of Chicago Press.

Sahagun, Bernardino de. 1953. *Florentine Codex: General History of the Things of New Spain. Book 8 – Kings and Lords*. A.J. Anderson and D. E. Dibble, trans. Santa Fe, N.M.: School of American Research and University of Utah.

Sahlins, Marshall. 1968. *Tribesmen*. Englewood Cliffs, N.J.: Prentice-Hall.

1972. *Stone Age Economics*. Chicago: Aldine.

1977. *Culture and Practical Reason*. Chicago: University of Chicago Press.

Santa Cruz, Antonio. 1960. Acquiring Status in Guajiro Society. *Anthropological Quarterly* 33:115–27.

Schaedel, Richard P. 1978. Early state of the Incas. In *The Early State*, pp. 289–320. J. M. Henri and Peter Skalnik, eds. The Hague: Mouton.

Schapera, Isaac. 1930. *The Khoisan Peoples of South Africa: Bushmen and Hottentots*. London: Routledge & Kegan Paul.

Schapera, Isaac, and E. Farrington. 1933. *The Early Cape Hottentots*. Westport, Conn.: Negro Universities Press.

Schildkrout, Enid. 1979. The ideology of regionalism. In *Strangers in African Society*, pp. 183–210. William Shack and Elliot Skinner, eds. Berkeley: University of California Press.

Schwartz, R., and J. Miller. 1964. Legal evolution and societal complexity. *American Journal of Sociology* 20:159–69.

Seligman, C., and B. Seligman. 1932. *Pagan Tribes of the Nilotic Sudan.* London: Routledge & Kegan Paul.

Shack, William, and Elliot Skinner. 1979. *Strangers in African Society.* Berkeley: University of California Press.

Silas, Ellis. 1926. *A Primitive Arcadia; Being the Impressions of an Artist in Papua.* London: Unwin.

Singh, Indrajit. 1944. *The Gondwana and the Gonds.* Lucknow, India: Universal Publishers.

Skeat, Walter, and Charles Blagden. 1906. *Pagan Races of the Peninsula.* London: Macmillan.

Skinner, Alanson. 1911. *Notes on the Eastern Cree and Northern Saulteaux.* Anthropological Papers of the American Museum of Natural History, vol. 9, part 1. New York-American Museum.

Skrefsrud, Lars O. 1942. *Traditions and Institutions of the Santals.* Oslo: Oslo Etnografiske Museum.

Smith, M. G. 1960. *Government in Zazzau 1800–1950.* London: Oxford University Press.

Smith, W., and J. Roberts. 1954. *Zuni Law: A Field of Values.* Cambridge, Mass.: Harvard University Press.

Southwold, Martin. 1965. The Ganda of Uganda. In *Peoples of Africa,* pp. 81–118. J. Gibbs, ed. New York: Holt, Rinehart and Winston.

Spencer, Walter, and F. Gillen. 1927. *The Arunta: A Study of Stone Age People.* London: Macmillan.

Stanner, William. 1953. *The South Seas in Transition.* Sydney: Australasian Publishing Company.

Starr, June. 1978. *Dispute and Settlement in Rural Turkey.* Leiden: Brill.

Stevenson, Henry. 1944. *The Hill People of Burma.* London: Longmans, Green.

Stevenson, Matilda C. 1904. *The Zuni Indians: Their Mythology, Esoteric Fraternities, and Ceremonies.* Washington, D.C.: Bureau of American Ethnology.

Steward, Julian, and Louis C. Faran. 1959. *Native Peoples of South America.* New York: McGraw-Hill.

Steward, Julian, and Alfred Metraux. 1948. The Jivaro. In *Handbook of South American Indians,* vol. 3., pp. 617–27. J. Steward, ed. Washington, D.C.: Government Printing Office.

Stewart, Omer. 1943. *Notes on Pomo Ethnogeography.* Berkeley: University of California Press.

Stirling, Matthew. 1938. *Historical and Ethnographical Material on the Jivaro Indians.* Washington, D.C.: Government Printing Office.

Stirling, Paul. 1965. *Turkish Village.* London: Weidenfeld and Nicholson.

Sumner, Colin. 1979. *Reading Ideologies: An Investigation into the Marxist Theory of Ideology and Law.* London: Academic Press.

Sverdrup, Harald. 1938. *Hos Tundrafollcet* (With the People of the Tundra). Oslo: Gyldendal Norsk Forlag.

Szyliowicz, Joseph. 1966. *Political Change in Rural Turkey Erdemli*. The Hague: Mouton.

Taylor, Douglas. 1938. *The Caribs of Dominica*. Bureau of American Ethnology Bulletin 119. Washington, D.C.: Government Printing Office.

———. 1946. Kinship and social structure of the Island Carib. *Southwestern Journal of Anthropology* 2:18:–212.

———. 1951. *The Black Carib of British Honduras*. Viking Fund Publication in Anthropology, no 17. New York: Wenner-Gren Foundation.

Temple, Richard, 1903. *The Andaman and Nicobar Islands: Report on the Census*. Calcutta: Office of the Superintendent of Government Printing.

Terray, Emmanuel. 1972. *Marxism and "Primitive" Societies: Two Studies*. New York: Monthly Review Press.

Thompson, Eric. 1933. *Mexico Before Cortez: An Account of the Daily Life, Religion, and Ritual of the Aztecs and Kindred Peoples*. New York: Scribner.

Tucker, Robert, ed. 1972. *The Marx-Engels Reader*. New York: Norton.

Tuden, Arthur, and Catherine Marshall. 1972. Political organization: cross cultural codes 4. *Ethnology* 9(4):436–64.

Tylor, E. B. 1958. *Primitive Culture*. New York: Harper Torchbooks. (Orig. pub. 1871.)

Vaillant, George C. 1944. *Aztecs of Mexico: Origin, Rise and Fall of the Aztec Nation*. London: Penguin Books.

Veniaminov, Ivan. 1840a. *Zapiski op Ostrovakh Unalashkinskao Otdiela* (Notes on the Islands of the Unalaska District), vol. 2. Innokentii: Metropolitan of Moscow.

———. 1840b. *Zapiski op Ostrovakh Unalashkinskao Otdiela* (Notes on the Islands of the Unalaska District), vol. 3. Innokentii: Metropolitan of Moscow.

Villaverde, Juan. 1909. The Ifugaos of Quiangan and vicinity. Dean Worchester, trans. *Philippine Journal of Science* 4:237–62.

Vorren, Ornulu, and Ernest Manker. 1962. *Lapp Life and Customs: A Survey*. London: Oxford University Press.

Waterman, Thomas T. 1920. *Yurok Geography*. Berkeley: University of California Press.

Weber, Max. 1954. *Law in Economy and Society*. Max Rheinstein, ed. New York: Simon and Schuster. (Orig. pub. 1925.)

Weltfish, Gene. 1965. *The Lost Universe*. New York: Basic Books.

Whitaker, Ian. 1955. *Social Relations in a Nomadic Lappish Community*. Oslo: Utgitt Av Norsk Folkenmuseum.

Whitely, Wilfred. 1950. *Bemba and Related Peoples of Northern Rhodesia*. London: International African Institute.

Wimberly, Howard. 1973. Legal evolution: one further step. *American Journal of Sociology* 79(1):78–83.

Wittfogel, Karl. 1957. *Oriental Despotism*. New Haven, Conn.: Yale University Press.

Yengoyan, Aram. 1968. Demographic and ecological influences on aboriginal Australian marriage sections. In *Man the Hunter*, pp. 185–99. R. Lee and I. DeVore, eds. Chicago: Aldine.

Yoe, Shway. 1927. *The Burman: His Life and Notions.* London: Macmillan.

Index